T0293617

ACADEMIC ENTREPRENEURSHIP
Creating the Ecosystem for your University

ACADEMIC ENTREPRENEURSHIP
Creating the Ecosystem for your University

Robert D. Hisrich
Kent State University, USA

Tony Stanco
National Council of Entrepreneurial Tech Transfer, USA

Helena S. Wisniewski
University of Alaska Anchorage, USA

World Scientific

NEW JERSEY · LONDON · SINGAPORE · BEIJING · SHANGHAI · HONG KONG · TAIPEI · CHENNAI · TOKYO

Published by

World Scientific Publishing Co. Pte. Ltd.

5 Toh Tuck Link, Singapore 596224

USA office: 27 Warren Street, Suite 401-402, Hackensack, NJ 07601

UK office: 57 Shelton Street, Covent Garden, London WC2H 9HE

Library of Congress Cataloging-in-Publication Data

Names: Hisrich, Robert D, author. | Stanco, Tony, author. | Wisniewski, Helena S, author.

Title: Academic entrepreneurship : creating the ecosystem for your university / Robert D Hisrich,
   Kent State University, USA, Tony Stanco, National Council of Entrepreneurial Tech Transfer,
   USA, Helena S Wisniewski, National Academy of Inventors, USA.

Description: USA : Worldscientific, 2020. | Includes bibliographical references and index.

Identifiers: LCCN 2019049846 | ISBN 9789811210631 (hardcover) |
   ISBN 9789811210648 (ebook)

Subjects: LCSH: Entrepreneurship--United States. | University-based new business enterprises--
   United States. | Academic-industrial collaboration--United States.

Classification: LCC HB615 .H573 2020 | DDC 338/.04--dc23

LC record available at https://lccn.loc.gov/2019049846

British Library Cataloguing-in-Publication Data

A catalogue record for this book is available from the British Library.

For any available supplementary material, please visit
https://www.worldscientific.com/worldscibooks/10.1142/11561#t=suppl

Desk Editors: Aanand Jayaraman/Sandhya Venkatesh

Typeset by Stallion Press
Email: enquiries@stallionpress.com

Preface

Today, perhaps more than ever before, colleges and universities throughout the world are looking for new sources of revenue partly to replace the decrease in traditional funding sources such as federal and state funding; a decline in the number of domestic and particularly international students and the resulting tuition revenue; a decrease in corporate and alumni donations; and corporate and government contracts. One source of new revenue is by commercializing the science and technology of the university that is created by its students, staff, and faculty. This was traditionally done through the technology transfer office where these new technological ideas were transferred to another entity; usually a company with a licensing agreement where the revenue is shared by the two parties. The new emphasis is for the university to create its own company spinoffs to better satisfy the third mission of the university — economic development and well-being of the region in which the university operates. This requires the establishment of an ecosystem at the university that encourages and supports the academic entrepreneur (the student, faculty, or staff) to go beyond the creation of a new technology to the creation of a technological idea that is the basis for a successful business.

To provide an understanding of this academic entrepreneur and the elements of the ecosystem, this book is divided into 10 chapters and an appendix.

Chapter 1 introduces the concept, its importance and history, as well as the impact of academic entrepreneurship on the regional economic environment, the culture, and revenue stream of the university.

Chapter 2 introduces the concept of an ecosystem for encouraging and supporting the process of business creation and its management.

Chapter 3 discusses the first element of the ecosystem — the role of patents.

Chapter 4 presents the second element of the ecosystem — identifying markets and opportunities for the ideas and technology created by the academic entrepreneur.

Chapter 5 discusses all the aspects of a business plan for the technological idea needed for starting, launching, and growing the new venture.

Chapters 6 and 7 discuss one of the most important and difficult aspects of creating an ecosystem — the funding sources. The sources discussed include angel networks and funds, corporations, government grants, university angel groups, and the national angel network.

Chapter 8 presents the role of incubators and accelerators in creating a new business in the ecosystem formation and operation.

Chapters 9 and 10 appropriately conclude the book by presenting the differences in creating a business venture and technology transfer through licensing in terms of their aspects, difficulties, and revenue stream, as well as managing and creating the results of the ecosystem established. The chapter and book conclude with a discussion of the ownership and royalty policies of several universities.

The appendix contains 20 profiles of academic entrepreneurs in various types of universities throughout the United States.

To make *Creating an Ecosystem for Academic Entrepreneurship* as meaningful and useful as possible for both academic entrepreneurs and administrators developing and managing the ecosystem, each chapter begins with learning objectives and a profile of an academic entrepreneur (a student, faculty, or staff member) who started a business venture while employed by the university. This chapter includes numerous examples and illustrations of academic entrepreneurs and university ecosystems. Each chapter concludes with a synopsis of selected readings to further develop the chapter content.

At the end of the book is a selection of profiles of academic entrepreneurs from universities throughout the United States.

Many individuals — students, business executives, entrepreneurs, professors, and the publishing staff — have made this book possible. Special thanks go to Anit Kunwar and Ria P. Ancheta-Adrias for their assistance in obtaining and developing the profiles of the academic entrepreneurs which start each chapter and are listed in the appendix. Special thanks also to Garima Jha and Mary Bamer-Ramsier for their research and editorial assistance.

This book is dedicated to my wife, Tina, whose support and patience helped bring this book to fruition, and my children — Kelly, Kary, and Katy — and grandchildren — Rachel, Andrew, and Sarah — and their generations, some of whom may become academic entrepreneurs.

Robert D. Hisrich

About the Authors

 **Robert D. Hisrich** is the Bridgestone Chair of International Business and Director of the Global Management Center at the College of Business Administration at Kent State University, USA. He holds a BA from DePauw University and MBA and PhD degrees from the University of Cincinnati. Professor Hisrich's primary research focuses on entre- preneurship and venture creation: entrepreneurial eth- ics, corporate entrepreneurship, women and minority entrepreneurs, venture financing, and global venture creation. He teaches courses and seminars in these areas, as well as in marketing management and product planning and development. His interest in global management and entre- preneurship resulted in two Fulbright Fellowships in Budapest, Hungary, honorary degrees from Chuvash State University (Russia) and University of Miskolc (Hungary), and being a visiting faculty member in universities in Austria, Australia, China, Ireland, and Slovenia.

Professor Hisrich serves on the editorial boards of several prominent journals in entrepreneurship, is on several boards of directors, and is author or co-author of over 300 research articles appearing in journals such as *Journal of Marketing, Journal of Marketing Research, Journal of Business Venturing, Academy of Management Review, Strategic Management Journal, California Management Review, American Psychologist*, and *Entrepreneurship Theory and Practice*. Professor

Hisrich has authored, co-authored, or edited 46 books or their editions, including the following: *Marketing* (2000, 2nd edition); *How to Fix and Prevent the 13 Biggest Problems That Derail Business* (2004); *Technology Entrepreneurship* (2015, 2nd edition); *Entrepreneurial Finance* (2015); *International Entrepreneurship* (2016, 3rd edition); *Advanced Introduction to Corporate Venturing* (2016); *Effective Entrepreneurial Management* (2017); *Entrepreneurial Marketing* (2018); and *Entrepreneurship* (2019, 11th edition).

Tony Stanco, Esq. is the founder and executive director of the National Council of Entrepreneurial Tech Transfer and co-founder of National Angels USA. He works with researchers and universities to create and fund startups. Mr. Stanco was a senior attorney at the Securities and Exchange Commission. Previously he was the director of the Council of Entrepreneurial Tech Transfer and Commercialization (CET2C) of The George Washington University. At the School of Engineering and Applied Science at The George Washington University, Mr. Stanco worked with universities and governments around the world on innovation policy, startup finance policy, software policy, Open Source, cyber-security, and e-Government issues. He has an LL.M. from Georgetown University Law Center in securities regulation and is licensed as a lawyer in New York state.

Dr. Helena S. Wisniewski is Professor of Entrepreneurship and Department Chair at the University of Alaska Anchorage (UAA) and a Fellow of the National Academy of Inventors. She has executive and leadership experience in academia, industry, and government. As Vice Provost for Research at UAA and Vice President for Research and Enterprise Development at Stevens Institute of Technology, she led and created ecosystems of entrepreneurship and innovation, significantly increased patent portfolios, and launched multiple startups across diverse technological areas. She directed corporate-wide technological innovations as an executive at the Lockheed Corporation and as a Vice President at the Titan Corporation and ANSER. As Founder and CEO of Aurora Biometrics, she built an international business and later sold the company. At DARPA, she identified and directed many breakthrough advances in math and science as Manager of the Applied and Computational Mathematics Program. Among her awards is the 2002 Women in Technology Leadership Award for Entrepreneurship.

Contents

Chapter 1

The Importance, History, and Impact of Academic Entrepreneurship

Learning Objectives

- To understand the role and mission of universities past, present and future.
- To understand the nature of academic entrepreneurship.
- To understand the importance and future of academic entrepreneurship.

Opening Profile — Prabir K. Dutta

Q1. Submitter Information

Name of Nominee	**Prabir K. Dutta**
University the Nominee is representing	**The Ohio State University**
Email	dutta.1@osu.edu
Phone number	614 292 4532

Professor Dutta is a Distinguished University Professor at The Ohio State University in the Department of Chemistry and Biochemistry. He has published 262 referred manuscripts as an independent investigator, several book chapters, edited two books, is the author of 17 issued patents, eight patent applications, and been a mentor for about 100 postdoctoral and graduate research students. The Ohio State University has licensed several of Professor Dutta's sensor inventions to companies, most recent being Spirosure, a startup company in California that has translated Professor Dutta's invention into a breath monitor product for predicting asthma attacks. Professor Dutta has recently founded his own company, Zeo Vation, which is an applied materials company focused on Zeolitic microporous materials with added functionalities for environmental and consumer markets. On the pedagogical side, a significant contribution has been to develop a NSF-supported Ohio-wide effort to alter the curriculum of undergraduates taking chemistry courses with the goal of increasing the number of Science and Engineering graduate in the state of Ohio. The innovation was to introduce research into the laboratory curriculum, and this program has reached tens of thousands of students across Ohio. Professor Dutta is a Fellow of AAAS and National Academy of Inventors.

Q2: The nominee's position when they created the company. Describe the nominee's process with the university as they were creating the company. Be as detailed as possible.

Professor Dutta was Distinguished University Professor in The Department of Chemistry and Biochemistry at The Ohio State University (OSU) when he co-founded the company ZeoVation in 2016–2017. Over the past decade, Prof. Dutta has been active in patenting research coming from his laboratory. With the help of the Technology Commercialization Office (TCO) at OSU, many of these patents were licensed to companies including Nextech, Ceramatech, Measurement specialties, K&A Wireless, and Spirosure. Some of these companies have gone on to develop commercial products based on Prof. Dutta's technology. By interacting with these companies, Prof. Dutta gained considerable experience in writing patents, raising funds, IP protection and manufacturing issues with device fabrication and scale-up. In 2016, Dr. Bo Wang, a Ph.D. student in Prof. Dutta's laboratory got interested in commercialization of academic research and took a course in "Entrepreneurship" at OSU.

This course and his interactions with young entrepreneurs motivated Dr. Wang to consider forming a startup company based on his thesis research. Prof. Dutta encouraged Dr. Wang to proceed with his startup idea. Dr. Wang got in touch with Rev1, an inventor startup organization in Columbus, which acts as a hub to connect startups with corporate innovators.

Rev1 has a history of working with TCO to develop OSU technologies. Rev1 conducts a quarterly competition to determine which clients they will accept, and Dr. Wang applied for consideration. Prof. Dutta and Dr. Wang also started to develop their business model centering on the use of nano and hierarchical zeolites for consumer applications. OSU also filed patents on the synthesis procedures that Dr. Wang developed for nano and hierarchical zeolites. The initial product development focused on sunscreens and antimicrobials. Rev1 and TCO carried out a customer survey to determine the level of interest in the products proposed by Prof. Dutta and Dr. Wang. Based on the consumer analysis and presentations by Prof. Dutta and Dr. Wang, Rev1 decided to take the startup on as a client. This meant the startup could take advantage of the extensive legal, financial, and management network of Rev1 and OSU. Dr. Wang and Prof. Dutta incorporated the company as ZeoVation Inc.

Q3: Describe the nominee's experience working with the university in creating the company. What were the challenges? What support did they receive? Be as detailed as possible.

With the startup of ZeoVation, there were three immediate challenges: finalizing negotiations with OSU and Rev1, formalizing a 5-year business plan, and raising seed funding. ZeoVation needed a CEO in place, who had experience in the business. Rev1 and TCO were helpful in finding a CEO, Mr. Steve Jones, who had considerable business experience in both the US and Asia. Mr. Jones negotiated with OSU the patent licensing and with Rev1 regarding ownership. Mr. Jones also negotiated with nearly a dozen seed investors.

These legal negotiations and setting up the final version of the ownership of the company required considerable time, patience and business savvy decisions by Mr. Jones and the legal team.

Q4: What happened to the company the nominee created? Describe in detail where it is now and how is it doing. What is the history of the company? Be as detailed as possible.

ZeoVation is an advanced material company imparting novel functionality to the zeolite platform to generate consumer products. Early on, ZeoVation set up a website and started selling the nanozeolite and hierarchical zeolite (gram scale) for academic researchers. The goal was to generate a revenue stream that would facilitate product development. ZeoVation also obtained funding from the State of Ohio's commercialization efforts, Rev1 and individual investors. A process engineering company identified the unit operations and carried out an analysis of the requirements of a pilot plant capable of manufacturing the products at the ton level. In addition, funds were spent for developing the sunscreen and antimicrobial formulations. ZeoVation's business model is to interest both small and large companies to evaluate the present products, and then co-develop a product suited to the company requirements. ZeoVation has been successful in setting up relationships with five companies, including materials transfer agreements, and are in discussions with three other companies. The goal is to set up Joint Development Agreements (JDA) with these partners and begin manufacturing at the ton scale with toll manufacturers, based on the current pilot plant specifications. Once the JDAs are in place, ZeoVation will also seek series A financing, expected to occur in 2019. ZeoVation is also writing SBIR/STTR proposals with OSU as a partner. Being able to use OSU facilities for carrying out the base R&D associated with the products has also been a significant help for ZeoVation.

Introduction

As is indicated in the profile, academic entrepreneurship which will be viewed in this book as "a member of the university community (faculty, staff, or student) forming a new venture," is a process that is attracting the attention of policymakers, academic institutions, financial institution, economist, as well as the overall population. Questions that have been raised include: Is this the role of a university? Will farming and spinning off ventures in a university erode the intellectual mission of the university? Will the university as well as the economy and society benefit from these activities? How should the proceeds and ownership of this activity be divided? What role should a government or governmental agency play in this activity?

This chapter addresses these and other aspects of academic entrepreneurship by first addressing the history and role of universities. This is followed by discussing the impact of universities on the economy of the region, country, and world. After presenting the impact of universities, the chapter concludes with a discussion of academic entrepreneurship and an entrepreneurial university.

Origin and History of Universities

The term university comes from the Latin *Universitas Magistrorum et Scholarium* meaning a "community of teachers and scholars". The origin of a university as a formal institution was from a medieval Christian setting (Ruegg, 1992). Most of the first universities established had their roots in Christian cathedral schools or monastic schools where monks and nuns taught classes. These date back to the 6th century AD (Riche, 1978). Prior to the 12th century, the intellectual aspects of the culture of Western Europe occurred in monasteries and was mostly concentrated on prayer and performing literacy with only rare instances of investigation and intellectual understanding. The emphasis of the Gregorian Reforms was on canon law and the study of the sacraments resulted in Catholic schools being established mainly to train clergy in canon law and such aspects of administration as logic and disputation for use in theological discussion and preaching and accounting to help enlarge and control the finances of the institution. One figure emerged in the 11th century significantly impacted the transformation of these cathedral schools into the first European universities. Pope Gregory VII issued his 1079 Papal Decree that promoted and regulated these cathedral schools which transformed themselves into the first universities emerging in the 11th century (Ostereich, 1913).

Appropriately, the first university established was in the Holy Roman Empire in the Kingdom of Italy — the University of Bologna which had its charter granted formally in 1158.

Using the traditional definition of a university which is derived from the Latin *Universitas Magistrorum et Scholarium* meaning a "community of teachers and scholars," the seven (7) oldest universities in continuous operation are indicated in Table 1. Following the University of Bologna

Table 1.   List of oldest universities in continuous operation.

Year	University	Location Original	Location Current	Notes
1088 (charter granted 1158)	University of Bologna	Kingdom of Italy, Holy Roman Empire	Bologna, Italy	The oldest university in the world. A university in the sense of a higher-learning, degree-awarding institute, the word *university* (Latin: *universitas*) having been coined at its foundation. It received, in 1158, from Emperor Frederick I Barbarossa the "Authentica habita", which settled the rules, rights and privileges of universities.
1134 (charter granted in 1218)	University of Salamanca	Kingdom of León	Salamanca, Spain	The oldest university in the Hispanic world. The university claims to have been founded by Alfonso IX of León in 1218 (although James Trager's *People's Chronology* sets its foundation date as 1134), making it the third or fourth oldest university in continuous operation. It was the first European university to receive the title of "*University*" as such, which was granted by the King of Castile and León, Alfonso X, and the Pope in 1254. After being excluded from the University in 1852 by the Spanish government, the Faculties of Theology and Canon Law became the Pontifical University of Salamanca in 1940.
1222 (probably older)	University of Padua	Lombard League	Padua, Italy	Founded by scholars and professors after leaving Bologna.
1224 (1258)	University of Naples Federico II	Kingdom of Sicily	Naples, Italy	The first public university, founded by Frederick II, Emperor of the Holy Roman Empire. The university moved to Salerno in 1253, and its return to Naples in 1258 is sometimes considered as a refoundation. It is considered to be the oldest public and state university in the world.

University	Date		Location	Description
University of Cambridge	1209 (charter granted in 1231)	Kingdom of England	Cambridge, United Kingdom	Founded by scholars leaving Oxford after a dispute caused by the execution of two scholars in 1209. Its royal charter was granted in 1231. The University takes 1209 as its official anniversary. Inspired the establishment of Cambridge, Massachusetts, United States, with the first college in the United States, Harvard University named after one of Cambridge University's alumni, John Harvard.
University of Oxford	1096–1167 (charter in granted 1248)	Kingdom of England	Oxford, United Kingdom	The oldest university in the English-speaking world: Oxford claims its founding ("…teaching existed … in some form…") as early as 1096, and not later than 1167. Rashdall takes 1167 as the date when Oxford became a *studium generale*. In 1254, Pope Innocent IV granted Oxford a university charter by papal bull ("Querentes in agro"). Teaching was suspended in 1209 (due to the town's execution of two scholars) and in 1355 (due to the St. Scholastica Day riot), but was continuous during the English Civil War (1642–1651), when the University was Royalist.
University of Coimbra	1290	Kingdom of Portugal	Coimbra, Portugal	It began its existence in Lisbon with the name Studium Generale (*Estudo Geral*). *Scientiæ thesaurus mirabilis* ("the admirable treasure of knowledge"), the royal charter announcing the institution of the University, was dated 1 March 1290, although efforts had been made since at least 1288 to create this first university in Portugal. Papal confirmation was also given in 1290 (on 9 August of that year), during the papacy of Pope Nicholas IV.
University of Macerata	1290	Papal States	Macerata, Italy	Founded in 1290, possibly as a private law school rather than a university. Unknown whether this was in continuous operation, but there is evidence for a school (without degree awarding powers) in 1518. After petitions from the *commune* to the Pope from 1534, bull establishing a *studium generale* issued in 1540.

Source: Adapted from Wikipedia.

(chartered in 1,158), in terms of date of charter, are the University of Salamanca (chartered in 1218), the University of Padua (chartered in 1222), the University of Naples (chartered in 1224), the University of Cambridge (chartered in 1231), the University of Oxford (chartered in 1248), the University of Coimbra (chartered in 1290), and the University of Macerata (chartered in 1290). Each of these universities were already having activities before being chartered. Some notes on each university are also indicated in Table 1.

Impact of universities on economics

While each and every university has some impact on the economics of the area where it is located in terms of jobs, supplying companies, cultural and sporting events, and housing; two such universities in the United States will be discussed — Massachusetts Institute of Technology (MIT) and Stanford.[1]

Massachusetts Institute of Technology

MIT has a rich history in entrepreneurship and innovation which has a substantial impact on the economies of the region, the United States, and the world. In a report released in 2015, it was estimated that the more than 30,200 active companies of the entrepreneurial alumni employed more than 4.6 million people and had annual revenues of over $1.9 trillion which is more than the gross domestic product (GDP) of the 10th largest economy in the world. This is a substantial increase from the reported numbers of 2006 — 25,800 active companies worldwide employing 3.3 million people. The companies were founded in several sectors: biotechnology and medical devices, computer hardware, energy, engineering, manufacturing, and software. The software was the largest sector representing 18% of all alumni companies. A survey of alumni found that:

---

[1]For more details on the economic impact of each university go to the website of each university: MIT — http://news.mit.edu/2015/report-entrepreneurial-impact-1209; Stanford University — https://engineering.stanford.edu/news/alumni-survey-measures-stanford-s-economic-impact.

- 80% of alumni-founded companies survived 5 or more years and 70% survived 10 years.
- 25% of the alumni have founded companies with 40% being serial (repeat) entrepreneurs.
- 11% of alumni-founded companies within 5 years of graduation in the 2010s compared to 8% who founded companies in the 1990s versus 4% in the 1960s. MIT was instrumental in developing a corridor of entrepreneurial firms labeled Route 128.

Stanford University

Similarly, Stanford University has had a significant economic impact on its region by incubating ideas, educating entrepreneurs, and fostering breakthrough innovations. A report based on a 2011 survey indicated that more than 39,000 active companies have their roots in Stanford University. The $2.9 trillion revenue of these companies is more than the GDP of the 10th largest economy in the world, similar to MIT. These companies created an estimated 5.4 million jobs. Other interesting results of the survey include the following:

- 25% of the faculty respondents reported founding or incorporating a company.
- 55% of the respondents who became entrepreneurs in the last decade chose to study at Stanford due to its entrepreneurial environment.
- 18,000 firms created by Stanford alumni formed companies in California. These companies had revenues of $1.27 trillion and employed more than 3 million individuals.
- 25% of the entrepreneurs located their companies within 20 miles and 39% within 60 miles of Stanford. Stanford University was indeed the driving force behind the formation of what is labeled Silicon Valley.

The Entrepreneurial University

Recognized research universities have at least one characteristic in common — a commitment to the independent inquiry of their scholars to push the frontiers of the knowledge of their discipline and pass this knowledge on to successive generations. Circumstances today require that a university, in addition, needs to be managed more strategically using modern concepts and techniques to emerge as a new, organization and assist in the development of the economics in the region, country, and world in agriculture, industrial, and service sectors through innovation and problem-solving.

The goal to understanding this new role and purpose of higher education institutions (universities) has taken many directions since the musing of Newman about "the idea of a university" (Newman, 1852). This purpose is now centered on the civic and economic roles of universities. This new focus (in addition to continuing the focus on education and research) is best captured by the term "entrepreneurial university". The origin of this term is found in the book *Academic Capitalism* by Slaughter and Leslie (1997). The authors feel that an entrepreneurial university develops activity and energy to support the motion of enterprise. This means there will be risk taking in initiating new practices that have outcomes that may not be positive. These universities will be significant players on their defined dimensions allowing entrepreneurship as a process and outcome to flourish. This new form of a university will attract students such as was indicated in the case of Stanford University previously described. The result will be seen in outcomes in two areas: (1) academic entrepreneurship which focuses on the commercialization of knowledge and research findings (Klofsen and Jones-Evans, 2000) and (2) entrepreneurship education which links this third focus to the teaching mission (Gibb and Hannonn, 2006).

Since businesses, governments, societies, and universities are quite different throughout the world this task of creating an entrepreneurial university that does research, teaching, and commercialization is not an easy task and will take a wide variety of forms. Despite an increase in the number of books and articles on the topic, nothing definitive has been articulated. One area that needs significant attention is the institutional aspect of the third mission university problem. The entrepreneurial university as an institution is shaped by the environment in which it operates while it in turn is transforming this very environment.

While assisting in the development of more entrepreneurial universities, even government laws and incentives have come up short (for a discussion of thesis, see Lockett *et al.*, 2005). The Bayh-Dole Act of 1980 attempted to accelerate the diffusion of research and new technology by university and even more by several laboratories in the United States. Technology transfer offices (TTOs) were created in most universities to assist in this process by licensing the technology to organizations; mainly businesses outside the university. An annual "Technology Transfer" conference occurs yearly where individuals meet and present ideas and papers on the topic. It is estimated that over $10 trillion of technology lies hallow in various university settings. Leaders agree the revenue obtained, companies formed, and regional impact (Silicon Valley and Route 128) such as Stanford and MIT have moved towards but have not obtained the results of an entrepreneurial university.

Money has not been able to significantly affect this transformation process. Large multimillion-dollar grants from the Kauffman Foundation to several universities in the United States have not produced any significant results.

Attempts outside the United States have been equally frustrating. In the United Kingdom starting around 1988, British business leaders collaborated with the Thatcher government to build an enterprise culture in higher level education. Legislation such as the Science Enterprise Challenge, the Higher Education Enterprise Fund, and the University Challenge were enacted to: stimulate the commercialization of university-based research; develop public–private partnerships; and to create more innovation in small firms (Rasmussen *et al.*, 2014). Even with this cooperative effort and legislation, movement to add the third dimension of commercialization of research and teaching as exemplified in such universities as Cambridge; no entrepreneurial university emerged.

Similarly, in Norway, universities have attempted to incorporate this third dimension of commercialization as well. The ownership of intellectual property previous assigned to the university research scholar was transferred to universities starting in 2003 (Wigren-Kristolersan *et al.*, 2011).[11] In Sweden, the law of university teacher's exemption, allow researchers to retain full rights to their discoveries without having some percentage go to their institution — the University — remains

(Lockett *et al.*, 2014). Yet, one cannot describe the universities of the Chalmers University of Technology, The Arctic University of Norway, or Stavanger as being entrepreneurial universities. And, the list of countries, societies, economies, and faculty to establish an entrepreneurial university goes on. Given the complexity of the challenge, it is difficult to imagine an entrepreneurial university emerging in the near future if ever.

Academic Entrepreneurship

As was previously discussed, the substantial increase in the commercialization of science and technology has become of more interest in the last 10 years. The process of doing this by creating university spin-offs instead of the more traditional technology transfer has become even more important for universities throughout the world.

This new emphasis on business spin-offs is far different from the era when universities first established TTOs in the 1980s (Hisrich *et al.*, 2017). Up until the advent of entrepreneurship courses and programs and entrepreneurship itself as an academic discipline which is often cited as the first Babson Research Conference in 1981; the focus was patenting and licensing. Only recently has academic entrepreneurship and involvement in the economic aspects of the region became the third aspect of a university mission. This has only occurred at a few universities.

Entrepreneurship can be thought of as the ability to create something new of value by taking the necessary risks involved. The individual(s) doing this has an entrepreneurial mindset which involves "the ability to rapidly sense, act, and mobilize even under uncertain conditions" (Tijssen, 2006). With this entrepreneurial mindset, two entrepreneurial functions occur: identification and exploitation. These two functions vary in terms of the type of knowledge transferred, the risks involved, and the complexity of the activity. There are differences between university entrepreneurial activities based on the transfer of knowledge created by consulting or contract research, the transfer of technology through patents or licensing, and the transfer of products/services through spin-offs. Academic entrepreneurship in this book focuses on the transfer of products/services through spins or the exploitation point of entrepreneurship. More specifically academic entrepreneurship is "the formation of a new enterprise by someone employed by (faculty, research, or staff) or attending (student) the university". The academic entrepreneur goes through the commercialization process of idea generation, commercialization decision, prototype development, determination of technical and commercial validity, forming the founding team, determining the strategy and commercialization process, obtaining the needed capital, and launching the venture.

The academic entrepreneur can be: (1) an individual faculty member, researchers, staff, or student; (2) any of these partnering with an experienced entrepreneur; (3) any of these partnering with a business school professor or student; (4) any one of these partnering with any of the others such as faculty member partnering with a Ph.D. or postdoctoral student.

What are the usual problems encountered in having an abundance of academic entrepreneurship occur in the university setting? The first problem is the reward system by the university. There is a need for a university interested in creating an environment supportive of academic entrepreneurship to adopt promotion, tenure, and overall reward system to include commercialization activities. The first major university in the United States to reward commercialization in promotion and tenure was Texas A&M in 2006. Since then other universities have followed this practice. These include: Brigham Young University; George Mason University; New York University; Northern Arizona University; Ohio University; Oregon State University; University of Arizona; University of Maryland; University of North Carolina at Greensboro; University of Nebraska; University of Texas Health Science Center, Houston; Utah State University; and Wake Forest University, Health Sciences. The more commercialization can be an input into the reward system of a university the more academic entrepreneurship will occur by individuals particularly faculty and researchers employed there.

The second problem occurs when administrators of the university (presidents, vice presidents, deans, and even technology transfer officers) have little understanding and even less appropriate skills to develop and support commercialization strategies. Most upper-level university positions at the Vice President or President level are filled by individuals well versed in the arts and/or sciences with little or no knowledge of business and commercialization. And TTOs are challenged by a dual agency that does both licensing and spin-offs transfer of technology when previously the single focus was licensing. The more information and training that can be provided; the more academic entrepreneurship will occur when these groups are not only familiarized with but support the activity.

A third problem is the prospect of increased conflict when outside parties are introduced to the university. University administrators, faculty, researchers, students, and technology transfer officers have different and conflicting objectives and cultures. Their differences are amplified when angels, venture capitalists, and corporations add a further level of conflict. The more understanding that can occur between all these entities are needed for the resources, specifically funding, the more academic entrepreneurship will occur.

A fourth problem occurs in universities that are state-sponsored and those that are unionized. To flourish, academic entrepreneurship requires the opposite environment of control through state government and unions. A new ecosystem at the university needs to be established to encourage and promote academic entrepreneurship for the process to flourish and increase at the university level.

A fifth problem involves the amount of creativity that is encouraged and occurs at the university. It has been shown that education often hinders creativity by the courses and test administered rather than to encourage and support it. One story about a young girl in class illustrates this very well. A kindergarten teacher gave the class the assignment of drawing any flower they wanted. One young girl asked the teacher "what type of flower?" The teacher responded, "any flower you want to create." The young girl unsure of the assignment asked again, "what type of flower". The teacher response was "draw a red flower on a green stem." And, of course, the young girl handed her assignment — "a red flower and a green stem." I am sure each of you reading this book can produce numerous examples of the same situation. Creativity needs to be encouraged and supported in a university rather than hindered.

Finally, and perhaps one of the hardest to correct is the resistance to change. Members of the university, as well as the entire university itself, are steeped in tradition and established processes which lead to stagnant teaching and the lack of individuals to accept new ideas that will lead to change. This resistance and inability to change does not encourage or support academic entrepreneurship. This resistance needs to be dealt with through carefully selected information dissemination and discussions. In terms of academic entrepreneurship, the use of successful examples of academic entrepreneurship at other universities and the benefits that resulted.

Future

In spite of these issues, the future of academic entrepreneurship is very bright. Indeed, spin-offs need to be promoted from an institutional perspective either directly from faculty, researchers, staff, and students at the university or indirectly through graduates (alumni) of the university. Typically, the innovation policy of a university focuses on radical innovation with a high rate of uncertainty, risk, and failure. Entrepreneurship policy focuses on stimulating new ventures through innovations at all levels of uniqueness: radical (breakthrough), technological, and ordinary innovations. A new approach is needed to integrate both aspects so academic entrepreneurship can flourish and new venture spin-offs can occur. This may result in different institutional content that provides the framework and resources required to support academic entrepreneurship. Establishing and building a university ecosystem is the focus of the next chapter. The significant areas in entrepreneurship courses and programs, entrepreneurship centers, and university development officers indicate academic entrepreneurship has the opportunity to occur at universities throughout the world.

Summary

This chapter begins by focusing on the origin and history of universities to set the stage for the universities impact on the economies of the regional, national, and world economy. Two universities in the United States are discussed — MIT and Stanford University. Following a presentation of the entrepreneurial university is a discussion of academic entrepreneurship. The Chapter concludes with ideas for the future policy changes needed to occur in a university setting.

Selected Readings

(1) Siegel, D. S. and Wright, M. (2015). Academic entrepreneurship: Time for a rethink? *British Journal of Management*, 26(4), 582–595.

Academic entrepreneurship, which refers to efforts undertaken by universities to promote commercialization on campus and in surrounding regions of the university has changed dramatically in recent years. Two key consequences are more stakeholders have become involved in academic entrepreneurship and universities have become more "strategic" in their approach to this activity. The authors assert the time is ripe to rethink academic entrepreneurship. Specifically, theoretical and empirical research on academic entrepreneurship needs to take account of these changes, so as to improve the rigor and relevance of future studies on this topic. We outline a framework and provide examples of key research questions that need to be addressed to broaden the understanding of academic entrepreneurship.

(2) Wright, M., Siegel, D. S. and Mustar, P. (2017). An emerging ecosystem for student start-ups. *The Journal of Technology Transfer*, 42(4), 909–922.

New initiatives in student entrepreneurship programs are moving rapidly beyond traditional classroom teaching to experiential learning, which is associated with improved employment outcomes for students [Gosen and Washbush (2004). *Simul Gaming*, 35, 270–293]. Unfortunately, we lack a framework to understand the ecosystem required to enable our students to launch successful startups. In this article, we develop such a framework. The elements of this framework include university mechanisms to facilitate student entrepreneurship, along with a continuum of involvement from pre-accelerators through to accelerators; the involvement of a variety of entrepreneurs, support actors and investors; the particular nature of the university environment and the external context; and their evolution over time. We also consider the important issue of funding mechanisms.

(3) Hayter, C. S., Lubynsky, R. and Maroulis, S. (2017). Who is the academic entrepreneur? The role of graduate students in the development

of university spinoffs. *The Journal of Technology Transfer*, 42(6), 1237–1254.

Academic entrepreneurship, the establishment of new companies based on technologies derived from university research, is a well-recognized driver of regional and national economic development. For more than a decade, scholars have conceptualized individual university faculty as the primary agents of academic entrepreneurship. Recent research suggests that graduate students also play a critical role in the establishment and early development of university spinoff companies, but the nature of their involvement through the entrepreneurial process is not yet fully understood. Employing a case study approach, this paper investigates the role of graduate students in early-stage university spinoff companies from the MIT. We find that graduate students play role similar to that of individual faculty entrepreneurs in university spinoffs, both in terms of making the initial establishment decision and in reconfiguring the organization for marketable technology development. We also find that student entrepreneurs face unique challenges involving conflicts with faculty advisors and other students.

(4) Astebro, T. B., Braguinsky, S., Braunerhjelm, P. and Broström, A. (2016). Academic Entrepreneurship: Bayh-Dole versus the 'Professor's Privilege'. HEC Paris Research Paper No. SPE-2015-1118.

This article explores whether the Bayh-Dole intellectual property regime is associated with more, and more valuable academic entrepreneurship than the "Professor's Privilege" regime. Using data on US STEM Ph.D.'s becoming entrepreneurs during 1993–2006 and similar data from Sweden we present evidence showing that in both countries the entry rate into entrepreneurship is lower for those originating from academia than for those originating from non-university employment, and that the relative rate of academic entrepreneurship is slightly lower in the US than in Sweden. We also find that the mean economic gains for becoming an entrepreneur is negative, both for Ph.D.'s originating from academia and non-university alike in both countries. Further analysis indicates that in both countries there is selection from the bottom of the ability distribution among academics. The results suggest that policies aimed at screening entrepreneurial decisions by younger, tenure-track academics may be more effective than general incentives to increase academic entrepreneurship.

References

Gibb, A. and Hannonn, P. (2006). Towards the entrepreneurial university. *International Journal of Entrepreneurship Education*, 4(1), 73–110.

Hisrich, R. D., Peters, M. D. and Shepherd, D. A. (2017). *Entrepreneurship*, 10th edition. New York: McGraw-Hill Education, p. 11.

Klofsen, M. and Jones-Evans, D. (2000). Company academic entrepreneurship in Europe: The case of Sweden and Ireland. *Small Business Economics*, 14(4), 299–309.

Lockett, A., Siegel, D., Wright, M. and Ensley, M. D. (2005). The creation of spin-off firms of public-research institutions: Managerial and policy implications. *Research Policy*, 4, 981–993.

Lockett, A., Wright, M. and Wild, A. (2014). The institutionalization of third stream activities in U.K. higher education: The role of discourse and metrics. *British Journal of Management*, DOI: 10.1111/1467-8551.12069.

Newman (1852). *The Idea of an University*. London: Longmans, Green and Company.

Ostereich, T. (1913). Pope St. Gregory. In: Herbermann, C. (ed.), *Catholic Encyclopedia*. New York: Robert Appleton Company.

Rasmussen, E., Mosey, S. and Wright, M. (2014). The influence of university departments on the evaluation of entrepreneurial competence in spin-off ventures. *Research Policy*, 43, 92–106.

Riche, P. (1978). *Education and Culture in the Barbarian West From the Sixth through Eighth Century*. Columbia: University of South Carolina Press, pp. 126–127 and 292–298.

Ruegg, W. (1992). Forward: The University as a European Institution. In: *A History of the University in Europe, Vol.1: Universities in the Middle Ages*. London: Cambridge University Press, pp. xix–xx.

Slaughter, S. and Leslie, L. L. (1997). *Academic Capitalism: Politics, Policies, and the Entrepreneurial University*. Baltimore: John Hopkins University Press.

Tijssen, R. J. (2006). Universities and industrially relevant science: Toward measurement models and indicators of entrepreneurial orientation. *Research Policy*, 35(10), 1569–1585.

Wigren-Kristolersan, C., Gabrielson, J. and Kitagawa, F. (2011). Mind the gap and bridge the gap: Research excellence and the diffusion of academic knowledge in Sweden. *Science and Public Policy*, 38(6), 481–492.

Chapter 2

Establishing and Managing a University Entrepreneurial Eco-System

Learning Objectives

- Understand the concept of an entrepreneurial ecosystem.
- Learn the various models, features, and components of establishing a university entrepreneurial ecosystem.
- Gain knowledge of what makes a successful university entrepreneurial ecosystem.
- Understand elements involved in managing an entrepreneurial ecosystem.

Opening Profile — David Musial

Q1: Submitter information

Name of Nominee	**David Musial**
Email	David@ProfessorMusial.com
Phone Number	917-626-5956

Professor David Musial is an award-winning, entrepreneurial multimedia producer and educator with over 30 years of a wide variety of experience in the multimedia industry. Currently Prof. Musial is developing the Smart

Trax® at the Massachusetts Institute of Technology with the unique MusicTech Kids®, MusicTech Teens™ programs, and the NextGen Stars® Media Arts Lab & TV Show Series. In 2004, Stevens Institute of Technology engaged Professor Musial to create a BA Program in Music Technology applying his experience and knowledge to education. To facilitate the growth of the program and to attract students, Professor Musial launched Stevens Multimedia, LLC (SMM) with its first division — Castle Point Records (CPR) a student-run record label providing an experiential entrepreneurial experience for the program's students. The students became part of an actual company, provided its management, and learned aspects of the music industry. The students saw CPR as an opportunity to develop the necessary skills through hands-on corporate experience and as a great stepping stone to learn about the needs and work involved. CPR, became a multimedia startup corporation Stevens Multi Media, LLC, that Professor Musial started at Stevens, comprised of a publishing unit and a production company.

This experiential approach was successful. The program had over 60 full-time majors by 2012, and graduates pursued careers at major record labels, publishing firms, and radio stations. The curriculum Professor Musial designed for the Music Technology degree, won second place in America in 2012 by "Best Colleges" as "The Most Innovative College Music Programs Changing the Industry." Castle Point Records and Musial's approach to the music technology program illustrates with the right guidance and mentoring, *students can learn and execute successful entrepreneurial efforts from within the classroom to beyond the classroom* leading to career goals. Also, such efforts can result in increased enrollment for the programs at the university and as equally important — retention of students.

In 2011, Prof. Musial inspired and produced "Project Eleven" with students from all over America, including those from CPR. The live concert was on the USS WASP Aircraft Carrier in May 2012 that was aired nationally on SIRIUS XM featured on *FOX News.* His education included a full artistic sponsorship to the Juilliard School of Music and NYU for his first masters and a full-teaching fellowship to NYU for his second masters. His numerous honors include an award from the US

Department of Justice commending the lifetime success of his educational positive message media company "Smart Trax®." His "Take A Stand" project for the United States Department of Education earned an Emmy Award in MTV. His music video "Brave New American Heroes" was inducted into the 9/11 National Memorial, and Musial was inducted into the prestigious "Buffalo Music Hall-Of-Fame", along with his mentor Bob Moog, and entertainers like Aretha Franklyn and Rick James.

Q2: The nominee's position when they created the company. Describe the nominee's process with the university as they were creating the company.
Professor Musial was the founding head of the Music Technology BA Program, when he founded Stevens MultiMedia, (SSM) LLC and Castle Point Records (CPR). He performed dual roles in creating the company. One was to grow the Music Technology Program and the other was to establish CPR and tie into the classroom experience. This provided a means to grow the program, enhance the music industry learning experience, and prepare students for careers in the recording industry by experiencing various aspects of the music industry.

As part of the process, Musial met with Dr. Helena Wisniewski, who was the Vice-President of University Research and Enterprise Development, to discuss his ideas for the company and the program. She enthusiastically encouraged and supported CPR, working with Musial and the students to establish the program. She provided initial funding as well as guidance on the business plan and the structure. She stayed involved to encourage students and became one of its Directors. Both SMM and CPR then became part of the Stevens "Technogenesis™" portfolio of companies. The Executive Director & Producer of SMM was Prof. Musial. To provide additional guidance and real-world experience he chose external mentors. Carlos Alomar, a top performing artist and lead guitarist for David Bowie with 32 platinum records and Robert Harari, a producer, and composer who owns a production studio in NJ called HarariVille to provide corporate experience and skills necessary for the recording industry. The students ran the record label. The company Presidents were seniors and juniors, the VPs juniors, and other officers' were undergraduate students involved throughout their undergraduate years as part of their learning experience.

Q3: Describe the nominee's experience working with the university in creating the company. What were the challenges? What support did they receive?

A challenge was convincing some of the senior administration about the benefits of CPR for the students and for the Music Technology & Art Technology Programs. In addition to convincing students of CPR's benefits; CPR experienced success quickly. The Vice-President for Research and Enterprise Development, Dr. Wisniewski, encouraged and supported CPR from the start; working with the students and their mentors to make it successful. She felt CPR exemplified what Steven's learning environment was about — students collaborating with faculty and professionals in an industry to create new sustainable, market-based initiatives, and enrich the learning environment for current and future students. However, *the main challenges* Prof. Musial faced were to convince the university to provide additional funding for CPR and to build a recording studio/facility. He felt CPR and the program needed recording facility to reach the program's full growth potential. It would both attract and retain students while providing the needed professional infrastructure for growth. Despite providing strong justification the university did not provide the facility.

Q4: What happened to the company the nominee created? Describe in detail where it is now and how it is doing. What is the history of the company?

Its history can be best described from the fact that it was successful in achieving its objectives, CPR continued to experience many successes through the years, and the Music Technology Program continued to grow. The students participating in CPR went on to pursue careers they desired in the music, recording and related industries; using skills they learned from CPR. These careers include major record labels, publishing firms, and radio stations: SkyRoom Studios, Warner, Universal, ABC TV, SPIN, *Rolling Stone*, *TIME Magazine*, Atlantic, NYC Radio Stations, SIRIUS Satellite Radio, and firms in Hollywood while others went on to record songs that made the Billboard Charts. In addition, many of the artists they discovered did well. Under the guidance of Musial and their external mentors, Carlos Alomar and Robert Harari; the students' experience included how to recognize talent, how to find and contract new talent from clubs in NJ and NYC, as well as recorded, developed, and implemented marketing and sales strategies. The students initially signed NYC area bands — Last Perfect Thing and John Connor for their first CD — *Delusions of Grandeur.* Subsequently, they added WMD and Cori Yarkin who would later be featured in *Rolling Stone.* Rob Harari provided use of HarariVille to record and mix tracks for the students to produce their CDs, and teamed up with Carlos Alomar to produce the recording sessions. Musial introduced CPR to his Grammy award winning associate Scott Hall who mastered the album. A kickoff event for the CD was at Maxwells, a popular club in Hoboken, NJ. As part of their marketing campaign, CPR organized a concert that featured Cori Yarkin; sold CDs and memorabilia; they had a deal with Tower Records to sell their CDs; and later migrated to iTunes. *Status:* The Music Technology Program discontinued despite successes, the University closed CPR in 2012. Since then, CPR has evolved into the Audio Engineering Club, a very successful Student Government Organization on Campus under the guidance of Rob Harari, who since 2005 has been an Industry Associate Professor in Music & Technology at Stevens.

Introduction

Over the last two decades, the majority of job creation in the United States has occurred in young, startup companies. In addition, innovation and its real-world application, is all around us. From breakthroughs in medicine and genetics to clean technologies, social media, or education technologies; innovation is becoming a more critical part of all of the products and services available today. While the United States remains the global leader in innovation and entrepreneurship, there is constant competition from around the world to maintain that leadership.

In response, universities are taking a more prominent role in advancing economic development and many universities are developing entrepreneurial ecosystems. These ecosystems are becoming increasingly important in facilitating innovation and entrepreneurial opportunities in today's knowledge-based economies.

This emerging role of universities as entrepreneurial ecosystems requires institutions to develop a new culture of enterprise and innovation and new strategic directions regarding academic entrepreneurship. The creation and maintenance of a transformational and progressive entrepreneurial ecosystem within the university environment is essential to foster, support, develop, and commercialize new technologies.

This chapter focuses on the elements needed in a university ecosystem for encouraging, developing, and monetizing innovation for the university. It concludes with a discussion of the aspects of establishing and implementing the innovation of the university.

The process of technology commercialization by universities has changed dramatically in the last few years. Many universities are contributing to social impact and wealth in their regions through the commercialization of their technology. Academic entrepreneurship is becoming part of the strategic mission of many universities, and the breadth of stakeholders involved has expanded to develop entrepreneurial ecosystems that connect entrepreneurship and innovation. Raising capital, finding talent, and overcoming bureaucracy are three of the top challenges entrepreneurial universities face.

Overview: The Concept of Entrepreneurial Ecosystems

The idea of an entrepreneurial ecosystem was proposed by Daniel Isenberg in 2010, in the *Harvard Business Review*. It is a complex, adaptive system — a constellation of connections between components of ecosystem where relationships between individual elements are non-linear thus dynamic. An ecosystem is a dynamic structure that is formed by interconnected organizations which could be the new ventures, large corporations, government, industry associations, individual investors, public sector organizations, universities, and research centers. The system is complex as macrolevel and microlevel interactions among individual elements influence each other (see Figure 1).

However, there is no set definition of an entrepreneurial ecosystem, as each is unique, but there are some commonalities exhibited by successful

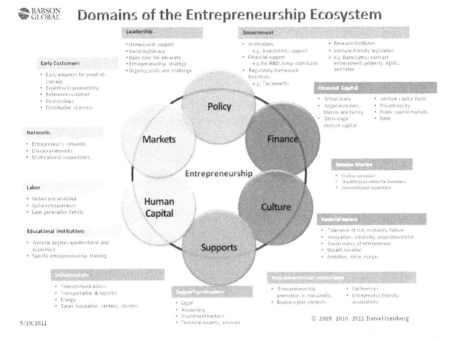

Figure 1.   Isenberg's model of an entrepreneurship ecosystem (Forbes, 2011; Mason and Brown, 2014).

ones. Isenberg identifies six domains within the entrepreneurial system: a conducive culture, enabling policies and leadership, availability of appropriate finances, quality human capital, venture friendly markets for products, and a range of institutional supports (Figure 1). At the center of this diagram is the entrepreneur. He emphasizes the importance of context: each ecosystem emerges under a unique set of conditions and circumstances.

Entrepreneurial ecosystems can be industry specific or may have evolved from a single industry to include several industries. They are geographically bounded but not confined to a specific geographical scale (e.g., campus, city, region), and they are not related to particular sizes of city. According to Isenberg, this approach potentially "replaces" or becomes a "precondition" for the successful deployment of cluster strategies, innovation systems, knowledge economy, or national competitiveness policies. This model may be modified for particular universities or institutions, but the basic six domains of the model are followed.

Elements of a University Entrepreneurial Ecosystem

Most people are familiar with the traditional centers of university-based innovation and entrepreneurship such as the Massachusetts Institute of Technology (MIT) and its connection to the Greater Boston entrepreneurship ecosystem, or Stanford and Silicon Valley. But over the last decade, more universities have embraced innovation and entrepreneurship as critical to their mission and role in their communities.

Historically, a large portion of America's investments in innovative companies has been centered in the metropolitan regions of San Francisco/Silicon Valley; Greater Boston; New York/New Jersey; Austin, TX; Seattle, WA; Washington D.C.; and San Diego. However, universities outside of these areas are now leading the charge to model new entrepreneurial ecosystems, according to the National Advisory Council on Innovation & Entrepreneurship (NACIE). For example, the University of Michigan's efforts in Michigan, Arizona State University's impact in the Phoenix area, the University of Akron's work in Ohio, and the University of Southern California's efforts in the Los Angeles area. In addition, hundreds of colleges and universities across the US are creating entrepreneurship programs with the short-term objective of creating educational value for their students and the long-term objective of driving economic growth in their communities through locally developed enterprises.

Pillars of innovation and entrepreneurship

A McKinsey Global Institute (2011) (MGI) Report on *Entrepreneurship* indicated there are three pillars to the platform that enables innovation and entrepreneurship to flourish, and universities are increasingly driving or involved in each of these factors as follows:

- developing innovation ecosystems,
- creating an entrepreneurial culture,
- providing sustained financing for new ventures.

○ **Developing an Innovation Ecosystem:** This is critical for the long-term success and quality of entrepreneurial activity. It is important to have a strong local base for entrepreneurship that is supported by regional economic development plans. American colleges and universities are often the centerpieces of regional economic development strategies not only because they are often the main source of innovation, but also train the local talent base and workforce to connect various networks to achieve a common agenda.

○ **Entrepreneurial Culture:** To achieve and sustain an entrepreneurial innovation ecosystem often necessitates cultural change on campuses and within communities. This includes making change a priority and incorporating into the university goals, as well as ranging from targeted entrepreneurship education to greater ties with local industry.

○ **Sustained Financing for New Ventures:** This factor is the importance of available financing, in particular, early-stage and sustained financing. While colleges and universities traditionally have not provided financing for company startups, they have begun creating their own investment funds to support their home-grown entrepreneurs. Sometimes these funds are created through university endowments, specialized donations, or sponsorships.

Models for university entrepreneurial ecosystems

Some models that universities have employed for developing successful ecosystems are as follows:

According to the MIT: Skoltech-entrepreneurial-ecosystems-report-2014 (Graham, 2014), most universities have employed one of the two following models: community led or university led.

• **Community-led model:** *Catalyzed by students, alumni and entrepreneurs in the regional economy.* This model is created through strong partnerships of trust between the regional entrepreneurial community and the university. The investment is focused on regional rather than institutional capacity; universities often downplay the importance of IP ownership and startup affiliation, regarding these as secondary to the overarching goal of developing the broader ecosystem. Community-led responds to economic and societal challenges, and entrepreneurship and innovation development. It is triggered by a desire to stimulate regional economic growth, and thereby create graduate jobs, research opportunities, and broader avenues for university support through the creation of a vibrant localized entrepreneurial ecosystem.

- **University-led model:** *Working through established university structures.* This model builds on established university research strengths, and offers a robust and fully institutionalized approach. It is typically triggered by the desire to realize income from university research with the entrepreneur, an innovation agenda driven by and focused on a strong technology transfer office (TTO) (or equivalent), and senior administrative support. However, there is a danger that the university's entrepreneurial and innovation policies become "synonymous" with those of the TTO, leading to a culture where "only university-protected IP is seen as worthwhile." Thus marginalizing student, alumni, and regional entrepreneurial communities.

Common Factors in Establishing Entrepreneurial Ecosystems at Universities

Despite choice of model, as well as geography, culture and institutional profiles, there are common factors among universities that have been successful in establishing entrepreneurial ecosystems. The National Advisory Council on Innovation & Entrepreneurship (NACIE) (The Innovative and Entrepreneurial University, 2013) and other organizations have identified focus categories at the heart of the innovation and entrepreneurship ecosystem activities within America's universities. These categories include the following:

- promoting student innovation and entrepreneurship,
- encouraging faculty innovation and entrepreneurship,
- supporting the Technology Transfer Function,
- facilitating Industry collaboration,

- engaging in regional economic development,
- creating a culture of innovation and entrepreneurship.

All these points provide methods to help achieve entrepreneurial ecosystems, and they also involve support from the senior management who made it a priority and part of the university's mission.

Promoting student innovation and entrepreneurship

Many universities are expanding their educational curricula and programs to foster innovation and entrepreneurship. They offer courses and programs in entrepreneurship and related fields for undergraduate, graduate, and postdoctoral students. Students develop a better understanding of innovation and entrepreneurship, through majors, minors, and certificate programs and through educational programs that emphasize hands-on learning. Student clubs, centered on multi-dimensional entrepreneurship activities, also are on the rise. Most campuses run a variety of business plans and venture competitions that offer students mentors and training seminars to help students further develop their innovative ideas.

Courses and degree programs in innovation and entrepreneurship: Many universities are consistently seeing an increase in student demand for innovation and entrepreneurship, and are broadening course and program offerings. Entrepreneurship courses and programs equip students with a wide range of valuable skills including business-plan development, marketing, networking, creating "elevator pitches", attracting financing (such as seed capital), and connecting with local business leaders. Some universities are offering bachelor's and master's degree programs and concentrations in innovation and entrepreneurship. Some business schools are breaking down traditional barriers and encouraging entrepreneurship through multi-disciplinary courses and programs to students of all academic disciplines. For example, the University of Colorado's Innovation and Entrepreneur Degree Program offers a Bachelor's degree in Innovation, which provides a unique multi-disciplinary team.

Experiential learning: This actively engages students in innovative and entrepreneurial activities through workshops, conferences, internships, hands-on experience, and real-world projects. It uses specialized internship programs focused on entrepreneurship education and technology innovation that match students directly to startup projects, TTOs, venture capital firms, and industry. For example, students at the University of Alaska Anchorage, as part of their entrepreneurship courses, create an investor pitch based on a startup and present it at community events such as 1 Million Cups that was developed by the Kaufman Foundation or they work with CEOs of local startups. This variety of educational opportunities allows students to address real-world challenges in a supportive educational environment. For example, the University of California at San Diego's Rady School of Business requires its management students to take a course entitled "Lab to Market." In Lab to Market, MBAs create new products or services and go through the commercialization process, with advice from faculty and business mentors.

Competitive opportunities: Competitions are an excellent way to actively engage faculty and students in the learning process. As a whole, business plan competitions are geared toward teaching students how to think outside the classroom, foster collaborations across disciplines, and increase access to businesses. Competitions provide an exciting platform for students to learn practical skills such as how to craft a business plan, access venture funding, and pitch ideas. Sequential competitions build upon project ideas, ultimately leading to completed business plans that are ready for possible funding from investors. Universities understand this and are transitioning away from single monetary rewards for competitions while increasingly recognizing milestone achievements with a multitude of prizes, including non-monetary resources such as incubator space and mentorships. Rice University makes over $1.2 million available in cash, prizes, and in-kind resources to winners that provide seed funding to launch their companies. These funds serve as seed funding for many of the winning teams. Florida Atlantic University (FAU) provides the winner of their business plan competition with free space in the incubator for half a year.

Entrepreneurial and innovation collaboration spaces: Entrepreneurial and innovation "living spaces" are a unique trend in motivating student involvement outside the classroom setting. These spaces use the power of proximity to promote student engagement in developing innovative ideas and starting businesses. Entrepreneurial spaces facilitate student access to learning and networking opportunities with local entrepreneurs and innovators. These spaces also host a variety of student entrepreneur clubs that serve as a premier resource for aspiring student entrepreneurs and foster a community of like-minded peers. These clubs are geared toward building financial literacy and leadership skills, as well as encouraging students to pursue commercialization opportunities for innovative ideas and technologies.

Encouraging faculty innovation and entrepreneurship

Rewarding and incentivizing faculty innovation and entrepreneurship: Universities and colleges are celebrating faculty achievements in innovation and entrepreneurship. These acknowledgments include campus-wide prizes and award ceremonies that bring the faculty community together to recognize and learn about the accomplishments of their peers across academic disciplines. Awards such as "Innovator of the Year" and "Faculty Entrepreneur of the Year" are popular as they reward faculty for achievements that reach beyond traditional research and teaching accomplishments. In addition, some universities have established a "Patent Wall of Fame" for when a faculty or student's patent is issued; they are inducted at a ceremony held once a year and a patent plaque of their first page of their patent describing their invention is placed on the wall of fame to inspire others. Some universities have Membership in the National Academy of Inventors to create a Chapter of the National Academy of Inventors at their university. They induct faculty and students as Chapter Members at a special ceremony that often includes community leaders, and both Fellows of and Board Members of the NAI.

Universities and colleges are updating tenure and sabbatical leave guidelines to encourage faculty to pursue collaborative and entrepreneurial endeavors, such as launching a startup company. Some programs allow faculty time-off to engage in innovation and entrepreneurial activities, without incurring any penalty toward tenure and promotion. Providing leave to pursue entrepreneurial activities increases the potential for the successful technology development and commercialization of research.

This flexibility also improves the focus of R&D efforts and facilitates public engagement by encouraging faculty to commercialize their research. Some universities provide funding to encourage entrepreneurship and innovation.

For example, the University of Southern California — promotes faculty entrepreneurship and innovation by supporting, rewarding, and funding the work of faculty members. The Lloyd Greif Center for Entrepreneurial Studies (The Innovative and Entrepreneurial University, 2013) presents three faculty members with research grants totaling $11,000 as part of their annual Faculty Research Awards. The Center also rewards entrepreneurial-minded faculty with the annual Greif Research Impact Award, which is given to the faculty member who has written an article that has the most effect on the area of entrepreneurship.

The University of Alaska Anchorage instituted the Innovate Awards to inspire research, creative works, and innovation. These awards provide $100,000 annually in funding to launch critical endeavors, interdisciplinary collaborations, and inventions. Faculty receive $10,000 for individual awards and $25,000 for a collaborative team; with 7–10 awards given. These have resulted in patents, the basis for startups, and received a six-fold financial return on research investment through external grants acquired by award recipients. Students are often included as part of a team. UAA also has a Patent Wall of Fame to recognize inventors.

Engaging with industry: A common theme developing across campuses large and small is the importance of creating connections between faculty and the outside world. Faculty is increasing its engagement with industry to obtain research and technology development ideas, capital, and other types of support. Many universities host events to bring faculty, industry, angel investors, and venture capitalists together for networking opportunities. These events give industry an early look at R&D activities on campus, while providing faculty with networking and funding possibilities. Examples of such events include lunch-and-learn series, rapid-fire networking programs, seminars, and workshops. In addition, universities are hosting special events for World IP Day. These events include speakers from venture firms, entrepreneurs, community leaders, and best ideas contests to acknowledge innovation, invention and IP, as well as connect the university with the community. Often community organizations and local companies will co-sponsor the events.

Actively supporting the university technology transfer function

University TTOs and Technology Licensing Offices (TLOs) have traditionally been the hubs within universities where innovators and outside business leaders engage to commercialize inventions. The recent increase of entrepreneurship on campuses has greatly expanded the role of the TTOs and TLOs. Instead of merely focusing on the commercialization of individual technologies, these offices now act as a central point where students, faculty, alumni, entrepreneurs, investors, and industry can connect with each other.

Effectively transforming research and ideas into marketable products and services is often a lengthy and complex process requiring substantial resources. A TTO at a college or university helps protect and promote the research developed by its faculty and students through commercialization and patents. The process begin with an invention disclosure, then discusses whether the inventors should apply for a patent, followed by the protection of IP, and whether to form a startup or license which are described in Chapter 3.

Reducing technology transfer barriers: A high priority for the nation's university and college system is to streamline the technology transfer process, to more effectively identify research with market potential, and to move from the lab to the marketplace. An emerging trend in technology transfer is the establishment of "one-stop-shops" that provides assistance, mentorship, and information on patenting and licensing processes to faculty and student inventors. These "shops" streamline the technology disclosure process and integrate all technology transfer functions into one facility. Some universities have created a commercialization infrastructure to streamline processes and provide a focus for faculty and students. Figure 2 illustrates an example of such an infrastructure that the author had created at UAA. Seawolf Holdings, LLC is a wholly owned subsidiary of UAA housed in the Office of Research and Graduate Studies (ORGS) that also has the TTO. It streamlines processes and provides support structure for commercialization to the faculty. It provides a corporate interface between UAA and its enterprise companies and licenses UAA's

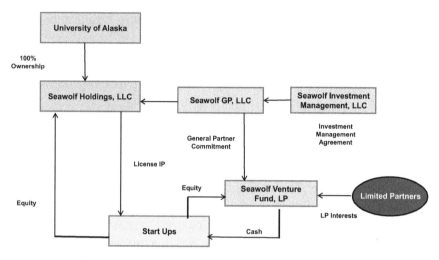

Figure 2. UAA technology commercialization infrastructure.

intellectual property to any entity interested in licensing. It also licenses IP to startups and holds equity shares in those companies on behalf of the university. It insulates the university from liabilities and is managed by an independent Board of Directors consisting of industry leaders and entrepreneurs. This infrastructure includes Seawolf Venture Fund established to provide UAA's startups with early-stage funding. Using this infrastructure, together with incentives from the Innovate Awards and Patent Wall of Fame, ORGS had spearheaded dramatic growth in intellectual property and forming startups.

TTOs are also involved in identifying and supporting entrepreneurship on campus and nurturing inventions and innovation by working closely with faculty and students to recognize patentability in their research or invention and to help them through the process. They assist faculty and students with startup potential for their inventions, provide support for the formation of their startup, help to develop a successful business model and plan, provide guidelines for startups (Figure 3), provide marketing materials, connect them with potential investors, and create companies that will be based in the communities around the university. TTOs provide guidance in navigating licensing processes and commercialization opportunities for innovative work.

Dr. Helena's Top 10 Business Rules for Start Ups

- **Rule 1: Know What Business You Are In.**

- **Rule 2: Understand Who/what Your Competition Is.**

- **Rule 3: Does Your Product Fulfill a Critical Need? Or, is it a nice to have?**

- **Rule 4: Understand Who Your Customers Are.**
  - o Individual consumers, corporations, government, other.

- **Rule 5: A Good Business Plan.**
  - o Key are a strong business model, and a compelling value proposition.

- **Rule 6: Strong Management Team.**
  Most VC firms would rather fund:
  - o a "B technology and an A management team."
  - o Than an "A technology and B management team."

- **Rule 7: Flexibility.**
  - o Do not be tied to your technical concept.

- **Rule 8: Protect your Intellectual Property.**
  - o It is your chief commodity.

- **Rule 9: Have an Exit Strategy.**

- **Rule 10: If You Cannot Walk Away From the Deal, It Is Not a Good Deal.**

Figure 3. The author's top 10 rules for startups.

California Institute of Technology (CalTech) — Files a provisional patent application for every single disclosure that goes through their TTO and later evaluates the technical and business merits over the first year.

A fast growing trend in this area is the rise of Proof of Concept Centers, such as the MIT Deshpande Center for Technological Innovation and the Von Liebig Center at the University of California San Diego. These centers have a variety of programs that collectively achieve three goals: increase the volume and diversity of entrepreneurship on campus, improve the quality of startups and entrepreneurs on campus, and be increasingly engaged with local investors and entrepreneurs so that the university's startups stay local.

The success of these technology transfer efforts at universities is evident by an increase in licensing and startup activity. The Association of University Technology Managers (AUTM) illustrated how universities are driving the Innovation Economy through the following examples of academic technology transfer in numbers. From 1996 to 2015, up to $1.3 trillion was contributed to US gross industrial output; 4.3 million jobs supported; 380,000 invention disclosures and 80,000 patents were issued to research universities; 11,000 startups were formed; and since the Bayh–Dole Act, more than 200 drugs and vaccines were developed through public–private partnerships. Also, according to a licensing survey by AUTM in FY 2016, total license income climbed to almost $3 billion, an increase of 17.5% over 2015. Equity cash-out also contributed to this overall gain, increasing 89.1% as compared to 2015. Notably, this increase does not include the reported $1.14 billion sale of royalty rights in Xtandi® to Royalty Pharma from the University of California. New patent applications have been steadily increasing year after year. Provisional applications filed in the United States (12,114) increased 5.2% over 2015. The number of US-issued patents (7,021) grew 5.1% since 2015. In FY2016, there were 1,024 startup companies formed and research institutions received equity from 495 of these startups, an increase of 5.1% over 2015. In addition, 800 new products were introduced into the marketplace in 2016 by universities. These numbers show that innovations born out of academic research often lead to the formation of new companies that develop new products, create jobs, and spark economic growth.

Facilitating university–industry collaboration

University–industry partnerships are essential for further developing ideas and technologies derived from university research. These partnerships are crucial for directing investment toward commercially promising research and helping to bridge funding gaps that often exist at the technology development and marketing stages. Universities and industry have found that working together is mutually beneficial because knowledge and resources are shared to achieve common goals. Industry benefits from greater and earlier access to scientific expertise, intellectual property, and commercial opportunities; while universities benefit from enhanced educational opportunities for faculty and students, ways to connect their research and students' education to emerging industry interests, revenues from successful licensing agreements and ventures, and local and regional development.

Sharing resources and knowledge: To facilitate greater collaboration and innovation, universities are opening up their facilities, faculty, and students to businesses (small and large) in the hopes of creating greater economic value. Universities are strategically partnering with companies, offering internships and externships, sharing facilities with startups, such as accelerators, and creating venture funds and incentive programs funded by industry; all of which drive increased innovation and product development by university students, faculty, and staff.

Universities with specific strengths in the areas of manufacturing or energy research have established long-term partnerships with large corporations, such as BMW®, FedEx®, Johnson Controls®, IBM®, Cisco®, Proctor & Gamble®, and Minova®. These relationships allow students and faculty to engage in cutting-edge research while helping solve industry problems. As an example, 'Tulane University' works to establish partnerships with smaller local companies not only to support the university's research but also to engage with the local community in a mutually beneficial way.

Examples of university–industry partnerships (The Innovative and Entrepreneurial University, 2013): The University of Minnesota's IPrime (Industrial Partnership for Research in Interfacial and Materials Engineering) was created in 2000 and is a university/industry partnership based on two-way knowledge transfer. The partnership is a consortium of more than 40 companies supporting fundamental collaborative research on materials. Participation in IPrime affords companies the chance to scan a wide range of scientific and technological developments and delve into the fundamental science that undergirds their products. A principal goal of IPrime is the engagement of industrial scientists and engineers in a pre-competitive, non-proprietary, and collaborative environment that promotes hands-on participation by visiting industrial scientists with IPrime faculty, students, and postdoctoral associates.

Clemson University's International Center for Automotive Research (CU-ICAR) is an advanced-technology research campus where university, industry, and government organizations collaborate. In the university's labs and testing facilities — automotive, motorsports, aerospace, and mobility experts work together on R&D. The Center's focus on applied education and direct engagement with industry leaders includes cutting-edge curriculum development and research capabilities focused on current trends and related issues in the automotive industry. Partners, such as BMW®, Michelin®, and Koyo® work with students and faculty to focus on systems engineering through automotive R&D.

Creative ways to draw industry partners to campus: Universities, as regional hubs of innovation and entrepreneurship, are developing creative ways to draw industry partners to campus. Emerging trends to increase industry presence on campus and facilitate conversations on new ideas and technology include: web portals that provide industry with access to university resources, networking events such as breakfast forums and casual roundtable discussions, and structured/intensive student and faculty internships in the private sector. Stevens Institute of Technology held "Disruptive Technology Roundtables." These monthly luncheon forums were to inform the business community and investors in the tri-state area about the university's technology. Cornell University IP&Pizza™ and IP&Pasta™ host outreach activities to Cornell faculty, research staff, and students. The goal of these activities is to increase appreciation of the importance of making university research results useful to society, providing a basic knowledge and understanding of intellectual property issues, and creating an awareness of capturing and protecting valuable intellectual property and its importance to entice potential industry partners. This and other similar programs are run through Cornell's Center for Technology and Enterprise and Commercialization.

Industry speaker series are another popular tool for engaging university and industry scientists in discussions of commercialization opportunities available in the private sector. On some campuses, students and faculty members participate in semester-long internships with an industry to learn and solve scientific and technology development challenges.

Accelerators: Another emerging trend is the development of "accelerators" and related initiatives located in and around university campuses. These accelerators are partnerships between universities and companies that are designed to fast-track the innovation and commercialization process by providing access to world-class scientific facilities, technical personnel, and testing and diagnostics equipment — resources not readily available to many startups. Some accelerators focus on helping companies in the post-incubation period such as meeting the technical needs of startups and bridging funding gaps.

An example is Georgia Tech's — Flashpoint (The Innovative and Entrepreneurial University, 2013). Flashpoint is a startup accelerator that offers entrepreneurial education and access to experienced mentors, experts, and investors in an immersive, shared-learning, and open work-space. The program, the first public–private partnership of its type in the country, brings together resources from the university, private sector, and startup leaders to accelerate innovation and growth. A $1 million fund, created by an investment firm working with Atlanta angel investors, invested between $15,000 and $25,000 in startup funds for the company. In January 2011, Flashpoint held its first "demo day" with 15 startups from the initial Flashpoint group that included Georgia Tech faculty and students.

Engaging with regional and local economic development efforts

Historically, local economic development has been an important mission of the nation's large universities. Land-grant universities have always felt a strong responsibility for the betterment of their surrounding communities. Universities are increasingly focusing on innovation and entrepreneurship as key contributors to the growth and success of local communities. Universities are requesting the federal government to include commercialization and innovation-driven economic development in their grant programs. In addition, regional economic development planning now often starts with an assessment of a local university's research strengths. In turn, universities are seeking partners to supplement their strengths and overcome their weaknesses through partnerships with community colleges, non-profit economic development agencies, governments, and entrepreneurship groups.

Some of the most effective practices include Tulane University's Social Innovation and Entrepreneurship Program (The Innovative and Entrepreneurial University, 2013) that integrates the university with the surrounding economic ecosystem, thereby contributing to local economic development. Students are required to engage outside the campus with the community, often through entrepreneurial projects. Partnering among schools across the university has created many student-led organizations and social ventures that assist with moving students out of the classroom and into the New Orleans Community. Tulane has also created several university competitions including the Tulane Business Plan Competition, the Urban Innovation Challenge, PitchNOLA, and the NewDay Social

Innovation Challenge to engage students and community partners with local problems while providing them with financial and technical support to create solutions. These programs offer students the opportunity to access over $100,000 in funding annually.

Research corridors: Universities also are encouraging economic development through the creation of research corridors. These corridors reside within and across regions and often have a particular technology focus such as biotechnology, nanotechnology, health, energy, and advanced materials. Corridors offer a resource pipeline for local communities, universities, and colleges that have similar research interests and challenges. They attract the industry by providing technical support, access to capital, and a large network of experts. Some research corridors unite communities across state lines, which allows them to address issues of regional importance, such as green technology, job training for the unemployed, and small business creation. Overall, universities are extending their influence and better serving their communities by participating in research corridors that connect them with other local universities, thereby leveraging the talent and resources of all of the participating institutions.

Examples of research corridors: Pennsylvania State University I-99 Corridor Region has received funding from the NSF Partnership for the Innovation Program and the Commonwealth to leverage Penn State research and education strengths for job creation in nearby counties of Bedford, Blair, and Centre.

The University of Michigan's University Research Corridor (URC) is an alliance between Michigan State University, the University of Michigan and Wayne State University to transform, strengthen, and diversify the state's economy.

Iowa State University's Research Corridor stretches from Ames to De Moines and focuses on research and manufacturing in agriculture, metals, and other areas. ISU and technology companies such as DuPont® and Syngenta® contribute their expertise toward the effort.

The Florida High Tech Corridor Council is an economic development initiative of three of the country's largest research institutions: University of Central Florida, University of South Florida, and University of Florida.

The mission is to grow the high-tech industry, innovation, and the workforce to support the corridor in a 23-county region spanning the state. It facilitates collaborations between partners in academia, industry, and economic development to create communities with unlimited potential.

Innovation districts: Another way universities are involved in engaging with local economic development efforts is through innovation districts that align with the preferences of innovation-minded people and entities. There are different definitions of innovation districts. The following one is from the Brookings Institute. "Innovation districts are geographic areas where leading-edge anchor institutions and companies cluster and connect with startups, business incubators, and accelerators" (Bruce and Julie, 2014). They are physically compact, accessible by public and shared transportation, and feature a mix of housing, office, public spaces, and retail connected by bike paths, pedestrian friendly streets, and green areas. There are three basic models: The anchor plus model; the re-imagined urban areas model; and the urbanized science park. We will discuss the anchor plus model in this chapter, but for the other models and an informative description we refer the reader to the Brookings Article — *The Rise of Innovation Districts: A New Geography of Innovation in America* by Bruce and Julie (2014); and the book *The Smartest Places on Earth* by Agtmael and Bakker (2016).

The anchor plus model (Bruce and Julie, 2014), primarily found in the downtowns and mid-towns of central cities, is where large scale mixed-use development is centered around major anchor institutions and a rich base of related firms, entrepreneurs, and startup companies involved in the commercialization of innovation. The following are some examples of the anchor plus model and their associated institutions. Philadelphia's University City, anchored by The University of Pennsylvania; Kendall Square in Cambridge, MA, the anchor institutions are MIT and Mass General Hospital; in Philadelphia, PA, Drexel University and the University City Science Center; in St. Louis, Washington University, Saint Louis University, and Barnes Jewish Hospital. Other emerging districts include the Greater Oakland neighborhood of Pittsburgh around Carnegie Mellon University and the University of Pittsburgh Medical Center; Midtown Atlanta around Georgia Tech University; downtown and midtown Detroit around the Henry Ford Health System and Wayne State University; Roosevelt Island in New York. One of the newest is in Houston, this innovation district is located in midtown, and sits between downtown and the Texas Medical Center and is within three miles of five universities that include Rice University, and the University of Houston, on a Metro transit line and near an intersection of freeways.

Some Success Stories of Entrepreneurial Ecosystems in Universities

Universities operating within established technology-driven innovation hubs, such as Silicon Valley and Kendall Square in the US, offer robust models for success within these environments. However, an increasing number of universities located within more challenging environments are establishing strong entrepreneurship and innovation profiles and reputations, some of whom will undoubtedly become future national and international leaders in entrepreneurial ecosystems.

A component of a strong ecosystem is that aspiring entrepreneurs can see examples of others in the ecosystem succeeding — no matter how big or small. Success stories send a clear message to individuals that people from this community can be entrepreneurs. Harvard doesn't have this problem; Mark Zuckerberg's is prominent. However, most universities are not in communities with famous names. So having a team reach a key milestone — whether that means a strong performance in a business plan competition, getting angel investors, or launching a product successfully — is social proof to those in the community that they can do it too. Successes of any size serves as a beacon that draws other would-be-entrepreneurs out of the woodwork.

We will present success stories from MIT and Stanford and illustrate how they address the domain and shared factors presented in this chapter, and then proceed to examples from additional universities in the Conclusion.

MIT and Kendall square

To the point of creating academic culture, *at MIT they say that entrepreneurship is in its genes (Dunn, 2005).* MIT has developed dozens of programs and centers that foster the entrepreneurial spirit on campus. "Fifty years ago, there were no formal [entrepreneurial] organizations such as we have today. *But there still was the culture*", says Merton Flemings '51, SM '52, ScD '54, Director of the Lemelson-MIT Program, which supports invention. "Faculty were encouraged to do something with their ideas. It's in the charter that we're not only here to educate and do research but also to serve. Part of serving is interacting with industry."

University-led entrepreneurial activity and faculty and student incentives: *Invention Rewarded Entrepreneurship starts with novel ideas, and MIT is long on them.* Each year, according to the TLO, Institute scientists receive more than $750 million in sponsored-research funding, which leads to about 400 new inventions. The TLO has more than 3,000 patents in its portfolio. MIT routinely ranks among the top three universities in the country in patents received, according to the US Patent and Trademark Office. (In 2004, the top two were the University of California system and the California Institute of Technology.) The campus organization that most visibly promotes invention is the Lemelson-MIT program, established in 1994. Lemelson awards a $30,000 prize annually to an MIT senior or graduate student who shows promise as an inventor.

Students as entrepreneurs: The MIT Deshpande Center for Technological Innovation supports the creators of technology, and the Entrepreneurship Center (E-Center) at MIT's Sloan School of Management nurtures the businesspeople involved with invention. The E-Center's chief purpose is education. Since 1996, it has housed the two dozen entrepreneurship-related courses offered by Sloan, including the I-Teams course. All of the courses are open to students campus wide. "We make an effort to market courses around campus", says former E-Center program manager Bob Ayan, who was known to hand out business cards at places like science and engineering business club meetings.

Two of the E-Center's most popular courses, the Entrepreneurship Lab and the Global Entrepreneurship Lab, place students with real-world companies, where they work for course credit in teams to solve problems "that keep the CEO awake at night." Those problems have included devising a marketing plan for a pre-IPO company and coming up with ways a company could expand. The center also supports several student entrepreneurship groups — including the Venture Capital and Private Equity Club, the BioPharma Business Club, and the $50K — giving office space to some and advice to others. The $50K organizers are concerned that many engineering and science students continue to see the competition as a Sloan event, not one open to them. And it's yet to be determined what roles student-researchers can assume in the Institute spin-off companies they help form. *But entrepreneurship, by its nature, is about taking risks.* So MIT is coming up with new ways — including some that may not always work — to support and nurture its future entrepreneurs.

Entrepreneurial ecosystem: MIT has established itself as an entrepreneurial hub — a place where research and ideas are transformed regularly into products and businesses with broad economic and social impact. MIT's interdisciplinary approach to education helps fuel this entrepreneurial activity, which is often sparked by interactions between students and alumni from MIT Sloan and the Schools of Science and Engineering. *The resulting entrepreneurial ecosystem,* which encompasses Kendall Square and areas far beyond, play a vital role in the life of MIT Sloan and the Institute as a whole.

Stanford University and Silicon Valley

The following is a Stanford case study presented in the Kauffman Fellows publication, *Universities and Entrepreneurial Ecosystems: Elements of the Stanford–Silicon Valley Success.* According to this case study, based on a historical analysis of the roots of Stanford's entrepreneurial ecosystem, there are six conditions that helped create Stanford and Silicon Valley's entrepreneurship and technological innovation (see Figure 4). These are inclusive of those presented earlier. In the following, we discuss each factor in this section: Stanford's risk-taking culture, its student body, the culture of giving back, abundant capital, collaboration with industry, and government support.

Culture: *Stanford's Office of Technology Licensing (OTL)*, established in 1969, has aided in helping commercialize faculty and student research into profitable companies. OTL's goal is to "plant many seeds" by

Figure 4. Six conditions foster the rise of Stanford and Silicon Valley Image, designed by J. Wiguna. https://www.kauffmanfellows.org/journal_posts/universities-and-entrepreneurial-ecosystems-stanford-silicon-valley-success.

transferring technology to as many companies as possible; with hope some of these technologies will flourish. Since its founding, over 200 companies (including Google) have began around technology licensed through OTL. Today there are more than 18,000 invention disclosures, more than 10,000 patents filed, and more than 5,000 licenses granted. Stanford OTL strives to be a partner to students and professors rather than a threat to their startups. For example, the OTL hosts a semi-annual innovation farm team where Stanford students, affiliates, alumni, and inventors meet to discuss the "potential uses of Stanford University technologies as applied in a variety of industries." The benefits of participating in this program range from the "potential for founding a new company" to "actively learning about commercialization, startups, and technology development outside of a classroom."

Government support: An aspect of Stanford's success in research and innovation is the huge role government support has played in funding cutting-edge research (see Figure 4). "Stanford is fundamentally a research university. The primary, almost exclusive source of its research budget is the federal government, particularly the NIH, the NSF, the Defense Departments, and various other federal agencies." When Fredrick Terman was Dean of Engineering, he sought government funding because it was "less restrictive and [a] substantially larger source of funding for building academic research programs", as opposed to industry sponsors that "only wanted to fund work directly related to their own interests."

Stanford students looking to fund a startup have ample opportunities to present their idea or prototype to investors. There are numerous opportunities to meet and connect with potential investors, from startup competitions (BASES 150K / E-Challenge), to classes (Launchpad and Creating a Startup), to meeting with instructors outside of class to discuss potential startup ideas. Students can also develop their startups in several accelerators and incubators that are close to campus, whether it be the Stanford-founded StartX or at Y Combinator or Lightspeed Ventures Summer Fellowship Program. Many instructors on campus have ties to the venture capital industry.

Collaboration with industry: An examination of Stanford's entrepreneurial historical roots reveals that Stanford has instituted a close relationship with industry. For example, Frederick Terman, Stanford's Dean of the School of Engineering from 1945 to 1953 and Provost from 1955 to 1965, deliberately intended the school to have close connections with industry. His emphasis on close collaboration between industry and the university has continued to this day and has ensured that students not only work on pure research but also tackle real-world challenges.

Abundant capital: Funding is a crucial ingredient to help student ideas become reality. Stanford is fortunate to have many venture capitalists close to campus on Sand Hill Road and on University Avenue. Additionally, venture capital's roots also stem from Stanford. Kleiner Perkins Caulfield Byers (KPCB), one of the first funds in the Valley was founded with Stanford faculty. The Mayfield Fund, which started in 1968, was also established by Stanford faculty. The Mayfield Fund is a generous sponsor of its namesake the Mayfield Fellows Program, a 9-month work/study program that attracts the university's top undergraduate and coterminal student talent. The founders of Instagram (Kevin Systrom and Mike Krieger) are Mayfield Fellows alums.

Summary: As this study reflects, merely appropriating physical space and designating a research institute is not enough. To build a community such as Stanford's requires: prescient leadership; government funding; top students engaged in cutting-edge research; private sources of capital for entrepreneurs; collaboration between industry and academia; the development of multidisciplinary students; a community that seeks to help the next generation of entrepreneurs; and a risk-taking culture. These are just a few of the features of the Stanford–Silicon Valley community.

Managing an Entrepreneurial Ecosystem

Talent needs to be nurtured to flourish

Entrepreneurs and innovators need an enabling and empowering environments, which not only ensure that their game-changing ideas are translated into actionable pursuits, but also ensure these entrepreneurs have the necessary ecosystem in which they can thrive and prosper. This is where ensuring that all the success factors in the section in this chapter "Common Factors in Establishing Entrepreneurial Ecosystems at Universities" are applied through policies and processes, and play an active role in nurturing success.

Adaptive management

Ecosystem management occurs when management is applied to the whole ecosystem, not just to single startups or organizations. It requires an understanding of the role of people, talent, and money as components of the ecosystems and the use of adaptive management. Although driven by explicit goals and executed by policies and processes, ecosystem management needs to be adaptable. This adaptability is achieved by monitoring the interactions and processes necessary to sustain ecosystem structures and functions. The purpose of adaptive management is to manage areas in a variety of scales to ensure the ecosystem services and resources are preserved, while appropriate resource use is sustained. This includes engaging a variety of stakeholders including entrepreneurs, inventors, the government, bureaucracy, funders, and consumers. Ecosystem services are typically created in a variety of one-to-one inter-actions among ecosystem stakeholders and the information of the inner workings of the ecosystem tends to be embedded within the ecosystem itself. Therefore, one needs to engage those stakeholders to find out if the ecosystem is working.

Dynamic entities

Since entrepreneurial ecosystems are dynamic entities, they are subject to periodic disturbances and are in the process of recovering from some past disturbance. When an entrepreneurial ecosystem is subject to some sort of agitation, it responds by moving away from its initial state. Understanding the dynamic structure and having processes in place to deal with both internal and external disturbances so that the system is resilient (returns quickly to its initial state) is critical. From one year to another, ecosystems experience changes in their people, organizations, and environments. Longer-term changes also shape ecosystem processes, for example, a startup company makes a big exit releasing capital and talent to the startup ecosystem. The frequency and severity of disturbances determine the way they impact the startup ecosystem functions. Major disturbances like a startup bubble burst leaves behind an investment-dry environment.

Conclusion

While work on entrepreneurial ecosystems is still in its infancy there are already several empirical studies showing how a rich entrepreneurial eco-system enables entrepreneurship and subsequent value creation at the regional level (Fritsch, 2013; Tsvetkova, 2015). For example, Mack and Mayer (2016) explore how early entrepreneurial successes in Phoenix, Arizona have contributed to a persistently strong entrepreneurial ecos-tem based on visible success stories, a strong entrepreneurial culture, and supportive public policies. Similarly, Spigel's (2015) study of entrepreneurial ecosystems in Waterloo and Calgary, Canada suggests that while ecosystems can have different structures and origins, their success lies in their ability to create a cohesive social and economic system that supports the creation and growth of new ventures.

The MIT Skoltech Initiative Report experts identified common factors underpinning successful university-based ecosystems (Graham, 2014). The following are seven factors that were consistently present and examples at different universities that illustrate them.

(1) *Institutional Entrepreneurial and Innovation culture.* Institutional culture was almost universally described by experts as an "essential" ingredient of a successful ecosystem. For a number of the world-leading universities in entrepreneurial ecosystems, their ethos was seen to have been either "sewn into the fabric of the universities from their very foundation" (as credited to MIT and Stanford) or as having benefitted from a national "ethos to make things happen" (as credited to Technion). However, most of the feedback focused on other universities and the *challenges they faced in catalyzing a change* in their entrepreneurship and innovation culture. Many experts noted that "British universities are the most interesting examples" of those that had successfully implemented such a change. As one expert explained, "…they had excellent universities, but no venture industry, no internal industry, and not much entrepreneurial spirit. They have been able to overcome a lot of this." The University of Cambridge was noted as a primary, ongoing example of a university whose successful cultural change was challenged by "800 years of history" and "active hostility to setting up technology transfer activities." Through celebrating the achievements of faculty role models, a relatively unstructured mix of entrepreneurship and innovation activities across campus, and the freedom for faculty to devote time to entrepreneurial ideas; the university is now seen to enjoy an increasingly entrepreneurial culture.

(2) *Strength of university leadership.* The names of particular university leaders were repeatedly raised as playing a pivotal role in establishing a strong entrepreneurship and innovation strategy by having the vision to catalyze change in their university's culture; sowing the seeds of a vibrant university entrepreneurial ecosystem. Some such individuals

were seen as the driving force behind the establishment of new eco-systems such as the case of Pierre Lafitte at Sophia Antipolis. However, more frequently identified were leaders associated with changes in previously underdeveloped ecosystems. They were cred-ited with enacting a fundamental change in the university's entrepre-neurial, innovation culture, and strategy that led to a significant strengthening of ecosystem performance. For example, a name strongly associated with the strengthening entrepreneurship and inno-vation reputation of Imperial College London was Richard Sykes, who served as university Rector between 2001 and 2008. Previously CEO of GlaxoSmithKline, Richard Sykes brought a culture of "cele-brating the success of entrepreneurs, sending the message that aca-demics can get rich without losing their credibility as a world class researcher." Richard Sykes also exerted pressure on the existing TTO, Imperial Innovations, to "demonstrate the value of their activities." In the years that followed, Imperial Innovations was transformed into "something very unique — an independent company that handles the whole technology transfer process for the university."

(3) *University research capability.* Many expert ranking universities have a long history as international research powerhouses, and the quality and capacity is seen as a cornerstone of the ecosystem's success.

(4) *The local or regional quality of life.* The attraction of the locality is a major benefit to ecosystem growth. For example, many experts described the "gorgeous location" of Sophia Antipolis creating uni-versity-based entrepreneurial ecosystems. Evidence from emerging world leaders indicate Antipolis as the "key to its success." As one commented, "…it sounds trivial, but location and lifestyle is a big factor. They were taking the Silicon Valley summery lifestyle and set-ting it up in the south of France." The design of the park itself was also seen as an influencing factor — "…it is not a science park as you would expect. The buildings are scattered throughout the hills. It is like nothing else I have seen." The pre-existing tourist industry also made the region "open to the world", with international schools, an international airport, and high-speed train lines to the rest of Europe.

(5) *Government support.* Many universities featured in the successful rankings have clearly benefitted from significant external support for

ecosystem development in the form of generous government subsidies and advantageous regional policies. For example, the collaborations across universities, business, and local government in the city of Tomsk, Siberia, were seen as a major factor in the emerging entrepreneurship and innovation environment at Tomsk State University of Control Systems and Radioelectronics (TUSUR). When describing the growing vibrancy of this university ecosystem, one expert commented, "TUSUR did not do this alone. There was an openness between the university and the rest of the ecosystem. They have combined the general city facilities with the university facilities with business facilities." Through this mutually reinforcing collaboration, the city is seen to have become open and attractive; a place where "entrepreneurs would want to move their ideas."

(6) *Effective institutional strategy.* Experts described at length the university strategies associated with successful ecosystem growth. Some effective strategies appeared to be relatively independent of the university size, location, and profile. Examples included approaches where the institutional focus for entrepreneurship and innovation did not reside within a single group or center, but was allowed to emerge as multiple, and often unconnected, activities operating across and beyond the campus. Other strategies described were specifically tailored to the university context, often in direct response to the challenges faced in that environment. For example, the size and geographical isolation of New Zealand together with the absence of multinational companies led the University of Auckland to develop a strategy of "associating our capabilities with the needs of other nations." Experts pointed, in particular, to the performance of UniServices, an autonomous but university-owned institution managing all research contracts and commercialization activities for the University of Auckland. UniServices has focused on the development of long-term strategic partnerships with large multinational companies and positioned themselves in specific segments of markets. One expert described how they had created "a support environment in New Zealand that allows people to think globally about their business."

(7) *Student-led entrepreneurship.* "Student energy in entrepreneurship" was viewed as an increasingly prominent driver of ecosystem

development, particularly among emerging ecosystems and those operating in more challenging environments. One university highlighted was the recently established Aalto University in Helsinki. The university was formed through the merger of three highly regarded schools of business, engineering, and design, with an explicit focus on innovation based entrepreneurship. Experts commented that after only 2 years of operation, the "levels of student engagement in entrepreneurship and innovation are phenomenal", supported by an array of activities and resources across campus. The decreasing dominance of the major employers of Finnish graduates, such as Nokia, supported a wave of interest in entrepreneurial careers among student populations, with emerging national role models such as the developers of the game — Angry Birds.

An outcome of the entrepreneurial ecosystem is entrepreneurial activity, the process that creates opportunities for innovation. This innovation will eventually lead to new societal value, which is the ultimate outcome of an entrepreneurial ecosystem.

Summary

This chapter focuses on the elements needed in a university ecosystem for encouraging, developing, and monetizing innovation in the university. It begins with the general concept of entrepreneurial ecosystems and elements of a university entrepreneurial ecosystem. Common factors in establishing entrepreneurial ecosystems at universities are discussed to include promoting and encouraging both student and faculty innovation and entrepreneurship, actively supporting the TTOs, facilitating university-industry collaboration and engaging with regional economic development efforts, with examples of how particular universities have successfully implemented these activities. Success stories of entrepreneurial ecosystems, the necessary components of managing an entrepreneurial ecosystem, and the aspects of establishing and implementing these ecosystems are discussed. The Conclusion provides seven common factors sustaining successful university-based ecosystems with illustrations.

Selected Readings

(1) Van Agtmael, Antoine and Bakker, Fred (2016). "The Smartest Places on Earth: Why Rustbelts Are the Emerging Hotspots of Global Innovation", *Public Affairs*, 1st edition.

The remarkable story of how rust belt cities such as Akron and Albany in the United States and Eindhoven in Europe are becoming the unlikely hotspots of global innovation, where sharing brainpower and making things smarter — not cheaper — is creating a new economy that is turning globalization on its head. Antoine van Agtmael and Fred Bakker counter recent conventional wisdom that the American and northern European economies have lost their initiative in innovation and their competitive edge by focusing on an unexpected and hopeful trend: the emerging sources of economic strength coming from areas once known as "rust-belts" that had been written off as yesterday's story. In these communities, a combination of forces — visionary thinkers, local universities, regional government initiatives, startups, and big corporations — have created "brainbelts." Based on trust, a collaborative style of working, and the freedom of thinking, prevalent in America and Europe, these brainbelts are producing smart products that are transforming industries by integrating IT, sensors, big data, new materials, new discoveries, and automation. From polymers to medical devices, the brainbelts have turned the tide from cheap, outsourced production to making things smart in our own backyard. The next emerging market may, in fact, be the West.

(2) Cohan, Peter (2018). *Startup Cities: Why Only a Few Cities Dominate the Global Startup Scene and What the Rest Should Do About It*, 1st edition, Apress.

This book offers a comprehensive model for explaining the success and failure of cities in nurturing startups, presents detailed case studies of how participants in the model help or hinder startup activity, and shows how to apply these lessons to boost local startup activity. *Startup Cities* explains the factors that determine local startup success based on a detailed comparison of regional startup cities — pairing the most successful and less successful cities within regions along with insights and implications from case studies of each of the model's elements. It highlights factors that distinguish successful from less successful cities and presents implications for stakeholders that arise from these principles. This book is for key startup stakeholders including: universities (presidents; deans of faculty; provosts; professors of finance, management, and entrepreneurship; directors of international education), local policymakers, entrepreneurs (CEOs, chief marketing officers, chief financial officers, chief HR officers, chief technology officers), and capital providers (venture capital partners and associates, angel investors, bank loan officers, managers of accelerator operations).

References

Bruce, K. and Julie, W. (2014). *The Rise of Innovation Districts: A New Geography of Innovation in America*, Brookings Institute.

Dunn, K. (2005). *The Entrepreneurship Ecosystem*, www.technologyreview.com/s/404622/the entrepreneurship-ecosystem.

Entrepreneur, https://www.entrepreneur.com/article/333131.

Fritsch, M. (2013). New business formation and regional development: A survey and assessment of the evidence. *Foundations and Trends® in Entrepreneurship*, 9(3), 249–364.

Forbes: Introducing the Entrepreneurship Ecosystem: Four Defining Characteristics, May 2011, https://www.forbes.com/sites/danisenberg/2011/05/25/introducing-the-entrepreneurship-ecosystem-four-defining-characteristics/#5434b1c45fe8.

Graham, R. (2014). Creating university-based entrepreneurial ecosystems evidence from emerging world leaders, MIT Skoltech Initiative.

Mack, E. and Mayer, H. (2016). The evolutionary dynamics of entrepreneurial ecosystems. *Urban Studies*, 53(10).

Mason, C. and Brown, R. (2014). *Entrepreneurial Ecosystems and Growth Oriented Entrepreneurship*, https://www.oecd.org/cfe/leed/Entrepreneurial-ecosystems.pdf.

McKinsey & Company, "The Power of Many: Realizing the Socioeconomic Potential of Entrepreneurs in the 21st Century Economy", G20 Young Entrepreneur Summit, October 2011. See http://www.mckinsey.com/locations/paris/home/The Power of Many-McKinsey Report- 20111005.pdf.

McKinsey Global Institute (2011). See http://www.mckinsey.com/insights/mgi/research/labor_markets/an_economy_that_works_for_us_job_creation.

Spigel, B. (2015). The relational organization of entrepreneurial ecosystems. *Entrepreneurship Theory and Practice*, 41(1), 49–72.

The Innovative and Entrepreneurial University: Higher Education, Innovation & Entrepreneurship in Focus (2013), Department of Commerce, https://www.eda.gov/pdf/The_Innovative_and_Entrepreneurial_University_Report.pdf.

U.S. Department of Commerce, and the National Advisory Council on Innovation and Entrepreneurship (NACIE), (2013). *The Innovative and Entrepreneurial University: Higher Education, Innovation & Entrepreneurship in Focus.*

van Agtmael, A. and Bakker, F. (2016). *The Smartest Places on Earth*, Public Affairs, Perseus Books Group.

Chapter 3

The Role of Patents

Learning Objectives

- Learn the various types of patents and other forms of Intellectual Property (IP), and their associated types of protection.
- Understand the value of patent protection.
- Be able to discuss how to file a patent or copyright.
- Know the difference between what is patentable and what is not patentable.
- Understand when to file a patent and who can file a patent.
- Be able to decide whether to license or form a startup.
- After reviewing the infringement case examples, determine if we are seeing a possible business model shift from patents protecting products to patents which themselves are products.

Opening Profile — Dr. Zhaohui "Joey" Yang

Q1: Submitter Information

Name of Nominee	**Dr. Zhaohui "Joey" Yang**
University the Nominee is representing	**University of Alaska Anchorage**
Email	zyang2@alaska.edu
Phone Number	907-786-6431

Dr. Zhaohui "Joey" Yang, joined UAA in 2003. He is currently Professor of Civil Engineering and Chair of the Civil Engineering Department, and Director for the Geotechnical and Frozen Ground Engineering Research Laboratory. Dr. Yang's expertise is in geotechnical and earthquake engineering, he has maintained an active research program with particular interests on cold region-related engineering issues, and he has led projects that helped advance the carbon fiber-based deicing technology.

One of Dr. Yang's major research interests is roadway deicing. Since 2009, he has been active in research involving new generation of deicing technology by using carbon fiber. He has received research funding in geotechnical/earthquake engineering and cold region-related research from: NSF EPSCoR, US Geological Survey, US Department of Interior, US Department of Transportation via Alaska University Transportation Center, US Department of Energy via Alaska Energy Authority, the State of Alaska Department of Transportation and Public Facilities, and the Municipality of Anchorage. He is also a recipient of an Innovate Award at UAA which provided funding for his work in carbon fiber tapes.

In 2013, he founded CFT Solutions™ to provide an innovative and cost-effective approach to revolutionizing snow removal and deicing using carbon fiber tapes. Efficient heating of the carbon fiber tapes embedded under the pavement keeps the surface free of snow and ice. The idea that would lead to CFT Solutions™ began when Dr. Yang met Professor Song from the University of Houston. Song was experimenting with commercially available flexible carbon fiber to heat surfaces in his lab. However, the connection to deicing applications came when Dr. Yang's relatives were visiting from China. His father in-law went outside to take his daughter to school right after a typical Alaskan freeze–thaw–freeze cycle had occurred. He slipped on the ice and broke this thumb. This incident sparked the inspiration to use the carbon fiber tapes for deicing. Receiving a grant from the Alaska University Transportation Center, he decided to test flexible carbon fiber tape as a way to heat surfaces of walkways in the challenging Alaskan winter, by embedding it under the pavement to keep the surface free of snow and ice. After building a prototype and successfully testing the prototype, CFT was formed a few years later.

Dr. Yang is the lead inventor of US patents related to carbon fiber application: Designs and Methods for Self-Heating Concrete (US Patent

No. 9,829,202); and Self-Heated Enclosure with Carbon Fiber (US Patent No. 9,829,203), and has two patents pending. He is also a co-founder of another UAA startup — Rhizoform (biodegradable insulation a possible Styrofoam replacement), which won the Best University Startup in a national competition sponsored by NCET2. He was inducted into UAA's patent wall of fame and UAA's Chapter of the NAI. Dr. Yang has published 70 peer-reviewed papers and is Associate Editor of *ASCE Journal of Cold Regions Engineering*. He has a Ph.D. in Civil and Environmental Engineering from the University of California, Davis and a B.S., in Hydraulic Engineering, from the Chengdu University of Science and Technology, China.

Q2: The nominee's position when they created the company. Describe the nominee's process with the university as they were creating the company.

Position: Dr. Yang is a Professor of Civil Engineering, Director of Alaska University Transportation Center, and Director for the Geotechnical and Frozen Ground Engineering Research Laboratory. *Process*: He had been meeting with Dr. Helena Wisniewski, Vice Provost for Research and Dean, Graduate School regarding the patent application and filing for his work in carbon fiber. During those meetings, they discussed whether it was better to license the technology or form a startup company. After considering the criteria, presented in Figure 4, they decided to form CFT. The fact a prototype existed and was successfully tested on campus with a grant from Alaska University Transportation Center was also taken into consideration. Moreover, it was in the winter of 2011–2012, which was the worst snowfall in Anchorage, the road surface was kept snow and ice free. A patent for the invention was pending. They formed an LLC, and UAA through Seawolf Holdings (Figure 2 of Chapter 2), provided a royalty-free exclusive license to CFT to use the patent, and continued to pay for the patent costs through its process to the issued patent. Seawolf Holdings would hold equity in CFT on behalf of UAA and would have a seat on its board of directors. Dr. Yang would have equity as a founder, and if the company was sold, he would receive a royalty for the patent asset portion of the sale. He would have a seat on the board and be the initial CEO.

Q3: Describe the nominee's experience working with the university in creating the company. What were the challenges? What support did they receive?

Support: The Vice Provost, Dr. Wisniewski, together with Dr. Yang's input, did the formation filings, obtained a tax ID number, developed and provided marketing materials, the LLC agreement, licensing agreement, provide access to the patent attorney, and would help identify and negotiate investment in CFT. She made contact with potential investors in CT and helped develop the investor pitch for the meeting. She subsequently negotiated an investment deal with the Alaska Acceleration Fund and had the UAA attorney create the investment documents. Dr. Yang participated in negotiation meetings. She had Dr. Yang speak at events that included community leaders, such as the Innovate Awards winners, and in 2013 Dr. Lang was a recipient of a UAA's Innovate Awards for $10,000 for his carbon fiber deicing work. *Challenges*: The Vice Provost and UAA were supportive of CFT, the challenges were ones typically faced by startups like finding investors, which they eventually did.

Q4: What happened to the company the nominee created? Describe in detail where it is now and how it is doing. What is the history of the company?

Milestones and Status: CFT, LLC was formed in May 2013. Dr. Yang was the founder and is the inventor of the technology, and patents were issued in 2017. After the company was formed, CFT was installed in walkways on the UAA campus — the main entrance to the new Engineering Building and the north entrance to the University Lake Annex Building, which kept them ice and snow free throughout the Alaskan winters. CFT was also installed at the Cook Inlet Housing Authority at their senior housing for melting snow. He included his student, Ben Still in developing the technology and installing it at those sites. CFT received requests for additional installations but a UL Listing was needed before a commercially ready product, at a reasonable cost could be feasible. For the initial installations, UL certified the particular site adding to the cost of the project installation. CFT began the UL listing process. Product advantages included: easy installation at lower costs than other systems, significantly less expensive (50% less) to operate than other systems, turns on only when needed, and environmentally friendly.

The Vice Provost negotiated a deal with the Alaska Acceleration Fund for a total investment of $300,000, which required changing the LLC to an Inc., and the new name became Arctic Heat Technologies, Inc. An additional investment of $10,000 was also acquired from a private investor. UAA through Seawolf Holdings granted an exclusive, royalty free license to Arctic Heat for using the patent, and Seawolf received shares in Arctic Heat and a seat on the Board of Directors, which included Dr. Yang who has shares in Arctic Heat and is its Chief Technology Officer. Tim Allen is now the President. The product has evolved into one that is more easily installed — called Tundra Tape. Arctic Heat has received additional investments and is pursuing the UL Listing process. Once UL listing is achieved, the product will be commercially available.

Introduction

Innovation is a hallmark of the US economy. In the previous century, ideas developed at universities became products that underwrote corporate giants like Boeing, Ford, Google, and Intel. In the 21st Century, universities must work harder to maintain the US global lead in innovation, science, engineering, and creative works. To provide incentives for university researchers to contribute to economic development, in addition to furthering their advancement of knowledge, requires the deployment of methods for the protection of Intellectual Property (IP). Patents provide the ultimate assurance that the economic potential of research remains protected.

The reliance of universities on varied sources of funding, including government, industry and contract research, commercial activity in areas such as the life sciences that are deeply intertwined with biotechnology, and legislation such as the Bayh–Dole Act, have contributed to an explosion in patenting and licensing by US universities. Universities must be active in protecting and exploiting their IP by promoting faculty and student research, but also must determine how best to pursue any relationship with business clients. Rapidly progressing globalization requires universities to be open to business and international collaboration. This in turn requires that universities protect and manage research results by protecting IP. *Therefore, the protection of intellectual property is always a concern for a university.*

The role of patents and the selection of the technology to be patented is the focus of this chapter. However, it also examines other protections for IP such as copyrights, trademarks, and trade secrets. The chapter also discusses the benefits received by both the university and the faculty from IP, incentives for faculty to pursue IP protection, and university ownership policies.

Types of Intellectual Property (IP)

IP refers to creations of the mind that result from the expression of an idea. IP includes inventions, literary and artistic works, designs, symbols, names, and images used in commerce or other creations. Whether one is an inventor, an artist, or an entrepreneur; one can find the right protection for intellectual property. The ways to protect IP are as follows:

- patents,
- copyrights,
- trademarks,
- trade secrets.

These enable individuals and organizations to earn recognition and financial benefit from inventions or creations.

Patents

Overview

A patent is a property right. It gives an inventor the exclusive right to *exclude others* from making, using, selling, offering for sale, or importing the claimed invention for a limited term. A patent has the status of a "legal monopoly." Persons or entities infringing a patent can be forced to pay damages to prevent further acts of infringement.

This patent right is in the United States Constitution. Article 1, Section 8, Clause 8, Patent and Copyright Clause of the Constitution, states "The Congress shall have power ... To promote the Progress of Science and useful Arts, by securing for limited Times to Authors and Inventors the exclusive Right to their respective Writings and Discoveries." In addition, the Infringement of patents is addressed in 35 U.S.C. 271 (a) "... whoever without authority makes, uses, offers to sell, or sells any patented invention, within the United States, or imports into the United States any patented invention during the term of the patent therefor, infringes the patent."

In return for a period of exclusivity in the market, some conditions/limitations apply. A patent has a limited term. In the US, this term is for a duration of 20 years from the original US non-provisional filing date. The inventor must make a full disclosure that illustrates how to make and use it. There is no worldwide patent. Protection is only in the territory that granted the patent. A US patent only covers the United States and a separate patent is necessary in each country.

Although a patent gives the inventor the right to exclude others; it is not a right to practice or use the invention. A patent does not necessarily give the patent owner the right to exploit the patent. For example, if the invention is an improvement of prior inventions that may still be covered by someone else's patent. When an inventor obtains a patent on improvements to an existing, still under patent invention, then they need permission from the owner of the original invention before they can build the improved invention. *For example*, a mouse trap designer can only legally build an improved mouse trap design with permission from the patent holder of the original mouse trap.

Patents are assets

A patent can be sold, licensed, mortgaged, assigned, or transferred. It is an investment, which can be used to do the following:

- obtain a return-on-investment from licensing revenue,
- avoid litigation,
- apply leverage during negotiations,
- provide part of a company's valuation.

If one intends to start a company, one should include IP protection in any business plan as it has the following features:

- It influences a business model.
- It is a valuable company asset.
- It may provide a chief commodity and barrier to market.
- It protects the company's inventions against competitors (as an offensive weapon).
- It allows the construction of a defensive patent portfolio in case of litigation.

Entire business strategies can be based on patents. Focusing on not just the innovations in products but also on a protection plan for those concepts, can turn an innovation into something of greater value than just a good product feature. A directed focused R&D program can develop solutions to specific problems that are preventing the growth of certain sections of an industry.

What is patentable?

Title 35 of the United States Code for patent law states in §101 that "Whoever invents or discovers any *new* and *useful* process, machine, manufacture, or composition of matter, or any new and useful improvement thereof, may obtain a patent therefor, subject to the conditions and requirements of this title."

Therefore, a patentable invention is any *new* (means not known more than a year before filing the patent application in the US only) and *useful*:

- **Process:** "An act, or series of acts or steps."
- **Machine:** "A concrete thing, consisting of parts, or of certain devices and combination of devices."
- **Article of Manufacture:** "An article produced from raw or prepared materials by giving these materials new forms, qualities, properties, or combinations, whether by hand, labor, or by machinery."
- **Composition of matter:** "All compositions of two or more substances and all composite articles, whether they be the results of chemical

union, or a mechanical mixture, or whether they be gases, fluids, powders, or solids, or

- **Improvement** on any of the above.

Patent requirements/criteria

- usefulness,
- novelty,
- non-obviousness.

These are defined as follows:

- **Novelty** is strictly defined by patent law and essentially refers to the originality of the idea. Therefore, no prior art exists. This is in 35 U.S.C. Section 102, Patentability over the Prior Art.
- **Useful** means there must be utility or purpose to an invention, which furthermore can be made and be operable.
- **Non-obvious** means it would not naturally occur to someone having skill/expertise in the relevant field. Even if a new invention differs in one or more ways from another patented invention, a patent may still be refused if the differences would be obvious. Non-obviousness, requires a sufficient difference from what has been used or described before a person having ordinary skill in the area of technology, related to the invention, would not find it obvious to make the change. For example, sodium chloride (table salt) and potassium chloride (a chemically similar salt) can often be used interchangeably. However, a chemist working to improve road salt would consider it obvious to substitute potassium chloride for sodium chloride, so a formula that simply made this substitution in an already patented road salt formula would not be patentable.

What is not patentable?

- laws of nature;
- natural phenomena;
- abstract ideas;

- perpetual motion machines;
- signals.

"Laws of nature, natural phenomena, and abstract ideas" — these three terms are typically used by the courts to cover the basic tools of scientific and technological work, such as scientific principles, naturally occurring phenomena, mental processes, and mathematical algorithms.

In addition, a patent cannot be obtained if an invention was previously known or used by other people in the US, or was already patented or published anywhere in the world. Furthermore, publicly using or selling an invention more than a year prior to filing a patent application completely bars you from ever winning a patent on that invention. Be aware that less formal communications also count. Discussing the invention in a hotel lobby is considered a public disclosure, as is posting data onto a website, giving a departmental seminar, tacking up a poster, or publishing an abstract. Even winning a grant can prematurely end any potential patent rights, because the grant application itself is often made accessible to the public. Remember: The clock starts ticking as soon as you start talking about your invention.

Who can apply for a patent?

In the US, only the inventor may apply for a patent, with certain exceptions. For example, if the inventor is dead, the application may be made by legal representatives, that is, the administrator or executor of the estate. If two or more persons invent something jointly, they may apply for a patent as joint inventors. However, a person who makes only a financial contribution is not a joint inventor cannot be added in the application as an inventor.

An important change to US patent law occurred in March 2013. Before this date the US followed a "First to Invent" principle which meant that even if a patent had been filed by one entity, its validity could be challenged on the basis that some other entity could demonstrate priority in invention. As an example, the original patent for the laser went to researchers who described such an invention in a scholarly paper, rather than to the scientists at Bell Labs who first constructed a working device.

The change made to the law in 2013 changed the priority from a First to Invent to a First to File System, which means multiple entities may claim contributions to the invention, whoever files for a patent first has priority.

Types of patents

The United States Patent and Trademark Office (USPTO) issues several different types of patent documents offering protection for different types of subject matter as follows:

- **Utility Patent:** Issued for the invention of a new and useful process, machine, manufacture, or composition of matter, or a new and useful improvement thereof. It generally permits its owner to exclude others from making, using, or selling the invention for a period of up to 20 years from the date the patent application is filed. Approximately 90% of the patent documents issued by the PTO in recent years have been utility patents, also referred to as "patents for invention."
- **Design Patent:** Issued for a new, original, ornamental design for an article of manufacture. It permits its owner to exclude others from making, using, or selling the design for a period of 14 years from the date of the patent grant. Until the last few years, design patents were pretty much ignored by technology companies. Now companies are seeking out design patents to go with their utility patents to create a more impervious wall of protection around their successful products. It's even conceivable that a company could lose a patent fight over some critical bit of technology that makes a product work, but win damages from a competitor that copied a completely non-functional aspect of the design. We discuss some infringement cases later in this chapter.
- **Plant Patent:** Issued for a new and distinct, invented or discovered asexually reproduced plants including cultivated sprouts, mutants, hybrids, and newly found seedlings. It permits its owner to exclude others from making, using, or selling the plant for a period of up to 20 years from the date the patent application is filed.

- **Reissue Patent:** Issued to correct an error in an already issued utility, design, or plant patent, it does not affect the period of protection offered by the original patent.

There are also different types of patent applications which are as follows:

- provisional,
- non-provisional,
- international application under the Patent Cooperation Treaty (PCT).

Provisional patent application

A provisional application for a patent provides the means to establish an early effective filing date in a later filed non-provisional patent application filed under 35 U.S.C. §111(a), which is important for a first to file law. It also allows the term "Patent Pending" to be applied in connection with the description of the invention. A provisional application for patent (provisional application) is a US national application filed in the USPTO. A provisional patent is simpler and less expensive than a patent filing. No claims or prior art statements are required. It does require a written description of the invention and any drawings necessary to understand the invention.

However, the provisional application should be essentially the same as the corresponding non-provisional application, with the possible exception of claims and new subject matter developed after the provisional application filing. A non-provisional application must be filed within 12 months from the date of the provisional application. Benefits of the provisional include the following:

- Simplified filing with a lower initial investment with 12 months to assess the invention's commercial potential before committing to higher cost of filing and processing a non-provisional application.
- Establishes the official United States patent application filing date for the invention. You establish an early effective filing date for a patent claim and avoid an impending statutory bar to patentability.

- Permits authorized use of the "Patent Pending" notice for 12 months.
- Permits enable immediate commercial promotion of invention with greater security against having the invention stolen.

A provisional patent application allows marketing the invention without fear of losing patent rights; generating cash to proceed with development or further patent activities. The provisional patent application can be viewed as an interim step along the road to a patent. However, the 20-year term does not start with the filing of a provisional application, it is 20 years from the filing date of the non-provisional application.

A provisional application can be filed up to 12 months following an inventor's public disclosure of the invention. One should consider filing a provisional patent application as soon as your invention is concrete and tangible enough to describe. Figure 1 compares a provisional and non-provisional patent application.

Associated costs of filing a patent application

It takes 5+ years for a patent to get issued as a US Patent. The associated costs of filing include the following:

- Provisional: $2,000.
- Non provisional: $15,000 to $20,000.
- Issue fee.

Provisional:

- One year period then expires.

- Filed for filing date priority for later-filed non-provisional

- Not examined, so no patent.

- Not allowed for design.

Non-Provisional:

- Once issued, 20-year patent protection from filing date.

- Examined for patentability.

- Claims required.

Figure 1.   Types of patent applications.

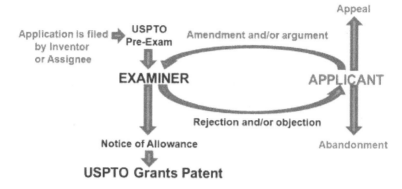

Figure 2.   Patent examination process overview.

- Maintenance fees at 3.5, 7.5, 11.5 years or — expiration.
- Term of patent — 20 years.

After you file a patent application, the patent examination process that takes place is illustrated in Figure 2.

Deadlines for filing a patent

Quick answer — as soon as possible after you have an invention. In March of 2013, the United States changed from a First to Invent to a First to File System. If a person only wants US protection, then they can file a within a year after their public disclosure. However, with the new patent system, filing early will be more critical than ever before. The following are a few examples of why.

If two people create the same invention and there has been no public disclosure of the invention, and both describe and claim that invention in separate patent applications, the inventor that filed his patent application first will get the patent. Previously, if the same scenario had occurred the person who was the first to invent got the patent.

Given the new law, provisional patents will be playing a more important role since they hold the filing date for one year and are easier to file. An inventor should consider filing a provisional application as early as possible. However, the best practice is to file a provisional application before any public disclosure.

If the inventor is looking for international protection, they must file before a public disclosure. Although there is no such thing as an international patent, an international agreement known as the "patent cooperation treaty" (PCT) provides a streamlined filing procedure for most industrialized nations.

Patent cooperation treaty

The PCT is an international treaty with more than 150 Contracting States. The PCT makes it possible to seek patent protection for an invention simultaneously in a large number of countries by filing a single "international" patent application instead of filing several national or regional patent applications. However, the granting of patents remains under the control of the national or regional patent offices in what is called the "national phase." Filing a single "international" patent application or PCT application preserves the applicant's right to seek patent protection for an invention in a large number of countries. Eighteen months after the PCT application is filed, the applicant must choose the specific countries in which to pursue patent protection and file applications in the national patent office of each one. Therefore, the PCT delays the need to file separate foreign applications in each country, providing the applicant with ample time to develop, evaluate, and market the invention before investing in the significant costs of international patent protection. Filings in individual countries can cost $40,000 or more. For additional information about the PCT, please refer to the WIPO website.

Patent wars and infringement case examples

Patents can also be used as both offensive and defensive weapons. Using patents as weapons is not new. Eli Whitney and his partner Phineas Miller brought many suits during the late 18th century to protect the market of the cotton gin. Inventors like Edison who helped build America's unparalleled dominance in Science and Technology regularly used patent challenges and litigation to attack competitors and secure General Electric's future. He developed the crucial devices that gave birth to four enduring industries: electrical power — Edison General electric (GE), recorded music, motion pictures, and a battery for an electric car, were among his 1,000 patents, and he created jobs — 13,000 persons worked in his NJ laboratory.

The following examples illustrate that patent wars have continued, and how corporations use patents not only to protect what they are currently doing, but also to set up roadblocks to keep competitors from moving down a particular line of research or product development. All of these examples point out the value of a properly developed patent portfolio as a business asset by focusing on not just the innovations in products, but on the underlying concepts of those innovations, and then implementing a strategically valuable protection plan for those concepts. They illustrate how to turn a solution to a problem into something of far greater value than just a good product feature.

After reviewing these cases, the reader can keep in mind the question: Are we seeing a possible business model shift?

- **Old Model:** Patents protect products.
- **New Model**: Patents themselves are products.

Example 1: Apple versus Samsung
The legal fight between Samsung and Apple started in 2011, when Apple alleged that several Samsung phones infringed the design and utility patents of its iPhone that raged on for 7 years. The latest twist in the seven-year-old smartphone patent trial between Apple and Samsung awarded the iPhone maker a final verdict of $539 million in damages, according to *Bloomberg*. The Jury concluded that Samsung infringed the Apple's design and utility patents covering aspects of mobile design like rounded corners, the rim of the front face of the iPhone, and the now-iconic app grid layout of the iOS home screen.

The case had been ongoing since 2011, and the countless appeals and verdicts made it one of the most complex corporate patent infringement trials in the history of the technology industry. Apple initially demanded Samsung pay $2.5 billion when the lawsuit began, but that figure was reduced to less than $1 billion in the initial 2012 verdict in Apple's favor. An appeals court ruled Apple could not legally trademark the iPhone's appearance in May of 2015, which meant Samsung was forced to pay only around $548 million. Samsung paid that amount in December 2015 after both companies agreed in 2014 to drop litigation outside the US.

Since then, a series of appeals have kept the case moving through federal court in California, resulting in a string of retrial attempts from Samsung that ultimately were aimed at trying to further reduce Apple's monetary awards. One of the two final cases between the tech giants concluded in November of 2017, pertaining to the iOS slide-to-unlock patent; resulting in an award of $120 million to Apple. Now with damages decided in this final case — a version of the original $1 billion Apple patent win from 2012 that moved through a number of reductions and appeals — the legal web between these two companies should be nearing a close.

Implications for Design Patents. Apple's courtroom victory over Samsung doesn't just mean a tougher road ahead for companies that want to clone the popular iPhone. It's a powerful lesson that patents aren't just for technology any more. The jury had found that three of the six patents Samsung had violated were design patents imitating the way an iPhone looked, not how it functioned. The verdict signaled the arrival of a once-obscure type of patent — the design patent.

Until the last few years, design patents were pretty much ignored by technology companies. Now companies are seeking out design patents to go with their utility patents to create a more impervious wall of protection around their successful products. It's even conceivable that a company could lose a patent fight over some critical bit of technology that makes a product work, but win damages from a competitor that copied a completely non-functional aspect of the design.[1]

Example 2: Google buys Motorola Patents
In August 2011, Google paid $12.5 billion for Motorola's U.S. smart-phone business. It did so to acquire Motorola's 17,000 patents and 7,500 patent application filings.

One month before the acquisition, Google's rivals — including Apple, Microsoft, and BlackBerry — had teamed up to acquire a coveted patent

---

[1] Forbes, April 9, 2012, Microsoft Buys 800 Patents for $1.1 Billion from AOL — But What's Next for AOL? Kelly Clay. Forbes, August 2012, https://www.forbes.com/sites/conniegug lielmo/2012/08/24/jury-has-reached-verdict-in-apple-samsung-patent-suit-court-to-announce-it-shortly/#d9609c0b7117.

portfolio at auction of 6,000 wireless patents for $4.5 billion from Nortel. This gave them a competitive advantage over Google in a global and ever-sprawling legal battle over smartphones.

The Motorola deal, gave Google a chance to counter-attack or at least hold its ground thanks to Motorola's intellectual property. It's not as if Motorola had some must-have patents for mobile phones. Instead, Google wanted an arsenal of patents to fight the similar arsenal collected by competitors of its Android operating system for smartphones. Motorola's patents have helped create a level playing field, which is good news for all Android's users and partners. Even though Google later sold Motorola, Google will retain the vast majority of Motorola's patents, which they will continue to use to defend the entire Android ecosystem.

The Motorola deal validates Google's strategy at a time when most patents are business weapons unrelated to actual innovation. The value of patents in software and hardware such as smartphones has everything to do with litigation risk and almost nothing to do with technology (Crovitz, 2011).

Example 3: Microsoft Buys AOL Patents

In April 2012, Wall Street cheered AOL's deal to sell 800 patents for $1 billion to Microsoft, sending the onetime Internet pioneer's stock soaring over 40% to levels not seen in nearly 2 years. For Microsoft, the deal highlights the premium that tech companies are willing to pay in order to bolster their intellectual property position and protect themselves as patent litigation continues to escalate across the tech industry. The deal increased the speed of the global gold rush in technology patents. The lofty price of $1.3 million for a patent reflects the crucial role that patents are increasingly playing in the business and legal strategies of the world's major technology companies, including Microsoft, Apple, Google, Samsung and HTC.

© Copyrights

A Copyright protects the expression of an idea, not the idea itself. It protects the original works of authorship that are fixed in a tangible medium of expression, including the following:

- literary;
- musical;
- recordings;
- dramatic;
- pictorial;
- graphic;
- sculptural;
- audio/visual works;
- layouts or typographical.

A copyright is a form of protection provided by US law to the authors of "original works of authorship" fixed in any tangible medium of expression. The subject matter of the copyright is extremely broad, including literary, dramatic, musical, artistic, audiovisual, and architectural works. Copyright protection is available to both published and unpublished works.

Under the 1976 Copyright Act, the copyright owner has the exclusive right to reproduce, adapt, distribute, publicly perform, and publicly display the work. In the case of sound recordings, the copyright owner has the right to perform the work publicly by means of a digital audio transmission. These exclusive rights are freely transferable, and may be licensed, sold, donated to charity, or bequeathed to your heirs.

It is illegal for anyone to violate any of the exclusive rights of the copyright owner. If the copyright owner prevails in an infringement claim, the available remedies include preliminary and permanent injunctions (court orders to stop current or prevent future infringements), impounding, destroying the infringing articles, and monetary remedies.

The exclusive rights of the copyright owner, however, are limited in a number of important ways. These can be found under the "fair use" doctrine, which has long been part of US copyright law and was expressly incorporated in the 1976 Copyright Act.

How to obtain a copyright

A copyright is secured automatically when the work is created, and a work is "created" when it is fixed in a "copy or a phono-record for the first time." For example, a song can be fixed in sheet music or on a CD, or both. No registration or other action in the Copyright Office is required to secure copyright. A copyright lasts the entire life of the author, plus 70 years.

Although registration is not required to secure protection, it is highly recommended for the following reasons:

- Registration establishes a public record of the copyright claim.
- Registration is necessary before an infringement suit may be filed in court (for works of US origin).
- If made before or within 5 years of publication, registration establishes *prima facie* evidence in court on the validity of the copyright and the facts stated in the certificate.
- If registration is made within 3 months after publication of the work or prior to an infringement of the work, statutory damages and attorney's fees will be available to the copyright owner in court actions. Otherwise, only an award of actual damages and profits is available to the copyright owner.
- Registration allows the owner of the copyright to record the registration with the US Customs Service for protection against the importation of infringing copies.

Be aware of myths around copyrights, for example, a "poor man's copyright" if you send the work yourself, the post mark means that the government has accepted your copyright. No such provision is at law. Also, be careful of Open Source, copyrighted materials freely used by others with author's permission; be sure to read the license agreement.

The following are examples of copyright and photo infringement suits in the music industry.

Example 1: Michael Jackson's Estate Sued ABC

Michael Jackson's estate sued ABC, arguing that the network aired a special about the pop singer's final days and used his songs and music videos without permission. The copyright infringement lawsuit, which also names ABC's corporate parent Walt Disney Co., as a defendant, was filed in Los Angeles federal court and took aim at "The Last Days of Michael Jackson," a two-hour show broadcast.

Example 2: Estate of Marvin Gay vs Robin Thicke and Pharrell

While Pharrell and Thicke admitted to being *inspired* by Marvin Gay's work, they swore that "Blurred Lines" — one of the biggest hits in 2013 — was an original all on their own. A court agreed the song was more than "inspired" by Gay's earlier work; the court ruled it was an outright copy of the 1977 song "Got to Give It Up." The court ordered Robin Thicke and Pharrell to hand over more than $7 million dollars in unpaid licensing fees plus a portion of their profits from the song.

Example 3 — Naruto versus David Slater

Meet Naruto, a rare crested macaque who lives on a nature reserve in Indonesia and who took a bunch of selfies. The macaque selfie photographs appeared in a book titled *Wildlife Personalities* that Slater had published, via San Francisco-based self-publishing company Blurb, Inc.. On 22 September 2015, People for the Ethical Treatment of Animals (PETA) filed a lawsuit against Slater and Blurb in the United States District Court for the Northern District of California. It requested that the monkey, whom they named Naruto, be assigned copyright, and that PETA be appointed to administer proceeds from the photos for the benefit of Naruto and other crested macaques in the reserve on Sulawesi. PETA did so by using the next friend principle, which allows persons to sue in the name of another person who is unable to do so. In November, Angela Dunning, the attorney for Blurb, noted that PETA may have been suing on behalf of the wrong monkey.

The dispute ended up at the United States Copyright Office on 21 August 2014. The Office decided the picture at stake was not susceptible to copyright protection, since "only works created by a human can be copyrighted under United States law. This excludes pictures and artwork created by animals or by machines without human intervention."

PETA continued to file appeals, and in March 2016, PETA filed an appeal to the Ninth Circuit Court of Appeals. However, in August 2017, before any proceedings took place, the lawyers of both parties notified the court that they had reached a settlement in which Mr. Slater would donate twenty-five percent of the revenues generated by the pictures to the animal organizations committed to the protection and preservation of the monkey's natural habitat.

Trademarks

A *trademark is a distinctive sign* or *indicator* used by an individual, business, or any other legal entity *to identify* for consumers that the products or services with the trademark appears originated from:

- a unique source;
- designed for a specific market;
- designed to distinguish its products from those of other entities.

A trademark is typically a name, word, phrase, logo, symbol, image, or a combination of these elements. A trademark may be designated by the following symbols:

- The letters "TM," for an unregistered trademark (a mark used to promote or brand goods).
- The letter "R" surrounded by a circle ®, for a registered trademark.

LEGO and Google are examples of a trademark using words, and logo, and Starbucks is an example of logo, words and picture.

Benefits of a registered trademark

Trade mark registration gives the proprietor the right to exclusively use the mark in respect of the goods or services covered by it. Possibly the most important reason for registration of a trademark is the powerful remedies against its unauthorized use. A trademark registration allows the proprietor to sue for infringement and to obtain very powerful rulings such as interdict, deliver up infringing articles and damages. At the same time, the trademark infringement provisions do not preclude a person. It can prevent others from using the same or similar mark if there is a likelihood of confusion.

The term for a trademark

The term for a trademark is 10 years with 10-year term renewal using the affidavit of use in commerce. Rights in a trademark can be lost through the action or inaction of the trademark's owner. Non-use of a trademark for three consecutive years creates a rebuttable presumption of abandonment of the mark.

There have been misuse or improper use of trademarks. Some examples are: Xerox, Aspirin, cellophane, escalator, and thermos. These sometimes occur on account of the failure to police the misuse. This can be harmful to branding and the company's reputation, in particular in the case of counterfeit good using the actual company's trademark.

Trade Secrets

A trade secret is any information that derives its economic benefit from not being generally known to the public. It is protectable as long as the information remains a secret or has been the subject of "reasonable" efforts to maintain secrecy. Information can mean: formula, pattern, compilation, program, device, method, technique, or process. Reasonable efforts to maintain secrecy includes employment agreements, building security, network security, restricted access, need-to-know basis, and employees continuously trained to appreciate proprietary information.

The benefit of using a trade secret to protect IP is no filings or registrations are needed to protect the trade secret. It does not require any registration costs and is not limited in time. It is immediately effective and it does not require disclosure or registration with government agency. Its term is infinite, forever, eternal ... until it's disclosed or someone figures it out. The negatives are that if it is disclosed or someone figures it out, the trade secret owner has no legal actions against a person who acquires secret through legal means. Also, competitors can reverse engineer and competitors can independently develop the trade secret.

A famous and extremely successful company that has been very effective at keeping its trade secret is Coca-Cola. It has been very effective in protecting its trade secret for several years more than the 20 years a patent protection would have provided. Its owners protect trade secret information by special procedures, as well as technological and legal security measures.

Some ways to protect secret formulas include:

- Restricting the key information to one or two trusted individuals.
- Legal protection includes non-disclosure agreements (NDA) and non-compete clauses.

The disadvantage of using a trade secret is there is no protection once information protected by trade secret is uncovered by reserve engineering. In contrast, a patent has a guaranteed time of protection, in exchange for disclosing the information to the public. A trade secret pitfall is that we have a "Culture of Connectivity"; a practice near compulsive sharing of information and detail through social media sharing, such as Facebook. We also have a perceived "Open Innovation" of sharing data and ideas that at times illustrate a disregard/lack of appreciation for ownership interests.

Important Legislation — Bayh–Dole Act

The Bayh–Dole Act fundamentally changed the way America develops technologies from federally funded university research and effectively secured the country's leadership position in innovation. The Bayh–Dole Act fundamentally changed the nation's system of technology transfer by enabling universities to retain the title to inventions and take the lead in patenting and licensing groundbreaking discoveries. Although patenting in US universities did occur prior to the passage of Bayh–Dole Act, patenting dramatically increased and became more systematic with processes, procedures, and infrastructures put in place.

The key change made by Bayh–Dole was in regards to ownership of inventions made with federal funding. Before the Bayh–Dole Act, federal research funding contracts and grants obligated inventors (wherever they worked) to assign inventions they made using federal funding to the federal government. Bayh–Dole permits a university, small business, or non-profit institution to elect to pursue ownership of an invention instead of the government.

The Bayh–Dole Act grew out of the Congress's efforts to respond to the economic malaise of the 1970s. One of Congress's efforts was focused on how best to manage inventions that were created with more than $75 billion a year invested in government sponsored R&D. *The Senate Judiciary Committee Report,* 12 December 1979, stated the following: "Ultimately, it is believed this improvement in government patent policy will lead to greater productivity in the United States, provide new jobs, create new economic growth, foster increased competition, and stimulate a greater return on the billions of dollars spent each year by the government on its research and development programs."

Internal Processes within Universities to Determine Patentability and Decide Whether to License or Form a Startup

University research is associated with the creation of tremendous economic value — it can potentially generate revenues for universities, create research connections between academia and industry, and enhance regional economic growth and development. Over the past two centuries, academic laboratories have played a critical role in the setting up entire industries including the synthetic dye industry (Murmann, 2003), the digital computer industry (Rosenberg and Nelson, 1994), and the biotechnology industry (Zucker *et al.*, 1998). In fact, large-scale empirical studies have found positive relationships between academic research and technology development (Jaffe, 1989) as well as between academic research and productivity growth (Adams, 1990).

To protect IP, identify commercial potential and stimulate economic development through the transfer of technologies to the marketplace, universities have put into place processes and infrastructure. Processes can vary but there are basic similarities; see example in Figure 3. The overseer

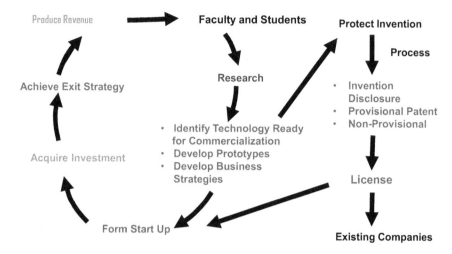

Figure 3.   Author's example of an internal university process.

of the process is usually the VP for Research, who oversees Technology Transfer Offices (TTOs) or Offices of Innovation and Commercialization (OICs). However, an important step is to build a culture of innovation, and to encourage and foster invention. To help determine if an invention is patentable, some universities have patent committees. These can be comprised of a variety of faculty — who have patents or patents pending, an expert in the field of the potential application, VP of Research, a patent attorney, etc.

The following are steps used by universities in the patent process and are illustrated in Figure 3.

Step 1: Submission of an Invention Discloser — The usual first step in the process is to have the inventors submit an invention disclosure form. This is a confidential document. It should fully describe the new aspects of the invention, including the critical solution it provides and its advantages and benefits over current technologies.

Step 2: Assessment of the Submission — Once the invention is disclosed; the VP, TTO or the patent committee will meet with the inventor to discuss the invention and evaluate its patentability. Prior art searches will be conducted to determine if they satisfy the patentability criteria of the USPTO — new, useful, and not obvious. An analysis of the market and competitive technologies is performed to assess the invention's commercialization potential. The assessment process will also guide the licensing strategy or form a startup. The decision to pursue invention protection is made.

Step 3: Invention Protection — If it is decided to pursue patent protection for disclosure; a consultation with a patent attorney to determine patentability is arranged. Preliminary discussion of the invention's marketing potential and determining whether to license a startup will begin. The TTO works with the inventor and attorney to file the patent applications. The inventor will be expected to evaluate previous patents and publications in the field, supply information to the patent attorney, and review draft patent applications.

Many universities encourage the initial filing to be provisional, due to first to file law. At the initial end of this process, the inventor will have the patent application filed and will have the patent pending. Subsequently, the patent is issued.

Step 4: License or Form a Startup — Once the decision is made to proceed and file a patent application, the next step is to decide whether to license the technology or form a startup. Criteria for this step are found in Figure 4.

If the license route is selected, then the TTO works with the inventor to identify companies in the field that would be able to fully exploit the technology's commercial potential. In addition, the university makes use of its own industry contacts to find and approach prospective companies.

If the startup route is selected, then the following steps are completed: the company is formed, the inventor and university enter into a license agreement for the startup to use the patent, the TTO helps with the business plan, marketing materials, and raising investment.

Figure 3 of Chapter 2 provides an example of the "Top Ten Rules for Startups," which can be used as a guide.

To License or Start-up?

LICENSE	START-UP
• **Technology represents an incremental improvement** to existing technology used by established companies.	• **Technology is disruptive**.
	• A platform technology.
• **Crowded field**, potential infringement risk.	• **Broad range of applications** for technology.
• **Customer loyalties** exist towards particular companies.	• Potential to mitigate risk (exit strategy).
• **Well-established distribution channels** have been created by existing companies.	• **New market** with high demand.
	• Clearly defined **need**.
• **Regulatory approvals required** – such as FDA approvals needed – high cost clinical trials.	• Can overcome barriers to entry.
	• Short time to market.
	• **Large market** with significant **growth**.
	• Significant **profit margins**.

Figure 4.   Author's license or startup determination.

Discussion of University Concerns

Publish or patent

Traditionally, advancement in universities by faculty has relied on the paradigm — Publish or Perish. Articles in peer reviewed journals, book chapters, proceedings at conferences, and other publishing forums have comprised the bulk of a faculty member's postdoctoral vita. Tenure and promotion have depended essentially on this research record. Patents in particular and IP protection in general, have rarely posed a significant contribution to faculty evaluation. However, with trends indicating that universities are concerned about economic development; patents and other IP protection will need to be included in the faculty record. Patents are an efficient way for university technology based on research to be introduced to the market, industry, and for the social good. In addition, there are financial benefits both to the faculty and the university resulting from the licensing and sale of patents, as well as from the sale of startups based on this technology. However, beyond this implied significance to IP for faculty, the university will need to explicitly acknowledge the value of a researcher's invention. Some universities realize this significance and are starting to treat patents as a research publication in tenure criteria.

Although universities for many years have been the source of innovation for startups and established industries; often university scientists and engineers do not realize the importance and benefits of patenting inventions. Given the emphasis of the importance of publishing research for tenure and promotion; applying for a patent is not often thought of as a path to follow. Yet, *research and patents are not mutually exclusive* but are closely linked. Furthermore, research has shown that increased licensing has led to research.

Building awareness

In the understandable rush to get published and funded, scientists tend to reveal their inventions too early and in too much detail to ever receive a patent. Yet, if inventors do not file a patent application within a year of disclosing the patent to the public, they may lose the right to stop others from exploiting their invention for their own gain. Then both the faculty member and the university would stand to lose the asset and any associated financial benefits yielded. An understanding of this information by faculty is important if universities want to grow their IP portfolio.

While the much deserved respect and recognition can be earned from technical communities by publishing in a highly regarded journal; being named an inventor on a patent opens different horizons and can offer valuable benefits. Also a patent filing does not preclude faculty from publishing. Once a faculty member files a patent they can also publish.

Incentivizing

To inspire faculty to purse innovation and IP protection, universities are beginning to establish faculty incentives. These incentives include recognition, awards, internal funding, a Patent Wall of Fame, university and inventor ownership, and royalty policies. To incentivize faculty they need to know that they have the support of the university and if they do pursue a patent, there is a way to bring it to fruition. Many universities have put in place commercialization infrastructures to streamline processes and nurture invention. Some of these structures are discussed in Chapter 2.

Conclusion

The protection of IP is critical for the US to maintain its title as the global leader in innovation and for the future growth of the economy. Also, it is an important asset for the individual inventor. It gives an inventor the exclusive right to exclude others from making, using, selling, offering for sale, or importing the claimed invention for a limited period of time. It has the status of a "legal monopoly." However, it is not a right to practice or use the invention. Patents are assets that can be sold, licensed, mortgaged, assigned, or transferred. Corporations not only use patents to protect what they are currently doing, but also to set up roadblocks to keep competitors from moving down a particular line of research or product line. The following are some trends that have been evolving as evidenced from the examples in the chapters. Previously, patents protected products but now patents themselves are products with design patents taking on more prominence and importance. Although patenting in US universities did occur prior to the passage of Bayh–Dole Act, patenting dramatically increased and became more systematic with processes, procedures and infrastructures put in place.

Many universities are increasing their prominent role in advancing local and regional economic development, and patents are an efficient way for university technology based on research to be introduced to the market, industry, and for the social good. To encourage faculty to purse innovation and IP protection, universities are establishing faculty incentives and increasing an awareness of the processes required to do so.

Summary

This chapter introduces the types of IP — patents, copyrights, trademarks, and trade secrets. It presents what is patentable, the types of patents, who can apply for a patent, the types of patent applications summarized in Figure 1, filing deadlines, and an overview of the patent examination process which is summarized in Figure 2. The chapter continues with examples of "patent wars," and examples of patent infringement cases. The next topic is copyrights — what it protected, how to obtain a copyright, followed by examples of copyright infringement cases, trademarks and trade secrets, and their benefits. Important legislation influencing patents such as the Bayh–Dole Act and the impact it had and continues to have on universities is presented followed by a discussion on some internal processes within universities to determine patentability and whether to license or form a startup illustrated in Figures 3 and 4. The chapter ends with a discussion on university concerns regarding the role of patents in universities.

Selected Readings

(1) Cullis, Roger (2007). *Patents, Inventions and the Dynamics of Innovation: A Multidisciplinary Study*, illustrated edition, Edward Elgar Pub.

This unique study investigates the path of innovation in the electrical, electronics and communications engineering industries. It presents a holistic, multi-disciplinary analysis of innovation based on case studies of paradigm-changing inventions — spanning 200 years — which altered the course of the global economy. The stimuli and constraints which control the dynamics of these innovations are pin-pointed in this book and applied in emerging technologies.

(2) Knight, H. Jackson (2013). *Patent Strategy: For Researchers and Research Managers*, 3rd edition, Wiley.

As individuals and companies realize the importance of their inventions, issues surrounding patent laws and practices are taking center stage around the world.

Patent Strategy introduces researchers to patent applications and patent portfolios. With minimum use of 'legal jargon' it provides the technical professionals with the assistance and advice they require to understand the legal complexities that they may encounter before and during a patent application. It also discusses the responsibilities of the researcher after patent applications have been filed and the role the researcher can play in the maintenance of a global patent estate.

(3) Morris, Edmund (2019). *Edison*, Random House.

Although Thomas Alva Edison was the most famous American of his time, and remains an international name today, he is mostly remembered only for the gift of universal electric light. His invention of the first practical incandescent lamp 140 years ago dazzled the world so much — already reeling from his invention of the phonograph and dozens of other revolutionary devices — that it cast a shadow over his later achievements. In all, this near-deaf genius ("I haven't heard a bird sing since I was twelve years old") patented 1,093 inventions, not including others, such as the X-ray fluoroscope, that he left unlicensed for the benefit of medicine.

(4) Evan, Hence, Andrea, *All About Inventing: Everything You Need To Know About Patents,* Purposely Created Publishing Group.

While inventors can have great ideas and know everything about their inventions, they often don't know how to go about protecting those inventions. They try to get patents to protect their intellectual property but make avoidable mistakes and spend unnecessary money — and sometimes invest their life savings in inventions that are not patentable or lose their intellectual property to invention scamming companies.

For people who need help navigating the patent office, *All About Inventing: Everything You Need to Know About Patents from a Former USPTO Patent Examiner & Patent Attorney* is invaluable. Andrea Hence Evans, former patent examiner at the USPTO and current patent attorney, has written this book to explain different types of patents, patent prosecution, how to avoid and correct rejections, and more! This book will help you understand your options to protect your invention and help you navigate your patent application through the USPTO.

References

Sites to search for prior art for patents:

- Google patents
  - Google.com/patents (US patents & published App)
  - Includes Google Scholar

- USPTO Databases
  - Patents
  - Published Applications
- European Patent Office
  - ep.espacenet.com
- Lexis/Westlaw/Bloomberg

AUTM Insight Newsletter, Bayh-Dole Act, https://autm.net/about-tech-transfer/advocacy/legislation/bayh-dole-act/.

Christina, S. and Inna, D. (2014). Turning your research into something more: Patents versus papers, *Mintz Insights*, https://www.mintz.com/insights-center/viewpoints/2231/2014-12-turning-your-research-something-more-patents-versus-papers.

Crovitz, G. (2011). Google, Motorola and the Patent Wars, *Wall Street Journal*, 22.

Jaffe, A. B. (1989). Real effects of academic research. *The American Economic Review*, 79(5), 957–970.

Jason Owen-Smith, W. W. *The Expanding Role of University Patenting in the Life Sciences: Assessing the Importance of Experience and Connectivity Forthcoming, Research Policy, Inclusive.* Powell University of Michigan Stanford University.

Kaufman Foundation, University Technology Transfer, https://www.kauffman.org/microsites/state-of-the-field/topics/technology-and-innovation/university-technology-transfer#litref-12.

Murmann, J. P. (2003). *Knowledge and Competitive Advantage: The Coevolution of Firms, Technology, and National Institutions*, Cambridge University Press.

Rosenberg, N. and Nelson, R. R. (1994). American universities and technical advance in industry. *Research Policy*, 23(3), 323–348.

University Licensing: Harnessing or Tarnishing Faculty Research? Jerry Thursby, Georgia Institute of Technology, Marie Thursby, Georgia Institute of Technology and NBER, Innovation Policy and the Economy, Volume 10, 2010, NBER.

Wisniewski, H. (2018). New structure at U Alaska generates improvements in disclosures, start-ups. TechTransferCentral.com/TTT, 12(8), 1124–1129.

World Intellectual Property Organization (WIPO). https://www.wipo.int/portal/en/index.html.

Zucker, L. G., Darby, M. R. and Brewer, M. B. (1998). Intellectual human capital and the birth of U.S. biotechnology enterprises. *The American Economic Review*, 88(1), 290–306.

Chapter 4

Identifying Markets and Opportunities for the Ideas and Technology

Learning Objectives

- To understand the aspects and process of creating a new venture.
- To understand the importance of early identification of markets for the technology.
- To know how to identify and access domestic markets.
- To be able to identify and evaluate international opportunities for the technology.
- To be able to create an opportunity assessment plan.

Opening Profile — Cindy Furse

Q1: Submitter Information

Name of Nominee	**Cindy Furse**
University the Nominee is representing	**University of Utah**
Email	cfurse@ece.utah.edu
Phone number	8016474174

Cynthia M. Furse (M'85–SM'99–F'2008) is the Associate Vice President for Research at the University of Utah and a Professor of Electrical and

Computer Engineering. Dr. Furse received her BS in Electrical Engineering with a Mathematics minor in 1985, MS Degree in Electrical Engineering in 1988, and PhD in Electrical Engineering in 1994 from the University of Utah. She has applied her expertise in electromagnetics to sensing and communication in complex lossy scattering media such as the human body, geophysical prospecting, ionospheric plasma, and aircraft wiring networks. She has taught electromagnetics, wireless communication, computational electromagnetics, microwave engineering, antenna design, introductory electrical engineering, and has been a leader in the development of the flipped classroom.

Dr. Furse is a Fellow of the Institute of Electrical and Electronics Engineers (IEEE) and the National Academy of Inventors. She is a past AdCom member for the IEEE AP society and past chair of the IEEE AP Education Committee. She has received numerous teaching and research awards including the 2009 IEEE Harriett B. Rigas Medal for Excellence in Teaching. She is a founder of LiveWire Innovation, Inc., a spin-off company commercializing devices to locate intermittent faults on live wires.

Q2: The nominee's position when they created the company. Describe the nominee's process with the university as they were creating the company. Be as detailed as possible.

Dr. Furse was an Associate Professor at Utah State University, where she was doing research on methods for locating faults in aging aircraft wiring. She received funding from the State of Utah to create a "Center of Excellence for Smart Wiring", which enabled her to further develop various technologies for wire fault location.

After developing, testing, and demonstrating a prototype device, it became clear that what the customer (Navair) was asking for wasn't actually going to solve the problem because the electrical faults occurred in flights (from vibration, condensation, etc.) and were often not there when the plane was on the ground. These "no fault found" conditions were extremely frustrating for maintainers and often resulted in disasters such as TWA800 and Swissair 111 air disasters. Several months later, she came up with the concept of using spread spectrum signals (used in your cell phone or GPS) as the test signals on the wires, which allows testing while the wires are live and in use (in flight). Her first PhD student helped build and test the prototypes for this method.

With the (strong) insistence of the Navy and Air Force, for whom she was doing research, Dr. Furse and her student founded LiveWire and began applying for Small Business Innovation Research (SBIR) funding to complete the development. The initial concept emerged around 1998/1999.

Q3: Describe the nominee's experience working with the university in creating the company. What were the challenges? What support did they receive? Be as detailed as possible.

At about this time (2002), Dr. Furse moved to the University of Utah. The movement of the IP from one university to another was uncertain, and costs from a lingering legal battle with a small company she was originally partnered with were a problem. After months (or years?), the two universities worked out an agreement on the existing and ongoing IP and agreed that any royalties from it would first pay off the legal fees before being distributed to the inventors. Dr. Furse continued research at this point, LiveWire (led by her now-graduated PhD student) continued to apply for (and eventually receive) SBIRs. The university hosted a display of university inventions and invited local entrepreneurs and investors. LiveWire won "best of the show" award and attracted numerous business prospects. Two experienced entrepreneurs joined the team and remained with the company for several years. There were numerous challenges in trying to break into the aviation field which was slow to adopt, highly regulated, etc. The startup had numerous false starts including being specked into circuit breakers (that partner canceled their circuit breaker program), aircraft (that partner canceled the aircraft), etc. They had technical challenges, business and market challenges, leadership team challenges, engineering team challenges, etc. The market kept changing rapidly and it was extremely difficult to keep up to understand it. For nearly a decade, they were funded by SBIR and other government grants; they were small but in the black. They had grants from Navair, US Air Force, Federal Aviation Administration, private companies, and others. Eventually, they changed leadership, including private investment and changed course to emphasize non-aircraft applications. Even though this was a good move, they continued to have challenges building a product that was "just right" for the applications. In time, they stumbled upon rail applications, where cable theft was a serious (expensive and dangerous) problem. They found an awesome new partner and started beta-testing the device. They were hopeful that this would finally be a large-scale product. In 2018, 18 years after the original concept, they shuttered the Salt Lake City arm of LiveWire and moved it to the UK partner's location and to CA; where their other partner was located. They also have an arm in Taiwan, with a young entrepreneur, who has also not done a lot.

Introduction

Most scientists and engineers do not envision being involved in anything but continually doing research furthering the science or application of the science with a focus on research and development. While this indeed is true for the majority of scientists, some like to try new things such as being a part of creating a new venture. As a scientist and developer of the technology, it is important to be familiar with the aspect of market opportunities and new venture creation.

Nature of Venture Creation

Many scientists and engineers enjoy the benefits of having their idea taken to market and/or actually have some part in the process. There are rewards for assisting the university by licensing your technology both monetarily and in creating goodwill. Besides, one may learn about the process of commercialization and business.

To follow this next step and assist more in creating a new university venture, the three necessary elements are the idea from the inventor/scientist, the business creation and implementation by the entrepreneur, and funds provided by an investor, fund, or government program (see Figure 1). Even if you are really interested in continuing research in the field of your choice, assisting in making your idea more appealing to an identified market can be rewarding in terms of your feelings of worth and reputation as well as monetarily. You may even decide to be a scientific

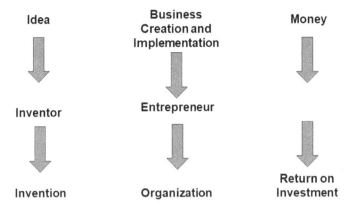

Figure 1. Elements of new venture creation.

advisor or be on the advisory board of the new venture created. You may be reluctant to be involved and fall into one of the three most frequently mentioned categories of decisions not to start a business. According to the Gallop Poll in 2015, three reasons are as follows: liking the security of a steady income (84%); not having enough savings (68%); worrying that the odds of success are low (66%). The latter is supported by the Bureau of Labor Statistics in 2015. The following survival rates by year were reported: 80% in year 2; 69% in year 3; 60% in year 4; 52% and 47% in year 6. And, these figures may be high due to the many Internet startups not in the official count and tracking system.

Ideas come in a variety of forms and their degree of uniqueness or innovativeness varies. The types of innovation in Figure 2 are shown in terms of their frequency of occurrences. As is indicated, ordinary innovations such as a slight modification of an existing product/service or an almost identical new product/service are the most frequent innovations launched in terms of the number of occurrences. These ordinary innovations are things such as "New and Improved Tide", another Pizza Parlor in the geographic area that already has one, a software system, or application that has little difference from all the ones presently available on the market.

Technological innovations are the second most frequent innovations that occur. Unlike ordinary innovations, there is a significant difference in the new product/service being offered but not as technologically and scientifically advanced as a breakthrough innovation. Technological innovations make meaningful advancements in their product/service area. Examples of this type of innovation include the following: a watch where the watch face could flip-up revealing a carrier for pictures (Hour Power LLC); a new system for quickly screening chemical compounds by pharmaceutical companies (Analiza Inc.); or a bird app that provides for the easy identification (sight or sound) of a bird, its habitat, and recording the time, date, and place of the sighting, and being able to send this information to anyone desired (Green Mountain Digital).

The final type of innovation — breakthrough innovation — is the one most desired, yet occurs the most infrequently of the three types of innovation (Figure 2). These innovations are extremely unique and often establish the base platform that is the foundation for the development of future innovations in the area. These innovations, whenever possible, are protected by patents or if not patentable covered by trade secrets or copyrights. Some breakthrough innovations include automobiles, airplanes, the computer, nanotechnology, and the Internet. There is frequent disagreement as to whether an innovation is a technological innovation or a breakthrough innovation due to the thin line between the two.

Another useful way for a scientist or entrepreneur to classify his/her new idea for a product/service is based on the consumer's (business or

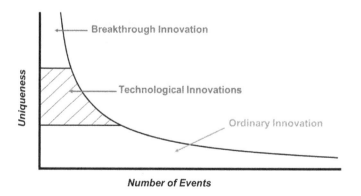

Figure 2.   Types of innovative idea.

individual) view of the innovation. From the consumer's perspective, a new product/service is often viewed in terms of its degree of awareness or its degree of disruption in how things are presently being done. A scale from having little or no disruption on the established ways of doing things (continuous innovation) to having a significant disruption or requiring a completely new way for doing things (discontinuous innovation). Why is this important? It will take the typical consumer longer to accept and purchase a discontinuous innovation (first cell phones, iPads, or even computers) due to the changes required than for continuous innovations (new year model of a car, the iPhone 7, package changes and/or size changes). By taking longer to be accepted — discontinuous innovations require more education, more unique marketing, and more capital for them to be successful.

Product Planning and Development Process

Once technological ideas emerge, there is a need for further development and refinement. This refining process — the product planning and development process — is divided into five major stages: idea stage, concept stage, product development stage, test marketing stage, and commercialization, which starts the *product life cycle* (see Figure 3) (Robert and Michael, 1991).

At each stage of the *product planning and development process*, criteria for evaluation needs to be established. These criteria should be all-inclusive and quantitative to screen the product carefully in this particular stage of development so that a *go/no-go* decision can be made. Criteria should be established to evaluate the new idea in terms of market opportunity, competition, the marketing system, financial, and development factors.

A market opportunity in the form of a new or current desire for the product/service idea needs to exist. The determination of market demand is by far the most important criterion of a proposed new product idea. Assessment of the market opportunity and size needs to evaluate the characteristics and attitudes of consumers or industries that may buy the product, the size of this potential market in units, the nature of the market

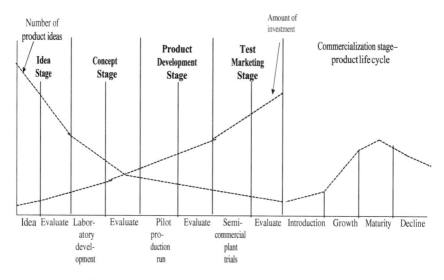

Figure 3.   The product planning and development process.

compared to its stage in the life cycle (growing or declining), and the share of the market the product could reasonably capture.

Competing products/services, prices, and marketing efforts should also be evaluated, particularly in terms of the impact on the probable market share of the proposed idea. The new idea should be able to compete successfully with products/services already in the market by having features that will meet or be better than the current and anticipated competition. The new idea should have some unique selling propositions when compared to the competitive products/services fulfilling the same consumer needs. Very, very few, if any, ideas fulfill a need that is not presently being met by something available on the market in developed economies. The idea is just meeting the needs with a better process.

Entrepreneurs, scientists, and inventors need to be concerned with formally evaluating an idea throughout its evolution. Care must be taken to ensure the idea can be the basis for a new venture. This can be done through careful evaluation of the results in a go or no-go decision at each of the stages of the product planning and development process, namely the idea stage, the concept stage, the product development stage, and the test marketing stage.

Idea stage

Developing a prototype and moving the idea forward can be costly. This is especially true if you need to hire a product design firm or a developer. "Don't go too far too fast without doing your homework on what your customers want and make sure there is not already an easy solution for the problem you're solving," says Jack D. Beasley, Managing Director of the USC/Columbia Technology Incubator and Senior Program Manager at the Office of Economic Engagement at the University of South Carolina.

One needs to simply ask potential customers whether your idea sounds appealing. Beasley advises doing in-person surveys of your target audience in a setting where you can find a lot of them. For instance, if you've dreamed up an app to help college students with time management, visit a campus to ask students about the need for your product, what problems they want to be solved by your app, what technology they already use, and what they might pay. No obvious place to go? Create a free survey on a site such as Survey Monkey, and ask people to provide information and share the survey with others.

Promising new product/service ideas should be identified and impractical ones eliminated in every stage but potentially the *idea stage*, allows maximum use of resources. One evaluation method successfully used in this stage is the systematic market evaluation checklist; each new idea is expressed in terms of its chief values, merits, and benefits. Potential customers are presented with clusters of new product/service values to assist with determining which, if any, new product/service alternatives should be pursued and which should not. Many potential new idea alternatives can be evaluated with this method, with only the promising ideas being further developed; resources are then not wasted on ideas incompatible with the market's value.

It is important to determine the need for the new idea as well as its value to the entrepreneur/company. If there is no need for the suggested product, its development should not be continued. Similarly, the new product/service idea should not be developed if it does not have any benefit or value to the entrepreneur or firm. To accurately determine the need for a new idea, it is helpful to define the potential needs of the market in terms of timing, satisfaction, alternatives, benefits and risks, future expectations, price-versus-product performance features, market structure and size, and economic conditions.

The need determination should focus on the type of need, it's timing, the users involved in trying the product/service, the importance of controllable marketing variables, the overall market structure, and the characteristics of the market. Each of these factors should be evaluated in terms of the characteristics of the new idea with the aspects and capabilities of the products/services currently available on the market for satisfying the particular need. This analysis will indicate the extent of the opportunity available.

Concept stage

After a new product/service idea has passed the evaluation criteria in the idea stage, it should be further developed and refined through interaction with consumers. In the *concept stage*, the refined idea is tested to determine consumer acceptance. Initial reactions to the concept are obtained from potential customers or members of the distribution channel when appropriate. One method of measuring consumer acceptance is the conversational interview in which selected respondents are required to review statements that reflect the physical characteristics and attributes of the product/service idea. Where competing products/services exist, these statements can also compare their related features. Favorable as well as unfavorable product/service features can be discovered by analyzing consumers' responses; the favorable features then being incorporated into the new product/service.

Features, price, and promotion should be evaluated for both studying the concept and identifying any major competing products by asking the following questions:

- How does the new concept compare with competitive products/services in terms of quality and reliability?
- Is the concept superior or deficient compared with products/services currently available in the market?
- Is this a good market opportunity for the firm?

Product development stage

In the *product development stage*, consumer reaction to the physical product/service is determined. One tool frequently used in this stage is the consumer panel, in which a group of potential consumers are given product samples. Participants keep a record of their use of the product and comment on its virtues and deficiencies. This technique is more applicable for a product than a service idea.

The panel of potential customers can also be given a sample of the product and one or more competitive products simultaneously. Then one of several methods — such as multiple brand comparison, risk analysis, level of repeat purchases, or intensity of preference analysis — can be used to determine consumer preference.

Test marketing stage

Although the results of the product development stage provide the basis for the final marketing plan, a market test can be done, particularly with business to consumer products, to increase the certainty of successful commercialization. This last step in the evaluation process, the *test marketing stage*, provides actual sales results which indicates the acceptance level of consumers. Positive test results indicate the degree of probability of a successful product/service launch and company formation.

At this point, a reality check is needed. Entrepreneurs and scientists are known for their optimism. The best way to determine if your enthusiasm is justified is to write a business plan, which is discussed in Chapter 6. This document typically includes a description of your product or service, your marketing plan, a market analysis, and financial projections. For assistance with the process, consult a good book or chapter on the topic or the BSA's Business Plan Tool at sba.gov.

Then get feedback from a mentor or an accountant who serves other businesses in the technology area. They can help figure out if all those components you expect are realistic. If not, you've got to give serious thought as to how to make it work because if it does not work out on paper, it probably will not work.

Getting the Idea to the Market

Regardless of whether the idea is an ordinary innovation, a technological innovation, or a breakthrough innovation or the market is a business-to-business market, a business-to-consumer market, or a business-to-government market, an entrepreneur of some type is needed to move the idea into a venture (business) and launch the idea in the market. As indicated in Figure 4, there are four types of entrepreneurs who can do this: individual entrepreneurs, corporate entrepreneurs, government entrepreneurs, or social entrepreneurs, each of which are defined below.

Entrepreneurship is the process of creating something new with value by devoting the necessary time and effort; assuming the accompanying financial, physical, and social risks; and receiving the rewards of monetary/personal satisfaction and independence.

Corporate entrepreneurship, which is often referred to as intrapreneurship or corporate venturing, is the process by which an individual inside an organization pursues opportunities independent of the resources they currently control; this involves doing new things and departing from the usual ways to create something new of value. Which in turn, results in the development, renewal, and innovation within that organization. Corporate entrepreneurship requires encouraging and facilitating entrepreneurial behaviors within an established business/organization. A system that enables individuals to be creative, invent technologies, and new ways of doing things.

Government (public sector) entrepreneurship, which is called governpreneurship, becomes more and more important when public revenues are

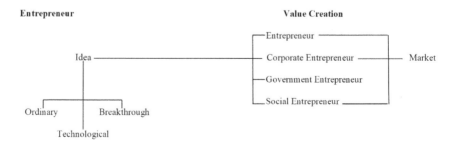

Figure 4.   Idea to the market.

reduced, catastrophes occur, and more services are requested. While there are no proven models for achieving public sector entrepreneurship, whether it can occur and the degree to which it does depends to a great extent on its internal and external environments. Since entrepreneurship is a universal concept, it can be a part of non-profit organizations as well as governments and other sector organizations. Governpreneurship is discussed in terms of framework, aspects and transforming, government entrepreneurs, managing internal and external politics, and building a coalition.

Social entrepreneurship has made significant contributions to communities and society in general by adopting business models to offer innovative and creative solutions to complex social issues. Despite increased interest in social entrepreneurship and the credence of the growing impact of social entrepreneurship, there has been somewhat limited research in the area.

Entrepreneur and Decision-Making

As a scientist/inventor, it is important to understand the decision-making aspects in starting a new venture is to take your idea to the market. As is indicated in Figure 5, a new venture starts with zero revenues and sales, and typically has one of the four outcomes (continue, initial public offering, sale, or create a family business) over a 7-year average and even longer for breakthrough technologies and biomedical ideas. A venture has a negative cash flow where cost is greater than revenue for a period of time until one of the most significant times for new ventures occur — its positive cash flow (the first-time revenues are greater than cost). This is particularly significant until positive cash flow occurs, the difference between the cost and revenues (if any) that occur needs to be financed outside the company. Sources of the financing (funding) are discussed in Chapters 8 and 9. It is extremely important that the time period from starting (launching) the venture and to when positive cash flow occurs should be as short as possible because one of the reasons causing a venture to fail (go belly up) is running out of cash (funds).

Once positive cash flow is reached, the venture continues to grow, becomes profitable, and then experiences a significant acceleration in

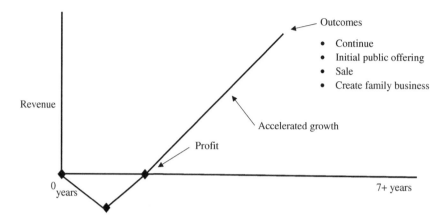

Positive Cash Flow = Revenue > Cost

Figure 5.   Entrepreneur decisions.

revenue growth. Each of these phases also needs to be carefully managed by the entrepreneur. Individuals who supply the capital during the phase before the venture has enough revenue to cover the costs usually want to have their investment money returned plus the return on investment, which requires some exit strategy such as issuing an IPO (an initial public offering) or selling the venture to another company or private equity firm, which is documented in Chapter 7.

The entrepreneurial process

The overall process of starting a new venture is outlined in the entrepreneurial process. An entrepreneur needs to first find, evaluate, and develop an opportunity and then overcome the forces that resist the creation of something new. The process has four distinct phases: (1) identification and evaluation of the opportunity; (2) development of the business plan; (3) determination of the required resources; and (4) management of the resulting enterprise (Figure 6). Although these phases proceed progressively, no one stage is dealt with in isolation or is totally completed before the work on other phases occurs. For example, to successfully identify and evaluate an opportunity (step 1), an entrepreneur must have in mind the resources, particularly the financial resources, needed.

Identify and evaluate the opportunity

Opportunity identification and evaluation are probably the most frustrating tasks. Most good business opportunities do not suddenly appear, but rather result from an entrepreneur's alertness to possibilities, or in some cases, the establishment of mechanisms that identify potential opportunities. For example, one entrepreneur asks at every cocktail party whether anyone is using a product that does not adequately fulfill its intended purpose. This person is constantly looking for a need and an opportunity to create a better product. Another entrepreneur always monitors the play habits and toys of her nieces and nephews. This is her way of looking for any niche toy products for a new venture.

Although most entrepreneurs do not have formal mechanisms for identifying business opportunities, certain sources are always beneficial: consumers and business associates, members of the distribution system, and technical people. How many times have you heard someone comment, "If only there was a product that would ..." This comment can result in the creation of a new business. One entrepreneur's evaluation of why so many business executives were complaining about the lack of good technical writing and word-processing services resulted in the creation of her own business venture to fill this need. Her technical writing service grew to 10 employees in 2 years.

Due to their close contact with the end users, channel members in the distribution system also evaluate product needs. One entrepreneur started a college bookstore after hearing students complain about the high cost of books and the lack of service provided by the only bookstore on campus. Many other entrepreneurs have identified business opportunities through a discussion with a retailer, wholesaler, or manufacturer's representative.

Finally, technically oriented individuals often conceptualize business opportunities when working on other projects. One entrepreneur's business resulted from seeing the application of a plastic resin compound in developing and manufacturing a new type of pallet while developing the resin application in another totally unrelated area — casket moldings.

Whether the opportunity is identified by using input from consumers, business associates, channel members, or technical people, each opportunity must be carefully screened and evaluated. This evaluation of the opportunity is perhaps the most critical element of the entrepreneurial process, as it allows the entrepreneur to assess whether the specific product or service has the returns needed compared to the resources required. As indicated in Figure 6, this evaluation process involves looking at the length of the opportunity, its real and perceived value, its risks and returns, its fit with the personal skills and goals of the entrepreneur, and its uniqueness or differential advantage in its competitive environment.

The market size and length of opportunity are the primary basis for determining the risks and rewards. The risk reflects the market, competition, technology, and amount of capital involved. The amount of capital needed provides the basis for the return and rewards.

Finally, the opportunity must fit the personal skills and goals of the entrepreneur. It is particularly important that the entrepreneur be able to put forth the necessary time and effort required to make the venture

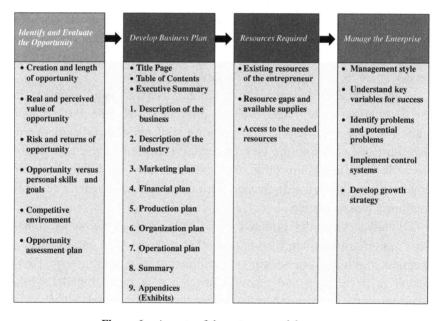

Figure 6. Aspects of the entrepreneurial process.

succeed. Although many entrepreneurs feel the desire can be developed along with the venture, typically it does not materialize. An entrepreneur must believe in the opportunity so much that he or she will make the necessary sacrifices to develop the opportunity and manage the resulting organization. This is his or her passion. The opportunity can be best evaluated using an opportunity assessment plan, which is discussed next in this chapter.

Develop a business plan

A good business plan must be developed in order to exploit the defined opportunity. This is a very time-consuming phase of the entrepreneurial process. An entrepreneur usually has not prepared a business plan before and does not have the resources available to do a good job. Although the preparation of the business plan is the focus of Chapter 7, it is important to understand the basic issues involved as well as the three major sections of the plan (see Tables 4–6 of Chapter 5).

Each of the three sections has a specific purpose. Section 1 contains the most important document when raising capital — the two-page executive summary. Section 2 is the main body of the business plan and needs to contain each of the following essential elements: description of the business, description of industry and market, technology plan, marketing plan, financial plan, production plan, organizational plan, operational plan, and summary. In some businesses, a non-technical service like a restaurant or an online service provider, there usually is no need for a technology plan or a production plan. Often, the production plan becomes an outsourcing plan since it is usually more cost effective and requires a lower capital to outsource any production for at least the first 3 years. One coaster manufacturing company started by outsourcing and has continued the practice today with revenues of about $800,000. The final section — Section 3 — contains the backup support material for Section 2. These include such things as résumés of the entrepreneur and management team, brief biographies of the board of advisors, market and industry statistics, list of suppliers, signed contracts and important articles on the industry, market, and their growth rates. No new materials should be introduced in Section 3. A good business plan is essential in developing the opportunity and determining the resources required, obtaining those resources, and successfully managing the resulting venture.

Determine the resources required

The resources needed for addressing the opportunity must also be determined. This process starts with an appraisal of the entrepreneur's present resources. Any resources that are critical need to be delineated from those that are just helpful. Care must be taken not to underestimate the amount and variety of resources needed. The downside risks associated with insufficient or inappropriate resources should also be assessed.

Acquiring the needed resources in a timely manner while giving up as little equity and control as possible is the next step in the entrepreneurial process. An entrepreneur should strive to maintain as large an ownership position as possible, particularly in the startup stage. As the business develops and more funds will probably be needed to finance the growth of the venture, requiring more ownership to be relinquished. Alternative suppliers of financial resources, the focus of Chapters 7 and 8, along with their needs and desires should also be identified. By understanding the needs of the resource supplier, the entrepreneur can structure a deal that enables the resources to be acquired at the lowest possible cost with the least loss of control.

Launch and manage the enterprise

After resources are acquired, the entrepreneur must use them to implement the business plan. The launch strategy and plan need to be developed and implemented. Focus, focus, focus is the key phase in doing this. The operational problems of the enterprise must also be examined. This involves implementing a management style and structure, as well as determining the key variable for success. A control system must be established so that any problem areas can be quickly identified and resolved. Some entrepreneurs have difficulty in managing and growing the venture they created.

Information sources

There are many sources of information both on competitive companies and products/services including the market size, characteristics, and growth rate available to the entrepreneur in identifying an appropriate opportunity. These will be discussed in terms of general assistance, general information sources, industry and market information sources, competitive company and product/service information, government sources, search engines, trade associations, and trade publications.

General assistance

Information and assistance are readily available for entrepreneurs, starting or growing a new venture. SCORE (www.score.org) is a nonprofit organization that provides free online and in-person assistance in about 400 chapter locations throughout the United States. The assistance takes the form of training, consulting, and mentoring provided mainly by retired executives and entrepreneurs.

Small business development centers

US Small Business Administration (SBA) (sba.gov/aboutsba/sbdaprograms/sbdc/sbdlocator/index.html) has small business development centers in over 1,100 locations throughout the United States. It provides counseling, training, and technical assistance on all aspects of starting and managing a new venture. Each location also has an on-site resource library. These centers are a part of the overall SBA (sba.gov), which also provides a wide variety of resources and tools for the entrepreneur. One of the helpful items in the SBA's resource library is the Small Business Planner, a step-by-step guide for starting your new venture. The SBA also has a Women's Business Center and a Minority Business Center.

General information sources

The US Chamber Small Business Center (uschamber.com/sb) provides startup assistance mainly through Web-based tools and resources. Its startup toolkit is very helpful in beginning a business as it focuses on everything from evaluating an idea to developing a business plan, accessing capital, and launching the venture. Other useful tools for various business documents, such as spreadsheet templates and other government forms, are also provided under the "Tools" section.

Other Websites providing useful information include the following:

1. *National Association of Small Business Investment Companies* (*nasbic.org*) — provides an online database of small venture capital firm members and a guide to obtaining SBIC financing.
2. *National Venture Capital Association* (*nvca.org*) — provides information on the venture capital industry as well as access to state and regional venture capital firms.
3. *National Business Incubation Association* (*inbia.org*) — provides information on the role of incubators, how to select the right incubator, and a listing of national and international incubators.
4. *FastTrac* (*www.fasttrac.org*) — funded by the Kauffman Foundation, provides educational programs for entrepreneurs throughout the United States.
5. *Active Capital* (*ACE-Net, activecapital.org*) — provides an opportunity for entrepreneurs to connect with accredited investors throughout the United States. Counseling, mentoring, and training are also provided.
6. *Collegiate Entrepreneurs' Organization* (*CEO, c-e-o.org*) — provides information on entrepreneurship programs at the undergraduate level in numerous colleges and universities.
7. *Consortium for Entrepreneurship Education* (*entre-ed.org*) — provides information on entrepreneurship programs and education throughout the United States.

8. *Ewing Marion Kauffman Foundation* (*Kauffman.org*) — provides resources for entrepreneurship education, research and lists the angel (private investor) groups throughout the United States.

Industry and market information

There are a wide variety of databases that provide significant information about the industry and market. These include the following:

1. *Plukett* — provides industry data, market research, trends and statistic on markets and forecasts.
2. *Frost & Sullivan* — provides industry-specific information on industries such as aerospace and defense, chemicals/materials, telecom/IT, consumer products, electronics, energy, healthcare, industrial automation, and transportation.
3. *Euromonitor* — provides consumer market sizes and marketing parameters as well as information on companies and brands.
4. *Gartner* — provides information on technology markets.
5. *Gale Directory Library* — provides industry statistics and a directory of nonprofit organizations and associations.

Competitive company and product/service information

Besides looking at the various products/service options presently available for satisfying the market needs through Google, several sources supply product/service information on competing products/services including the following companies:

1. *Business Source Complete* — provides company and industry information by scanning the Datamonitor reports.
2. *Hoovers* — provides information on both large and small companies with links to competitors in the same North American Industrial Classification System (NAICS) category.
3. *Mergent* — provides detailed company and product information on US and international companies.

Government sources

There are numerous information sources available from the US government including:

- Census Reports
  - o factfinder.census.gov/
  - o www.census.gov/population/international/
  - o www.census.gov/econ/ (ratios)
- Export/Import Authority
  - o UN Comtrade
  - o www.usa.gov/import-export
- North American Industrial Classification System and Standard Industrial Classification codes
  - o www.naics.com
  - o www.osha.gov/pls/imis/sic_manual.html
  - o Similar information is provided by governments of other countries as well.

Search engines

There are many key terms in order to search for the industry, market, and competitive information such as:

- Search: _____ and statistics
- Search: _____ and market share
- Search: _____ and industry
- Search: _____ and association

Trade associations

Trade associations in the United States and throughout the world are also a good source of industry data regarding a specific country. Some trade associations perform market surveys of the members' domestic and international activities and are strategically involved in the international standard issues for their specific industry.

Trade publications

There are numerous domestic and international publications specific to an industry that are also a good source of information. The editorial content of these journals can provide interesting information and insight on trends, companies, and trade shows by giving a more local perspective on the particular market and market conditions. Sometimes trade journals are the best source of information on competition and growth rates in a particular industry.

Summary

This chapter focuses on the importance and process of identifying a market for the newly developed technological idea. The basic types of innovation are discussed along with the product planning and development processes. Following a discussion of the entrepreneurial process, the chapter concludes with a discussion of the many sources of data available on competitive products/services and markets.

Selected Readings

(1) Hegde, D. and Luo, H. (2017). "Patent Publication and the Market for Ideas". *Management Science*, 64(2), 652–672.

In this article, we study the effect of invention disclosure through patent publication on the market for ideas. We do so by analyzing the effects of the American Inventor's Protection Act of 1999 (AIPA) — which required US patent applications to be published 18 months after their filing date rather than at the time the patent was granted — at the time the deals were licensed in the biomedical industry. We find that post-AIPA, US patent applications are significantly more likely to be licensed before granting of the patent and shortly after the 18-month publication date. Licensing delays are reduced by about 10 months, on average, after AIPA's enactment. These findings suggest a hitherto unexplored benefit of the patent system: by requiring inventions to be published through a credible, standardized, and centralized repository, it mitigates information costs for buyers and sellers and thus facilitates transactions in the market for ideas.

(2) Good, M., Knockaert, M., Soppe, B. and Wright, M. (2018). "The Technology Transfer Ecosystem in Academia. An Organizational Design Perspective". *Technovation*, 82–83, April–May 2019, 35–50.

University technology transfer (TT) has emerged as an important and standalone research field over the past few decades. Given the great challenges that are involved with transferring science to the market, many universities have established TT offices, science parks, incubators, and university venture funds — an organizational assemblage labeled the TT ecosystem. By reviewing the extant literature on the TT ecosystem and its components, this article aims at providing an understanding of the organizational design of the TT ecosystem. Surprisingly, the results of this review show that research considering this ecosystem as a whole is largely lacking. Specifically, the literature on the topic can be typified as atomistic, with a wide range of studies on the various TT components and a dearth of research studying holistically, the wider knowledge transfer ecosystem that reflects the evolution and impact of academic entrepreneurship. Consequently, this article presents an organizational design framework that sets out a future research agenda for studies taking a holistic approach.

(3) Gibson, I., Rosen, D. and Stucker, B. (2015). "Business Opportunities and Future Directions". In *Additive Manufacturing Technologies*. New York, NY: Springer, pp. 475–486.

The current approach for many manufacturing enterprises is to centralize product development, product production, and product distribution in relatively few physical locations. These locations can decrease even further when companies off-shore product development, production, and/or distribution to other countries/companies to take advantage of lower resources, labor, or overhead costs. The resulting concentration of employment leads to regions of disproportionately high underemployment and/or unemployment. As a result, nations can have regions of underpopulation with consequent national problems such as infrastructure being underutilized and long-term territorial integrity being compromised (Beale (2000). *Rural Cond Trends,* 11(2), 27–31).

References

Ejermo, O. and Toivanen, H. (2018). University invention and the abolishment of the Professor's privilege in Finland. *Research Policy*, 47(4), 814–825.

Gubitta, P., Tognazzo, A. and Destro, F. (2016). Signaling in academic ventures: The role of technology transfer offices and university funds. *The Journal of Technology Transfer*, 41(2), 368–393.

Hisrich, R. D. and Peters, M. P. (1991). *Marketing Decisions for New and Mature Products*. New York: Macmillan.

Kirchberger, M. A. and Pohl, L. (2016). Technology commercialization: A literature review of success factors and antecedents across different contexts. *The Journal of Technology Transfer*, 41(5), 1077–1112.

Chapter 5

Creating the Business Plan
for the Idea and Technology

Learning Objectives

- Understand the importance of a business plan.
- Identify the uses of the business plan.
- Understand the aspects of the business plan.
- Be able to prepare a business plan.

Javier Barcia Martinez

When Javier, co-founder of Rive Technology, found himself in a big dilemma whether to start an academic life as a professor or to get a job and work for a company to direct in the real world, he gathered some courage and decided to end up not losing any of them by taking a third way. He went on to establish a company to commercialize his invention which he considered a breakthrough in the molecular technology while working as a professor at the University of Alicante in Spain. He challenged the world that an academician does not have to sacrifice educational freedom for the opportunity to bring their discoveries to market.

I never found academic and entrepreneurial activities incompatible; in fact, I believe they go hand-in-hand — Javier Garcia

Javier was born and raised in Spain. He did his PhD in Chemistry from the University of Alicante, Spain and continued his postdoc in Chemical Engineering from Massachusetts Institute of Technology (MIT) as a Fullbright Scholar. He has also taken several short-term professional development programs from the world's best universities and also worked in the world's leading material science laboratories such as MIT, Caltech, Yale, Harvard, and the University of California, Berkley. Such involvement with faculty and friends from top universities helped him nurture his intelligence and creativity.

It was during his postdoc at MIT that Javier discovered a process which makes traditional zeolite catalysts more accessible to large hydrocarbon molecules. He recognized its commercial value and partnered with his friend who was pursuing an MBA at Sloan School of Management to develop the business plan and participated in the $50k (now $100k) Entrepreneurship Competition. Though the duo did not win the competition, the program helped Javier become familiar with the intellectual property business plan and sharpened his communication and fundraising skills.

He went back to Spain upon completing his postdoc and started working as a professor in 2004. Nevertheless, he was always keen on establishing his own venture to commercialize the invention he had made during his postdoc days. Recognizing the value of a new, commercially feasible product to a long-standing challenge, Javier patented the process and went on to found Rive Technology in collaboration with his friend.

They opened a small office in Cambridge, Massachusetts near MIT. Having an idea alone is not sufficient to generate money, investment is equally important. This reality was applicable in their situation as well. They struggled for a few years to manage funds for investment.

After 3 years of continuous effort and hard work, they were able to collect $14 million as capital, which they used to relocate into their large R&D facility in Princeton, New Jersey. They later started to commercialize their nanostructure zeolite catalysts for the production of diesel and gasoline when they secured $67 million from lending venture capitals and big firms. The company in Princeton, NJ, now employs over 30 technical team members from leading universities, catalyst manufacturers, and oil companies. The team is bringing its technology to the petroleum refining industry to collaborate with W.R. Grace, a global chemical manufacturing firm.

Javier currently is a faculty member at the University of Alicante, Spain and also the Director of the Molecular Nanotechnology Lab at the university. Javier has also served as an editor for *Nanotechnology for the Energy Challenge* (Wiley, 2010), a book about nanomaterials for energy production; and he has published more than 30 articles, three book chapters and two books on nanotechnology and energy.

He has published extensively in the areas of nanomaterials and energy and is the author of more than 25 patents. His latest books are *Nanotechnology for the Energy Challenge*, 2nd Ed. (Wiley, 2013) and *The Chemical Element: Chemistry's Contribution to Our Global Future* (Wiley, 2011). Javier has been recognized as a leader in nanotechnology and material science. He has received the Europa Medal in 2005, the Silver Medal of the European Young Chemist Award in 2006, the TR 35 Award from MIT's *Technology Review* Magazine, and in 2009, Javier was selected as the Young Global Leader. He is a member of the World Economic Forum Council on Emerging Technologies since 2010. Javier is fellow of the Royal Society of Chemistry, member of the Global Young Academy, and a Bureau Member of IUPAC.

Introduction

Being an effective, successful university entrepreneur requires taking the time to plan further research pertaining to the idea as well as the future activities of the business. There can be many forms of planning in both the short and long term, which provide a roadmap for the future of the idea and its development. The strategy involves developing a plan for the idea to prove its validity and then developing a plan for creating and operating a new venture by obtaining external and internal resources and aligning with the environment.

One aspect of developing and implementing a strategy is to develop at least a business canvas and, better yet, a business plan, which can act as effective tools for providing direction.

Business Model Canvas

An option for developing a business plan, particularly when funding is not the primary reason for development, is to develop a business model canvas, a strategic tool for developing a new business idea, or documenting and improving an existing one. Startup companies as well as large ones, such as Procter & Gamble, General Electric, and Nestle, use the business model canvas to evaluate their existing and new businesses in a structured manner. The business model canvas is a sound method for providing an understanding of the potential trade-offs by providing focus, flexibility, and transparency of all the core elements that drive the business.

A general framework for a business model canvas indicated in Table 1, can be applied to fit the particular business situation. The left side is the business and the right side is the customer which come together through the nine overall components.

The components of the business model canvas, as indicated in Table 1, are as follows:

- **Key Partners:** The key resources and activities needed from the partner and key suppliers need to be identified. These buyer–seller relationships necessary for the operation can be secured through business alliance with the partner through such vehicles as strategic and joint ventures.
- **Key Resources:** These are resources required to obtain the value proportions. These resources include financial, human, transportation, office, and any hosting requirements.
- **Value Proposition:** This identifies the points addressed by the value delivered to the customer. These value propositions can be more qualitative (customer experience) or more quantitative (price, efficiency, and ease of use). The value propositions should be listed based on the order priority and mode of delivery.
- **Customer Relationships:** The relationships maintained with each customer segment as well as the costs and methods for establishing and maintaining the associations need to be established along with the company's expectations from each segment.
- **Channels:** The channels required to reach the desired customer segment and their integration and cost need to be determined. These can be company or partner channels that are linked to a corresponding customer segment.

Table 1. The business model canvas.

Key Partners	Key Activities	Value Propositions	Customer Relationship	Customer Segments
	Key Resources		**Channels**	
Cost Structure		**Revenue Streams**		

Source: www.businessmodelgeneration.com.

- **Customer Segment:** The customer segment(s) targeted by the value propositions and the product/service offered to each should be identified as specifically as possible.
- **Cost Structure:** The most important cost drivers as well as the cost of the most expensive key resources and activities need to be determined. A company is usually cost driven (minimize all cost) or value driven (focus on delivering great customer value in terms of quality and low pricing).
- **Revenue Streams:** The amount and method of payment for each product/service revenue streams need to be determined as well as the price sensitivity to various levels of value and the price currently being paid.

By providing the necessary information on each component, the essential core elements are identified for a successful business that can be adjusted as needed.

Writing the Business Plan

Creating and building a successful enterprise requires effective planning (Trust & Estates, 2013). Indeed the process of developing the necessary strategies is important, the process and the discipline required in putting this in writing makes the thinking process more effective, thus giving the venture a better opportunity for success. Often something conceptualized in the mind of an entrepreneur does not make sense until it is committed to writing.

A frequently asked question is how drawn-out a business plan should be. (How many pages should it have?) Although there is no strict answer to this question, sometimes it is too long. The main body of the business plan, which is discussed later in this chapter, is usually about 30–40 pages. This does not include exhibits or appendices which contain additional market statistics, the actual patents, the resumes of the management team and scientists, and other material that can add another 20–100 pages of material. Moreover, a 2-page executive summary is essential as a door opener if capital needs to be raised (Kwicien, 2012). One factor that impacts the length of the plan is its purpose, which is discussed in the next section.

Even though the professors, staff, or students of the university needs to write the plan, they should get help with editing and laying out the plan in the most favorable way. No matter how good the content, the way the business plan looks and is presented affects its evaluation. Any spelling errors, mathematical errors, numbers not making sense, or poor graphics impact the evaluation of the plan to some extent. And, a knowledgeable investor will easily discern whether the plan was written, at least initially, by the entrepreneur or prepared externally by someone else.

Purpose of the plan

In providing a roadmap to achieve the goals of the enterprise, there are five general purposes of writing a business plan as indicated in Table 2. By far, the most frequent reason for writing a business plan is to obtain financing (Boni, 2012). Most entrepreneurs do not have all the resources (particularly financial) needed to launch and develop a venture. Usually, some external financing called "enterprise capital" is needed, which is discussed in Chapter 7. Each source of enterprise capital discussed in this chapter needs a business plan to make the decision to invest because in many cases only one or two out of the 100 business plans evaluated will receive an investment. The business plan needs to be very carefully crafted, particularly the executive summary which is often the only part that is actually read.

Table 2. Purpose of a business plan.

- **Obtain Finances**
- **Determine Resources Needed**
    - Determine existing resources
    - Identify resource needs
    - Determine suppliers of needed resources
- **Establish Direction for Firm**
- **Evaluate Results of Firm**
    - Management by deviation
    - Reporting results to stakeholders
- **Obtain a Joint Venture Partner**

Another purpose of a business plan is to determine all the resources needed to launch and grow the business. A careful review of the currently existing resources of the entrepreneur and the enterprise and the resources needed at various stages of development such as financial, human, technological, supply, or distribution help make sure these resources are available when needed (Cordeiro, 2013). Potential suppliers of the resources should be identified along with a solid approach to each supplier.

The third purpose of a business plan is to provide a direction for the new venture. In the development, launch, and growth of a venture, there are many different directions and opportunities available (Enman, 2013). A good business plan allows these to be more easily evaluated and the best direction or opportunity selected.

Being able to evaluate the results of the venture is the fourth purpose of a business plan (Rafael *et al.*, 2012). The results compared to the forecast in the business plan point out problems that need attention and focus. *Pro forma* income statements discussed later in this chapter present forecasted numbers, which eventually become actual numbers once the plan is implemented. There is always a positive or negative deviation between the numbers forecasted and the numbers achieved (Benson *et al.*, 2011). When this difference is large and negatively affects the ventures, corrective action is needed. Because an entrepreneur usually never has enough time or money, by focusing on these deviations, attention can be paid to the most critical problems. This is called management by deviation.

The final purpose of a business plan is to obtain a partner or outsourcer (Pollock and Sumner, 2012). A business plan lays out the guidelines for the business of prospective individuals and companies and helps them decide whether to be involved or not. Whether obtaining a member for the board of advisors, a firm in the distribution channel, a supplier firm, or a firm that could be a joint venture partner; the job is easier when a business plan has been prepared. Most seasoned entrepreneurs and individuals will not consent to be a member of an advisory board of a venture without having evaluated at least a preliminary business plan.

Benefits of a business plan

Since a business plan details the entrepreneur's vision and indicates the implementation strategy and the cost involved, it has several benefits and helps avoid some of the problems identified by successful entrepreneurs.

- *Determining the amount and timing of resources needed*: The business plan indicates the existing resources of the firm, the resources needed, and some potential suppliers of these resources. This allows the entrepreneur to determine how much money is needed at various times to obtain these resources and what approach to develop and use to obtain the money as well as any other resources. The money will be obtained from outside capital providers.
- *Establishing the direction of the firm*: Since the business plan is a comprehensive document, it fully treats all the major issues encountered in starting and growing the venture. This enables the entrepreneur to develop strategies and contingency plans to reduce the impact of any problems.
- *Guiding and evaluating*: By setting goals and milestones for the venture, the business plan lays out the intentions of the entrepreneur as well as his/her values. Accomplishments and results can be measured and any deviation to the plan is corrected in a timely manner. These results can be reported to all interested stakeholders and to outside providers of financial resources at least four times a year if not more frequently such as every month in at least the first year. By being put together by the entrepreneur and the management team, and being reviewed and revised frequently, the business plan can be used to guide decisions and help avoid conflicts.

Elements of a business plan

Although there are some variations, most business plans have the same elements. These can be grouped into three main general sections (Table 3).

Table 3.   Aspects of a business plan.

SECTION 1	• **Title Page** • **Table of Contents** • **Executive Summary**	
SECTION 2	**1.0 Description of Business** • Description of the venture • Product(s) and/or service(s) • Type of industry • Mission statement • Business model	**2.0 Description of Industry** • Future outlook and trends • Analysis of competitors • Industry and market forecasts
	3.0 Technology Plan • Description of technology • Technology comparison • Commercialization requirements	**4.0 Marketing Plan** • Market segment • Pricing • Distribution • Promotion • Product or service • Sales for the first 5 years

	5.0 Financial Plan
	• Sources and applications of funds
	  statement
	• *Pro forma* income statement
	• *Pro forma* cash flow statements
	• *Pro forma* balance sheet
	• Beak-even analysis
		6.0 Production Outsourcing Plan
		• Manufacturing process
		  (amount subcontracted)
		• Physical plant
		• Machinery and equipment
		• Suppliers of raw materials
		• Outsourcing aspects

	7.0 Organizational Plan
	• Form of ownership
	• Identification of partners and/
	  or principal shareholders
	• Authority of principals
	• Management team background
	• Roles and responsibilities of
	  members of organization
		8.0 Operational Plan
		• Description of company's
		  operation
		• Flow of orders and goods
		• Exit strategy
		9.0 Summary

SECTION 3	**10.0 Appendices (exhibits)** • Exhibit A: resume of principals • Exhibit B: market statistics • Exhibit C: market research data • Exhibit D: competitive brochure • Exhibit E: competitive price lists • Exhibit F: leases and contracts • Exhibit G: supplier price lists	

Section 1

Section 1 contains the title (cover) page, table of contents, and executive summary. The title (cover) page is an important part of every business plan because it has the following information:

- The company name, address, telephone, fax, e-mail address, and website.
- Name and position of each identified member of the management team.
- The purpose of the plan, the amount of money needed, and funding increments.
- At the bottom of the title page: "This is confidential business plan number _____." A low number should be placed in the blank space; a tracking system should be established of when and who received this numbered plan for a 30-day, 60-day, and 90-day follow-up. This statement, of course, does not bind the reader to confidentiality.

The first page after the title (cover) page is the table of contents. This follows the usual format and lists at least the major subsections in each section and the corresponding page numbers, as well as each figure, table, and exhibit. Preferably, each major subsection and smaller subsections can be labeled as 1.0, 1.1, 1.2, 2.0, 2.1, 2.3, and so on. The executive summary precedes the numbering and therefore has no number, smaller letters, or Roman numerals. The tables and figures should have a separate list as should the exhibits (appendices).

The last item in Section 1, following the table of contents, is the all-important two-page executive summary. This is by far the most important document in the business plan because it is the screening section. Many readers, especially potential providers of capital, never read beyond the executive summary. One head of a very successful venture fund, who is now managing his eighth fund, indicated that he receives about 1,500 business plans a year, discards 1,400 based on the cover page or executive summary, and, of the remaining 100, discards 80 based on an initial 1- to 2-hour examination. Of the remaining 20, about 4–6 will receive a term sheet and probably an investment from his fund. The executive summary needs to be really well written to invite a further reading of the business plan. Some capital providers only want to initially have a copy of the executive summary. If this passes the first evaluation, then the entire business plan is requested.

The executive summary should have the name of the company and address at the top just as it appears on the title (cover) page. It should begin with defining the nature and size of the existing problem. The more significant the problem, the better.

Your proposed solution should follow this problem. Again, this is making available several individuals who have had a background check and are capable and willing to do the task on a for-fee basis. In this section, all competitive ways to solve the problem should be discussed, showing the distinctiveness of the unique selling propositions of your solution. Following the solution is the size of the market, trends for at least 3–5 years, and future growth rates. The market needs to be large enough and accessible to deliver the sales needed for the profits and returns expected by investors.

The entrepreneur and team who will deliver these sales and profits needs to be described. The education, accomplishments, and industry experience of each known member of the top management team needs to be described.

The sales and profits should be summarized over a 5-year period in the following format:

	Year 1	Year 2	Year 3	Year 4	Year 5
Total revenue					
Cost of goods sold					
Gross margin					
Operating expenses					
Profit (loss) before taxes					

These numbers are taken directly from the *pro forma* income statement summary in the financial plan in Section 2. Note the exact calendar year is not used, but rather year 1, 2, 3, 4, and 5, with 1 indicating the first year of company operations after the investment is received.

The two-page executive summary closes with a statement of the resources needed, the increments of capital accepted, and contact information. Examples of executive summary are provided in Tables 4–6.

Table 4. Business plan (executive summary) — Himalayan Java Coffee Pvt. Ltd.

BUSINESS DESCRIPTION:

Himalayan Java Coffee is the first-of-a-kind specialty coffee shop in Nepal.

The target franchisee is incorporated as Namche Bazaar Coffee Pvt Ltd and operates in the name of "Himalayan Java." Himalayan Java is a first-of-a-kind specialty coffee shop in Nepal. The coffee chain was started in 1999 and has seen growth and progression for last 17 years, with over $5.5 million in revenue for the fiscal year 2014/15 across eight branches in Nepal. This coffee chain is the trendsetter in the Nepalese coffee shop market and has been very popular among the tourists who visit Nepal, as the first store was opened in Thamel, tourist Mecca of Kathmandu.

Current Products/Services

The following lists the various products and services of the coffee chain as a whole and the specific product of the target branch:

– The coffee shop caters to the needs of the growing number of coffee drinkers in Nepal. The coffee shop will have a variety of hot and cold coffee as well as tea of the highest quality available for the customers.
– The coffee beans are all produced organically in Nepal and are of the highest quality.
– The customer can buy coffee bags from the store. Again, the coffee is 100 percent organic and manufactured in Nepal. There are several packs and several roasts available.
– The shop also sells souvenirs for the visitors such as coffee mugs, photo hangers, magnetic photo frames. This is very popular among the tourists and requires an increase in the portfolios of the items that the store currently sells.

Proposed Expansion

The sales of souvenirs in this branch is significantly higher than other franchisees of this coffee chain. The plan is to get a souvenir manufacturer to produce souvenirs especially for this store and grow both operations.

Competition

The Namche Bazaar store will compete with the local coffee shops and souvenir shops in the respective markets located in this small town. The brand name of Himalayan Java will be very efficient in selling our products as it is a popular name among tourists coming to Nepal. There are no hybrid coffee shop and souvenir shops around the area and this store will be one of a kind

Primary Target Market

The town of Namche Bazaar is visited by tourists trekking in the Khumbu circuit and to the Everest base camp. It is a popular destination to take a one–two-day rest while visiting this area. Namche Bazaar has nice places to stay and some great places to eat, but the eateries are on the expensive side. This Himalayan Java coffee shop will be a great destination for tourists to get their morning cup of coffee and the destination to buy souvenirs from the base of the Himalayas.

USE OF FUNDS:

The Company is seeking funds to complete clinical trials, finalize product development, attain 510K clearance, conduct post-market studies, develop sales, marketing and operational efforts in the U.S., and prepare for manufacturing.

Business Plan– Himalayan Java Coffee Pvt. Ltd.

HEAD OFFICE
Tridevi Marg, Thamel
Kathmandu, Nepal
Phone: +977-1-4422519
http://www.himalayanjava.com/
info@himalayanjava.com

CAFÉ LOCATION
Namche Bazar - 2
Solukhumbu, Nepal

MANAGEMENT
Laxman Panthi – General Manager
Ganesh Bhandari - Operations
Ashish Hamal – Store Manager

ADVISORS
Robert D. Hisrich – Associate Dean, College of Business, Kent State University
Saurabh Sharma – Consultant, CBM International

INDUSTRY
Coffee Chain and Souvenir Shop

INCEPTION DATE
May 2015

EXISTING FUNDING SOURCES
Laxman Panthi
Everest Bank – Working Capital Loan

PRESEED FUNDS RAISED
$1M

SERIES A FUNDS SOUGHT
$500,000

Namche Bazaar P&L ($000)	2016	2017	2018	2019	2020
Revenue from coffee sales	23.00	25.30	27.83	30.61	33.67
Revenue from souvenir sales	32.00	38.40	46.08	55.30	66.36
COGS[a]	27.00	29.70	32.67	35.94	39.53
Gross profit ($)	28.00	34.00	41.24	49.97	60.50
Gross profit (%)	50.9	53.4	55.8	58.2	60.5
Operating costs					
Sales & marketing	3.00	3.35	4.05	4.28	4.79
G&A[b]	11.50	10.00	11.00	12.10	13.20
Total operating costs	14.50	13.35	15.05	16.38	17.99
EBITDA ($)	13.50	20.65	26.19	33.59	42.51
EBITDA (%)	24.5	32.4	35.4	39.	42.5

DISCLAIMER: This does not constitute the sale or the offer of sale of any securities. Any such offer or solicitation will be made only by means of a subscription agreement and other documentation to be entered into between IME and an Investor (the "Fund Documents"), which Fund Documents should be read In their entirety, including the risk factors and potential conflicts of Interest described therein.

Notes: [a]Cost of goods sold. [b]General and administrative expense.

Table 5.   Business plan (executive summary) — Mercury Biomed, LLC.

Robert D. Hisrich, Ph. D.

Do Not Distribute

BUSINESS DESCRIPTION:
Mercury Blamed, based in Cleveland, Ohio, is led by a team of world-leading experts in perioperative warming, medically induced hypothermia, bio heat transfers and human thermoregulation. Mercury was formed to design, manufacture, market and sell innovative and cost-competitive medical solutions for the rapidly growing, $2.8 billion, therapeutic patient temperature management market.

PRODUCTS/TECHNOLOGIES:
- A **Smart Temperature Management Platform** is supported by 2 issued US patent as well as 6 patent pending internationally. Our novel platform and unique approach represent a smarter, safer and more seamless way of moving heat into and out of the body than what currently exists. The system taps into, and utilizes the body's most efficient, intrinsic means of moving heat into and out of the body, whereas the competition relies on inefficient and/or brute force methods of heat transfer. We work with the body rather than against it.
- **WarmSmart**, an FDA Class II device launching in early 2017, will maintain normal body temperature and prevent hypothermia resulting from the administration of general anesthesia. The result is a reduction in infection risk to the patient, providing greater surgical site access, enhancing usability and making the O.R. more comfortable for surgeons and staff.

Mercury has partnered with Innovative Medical Equipment (IME) (owner of the ThermaZone technology) and has licensed the rights to use and modify IME's market proven Thermal therapy technology platform, its supply chain and existing manufacturing processes, as well as its expertise in Quality and Regulatory practices.

PRIMARY TARGET MARKET:
WarmSmart targets the perioperative warming market in hospitals, specifically the operating room. In the US alone, there are over 50 million inpatient surgical operations performed every year. Mercury's technology is a smarter, more effective and safer way of maintaining normothermia perioperatively. WarmSmart is associated with real-renowned thought-leaders in patient warming and is poised to take advantage of the new private payer and Medicare reimbursement requirements for perioperative temperature control (reduced payment if patient temperature is not above 35°C out of the OR). The Company's beachhead markets for the warming application include orthopedic and cardiovascular surgeries, operations involving implantable devices and ultra-clean surgical environments where surgical site infections result in devastating outcomes. Forced-air warming technologies, the current standard of care, are uniquely vulnerable in these market segments (particularly in orthopedic implant cases) because of the infection risk to the patient, as well as several other logistical drawbacks.

COMPETITION:
The Bair Hugger forced-air warming technology (acquired by 3M for $810M in 2010) and Mistral Air (Stryker) are our primary competitors in the patient warming space. Forced air warming has several drawbacks, including: disrupting air-flow patterns in the OR, allegedly increasing infections rates; a reliance on covering large surface areas of the body during surgery, which is not practical; and utilizing convective heat transfer via circulating air, one of the most inefficient means of heat transfer.

USE OF FUNDS:
The Company is seeking funds to complete clinical trials, finalize product development, attain 510K clearance, conduct post-market studies, develop sales, marketing and operational efforts in the US, and prepare for manufacturing.

Mercury P&L ($000)	2015	2016	2017	2018	2019	2020	2021
Revenue from Operations	.	.	577	3,180	12,770	29,072	60,988
COGS	.	.	140	719	2,891	6,350	12,284
Gross Profit ($)	.	.	438	2461	9,879	22,721	48,724
Gross Profit (%)			76	77	77	78	80
Operating Costs							
Sales & marketing	13	50	446	1,241	4,009	8,492	13,835
R&D	62	207	795	560	250	250	250
G&A	392	735	715	1,338	3,477	6,825	13,144
Total Operating Costs	467	992	1956	3,140	7,736	15,565	27,229
EBITDA ($)	(467)	(992)	(1,518)	(679)	2,144	7,155	21,495
EBITDA (%)					17	25	35

MERCURY**BIOMED**

29001 Cedar Road, Suite 326
Lyndhurst, OH 44124 216.777.1492
www.mercurybiomed.com
brad@mercurybiomed.com

MANAGEMENT
Brad Pulver – CEO
Jim Kuras – VP, Product Dev. Dr. Ken Diller – Inventor, Co-Founder & Chief Science Officer
Glen Guyuron – VP, Operations

DIRECTORS & ADVISORS
Brad Pulver - CEO
Brian Patrick - Co-Founder
Dr. Bahman Guyuron - Former Chair, Department of Plastic Surgery at Case Western Reserve University and University Hospitals
Terry Ozan - Former CEO of Ernst & Young Consulting
Dr. Ken Diller - Director of Biomedical Engineering Department, U. of Texas at Austin
Bob Kline – Founder, CEO of Medivance (sold to CR Bard 2011)
Dr. Daniel Sessler - CCF
Dr. Andrea Kurz —CCF
Dr. Alex Valadka – VCU

INDUSTRY
Medical Devices

INCEPTION DATE
February 2015

PATENT PORTFOLIO
2 issued, 6 pending

EXISTING FUNDING SOURCES
Brad Pulver
Bahman Guyuron
Terry Ozan
The State of Ohio – 3rd Frontier CALF LOAN

PRE SEED FUNDS RAISED
$1M ($300K convertible note, $700K CALF loan)

SERIES A FUNDS SOUGHT
$2M

DISCLAIMER: This does not constitute the sale or the offer of sale of any securities. Any such offer or solicitation will be made only by means of a subscription agreement and other documentation to be entered into between IME and an Investor (the "Fund Documents"), which Fund Documents should be read In their entirety, including the risk factors and potential conflicts of Interest described therein.

Section 2

Following the executive summary, the end of Section 1 of the business plan, Section 2 starts on a new page with its first section: Description of the Business.

Table 6.   Business plan (executive summary) — Wisr Inc.

Robert D. Hisrich, Ph. D.
Do Not Distribute

The Problem

Higher Education institutions are faced with increasing scrutiny to track and demonstrate **employment and degree outcomes** for students in proportion to increased tuition.

Career services offices are operating in the dark ages (excel, local databases, pencil/paper), to coordinate thousands of students.

Student retention is "the new enrollment", with millions in tuition revenue at risk on every campus. Universities and vendors only know how to accurately address financial aid gaps, but have not successfully addressed the **second largest factor, belonging**.

The Solution

- On-demand advisory board of successful alumni mentors.
- Mobile-first SaaS solution for Universities.
- Profile-matching & LinkedIn API connectivity.
- Boosts post-graduate success, retention, and alumni giving.

| Branded Mentor 'Hub' with matching | Alumni & Students join in via LinkedIn | Mobile-first, scheduling capabilities | University engagement dashboard |

Founders

Kate Volzer, CEO
- 5 Years admissions & career services leadership, overseeing UChicago increased applications by 84% and yield by 34%.
- VP business development at DecisionDesk; first 7-figure client contract and partnerships with Salesforce, Oracle, Parchment and Hyland.
- Chicago Booth MBA in Economics, Entrepreneurship, and Strategic Management.

John Knific, President/COO
- CEO/Co-Founder at DecisionDesk
- Oversaw growth rates between 50 and 110%; managed 25+ employees; Raised $7m+ angel, venture, and state capital.
- Entrepreneur in Residence at Oberlin College

Addressable Market

Seed/Beachhead | Ivy + and Coalition Cohort: 600, $15
Series A | Higher Education (4 Year/Grad): 4,700, $500 million
Series B | Corporate Education: 10,000+, $1b+

Pilot Customers

Late-Stage Pipeline

2016 Go-To-Market

- **Annual Subscription.** Targeting $30,000, 2-year term
- **Inside sales rep (ISR) driven sales.** Anticipated 3–4 month sales cycle
- **5 Pilot Development Partners.** Pre-pay for 2016 launch and access to product advisory board.
- **User Conference Launch.** UChicago sponsored user summit exclusively for the initial tranche of customers.

Fundraise

$750k–$1m Seed Round

Milestones:

- Recruit CTO/Lead Dev
- Initial 2–5 hires
- Successful launch 5 pilot customers
- Book 30 new customers by year-end 2017 projecting $1 million revenue
- Validate sales process in preparation for Series A.

Advisors

Jason Palmer
Deputy Director
Bill & Melinda Gates Foundation

Meredith Daw
AVP & Exec Director of Career Advancement
The University of Chicago

Deb Mills-Scofield
Management Consultant
Mills-Scofield, LLC

Description of the business

In this section, the nature of the venture is described to provide an understanding of the operation of the venture and the venture delivering the products/services to solve the problem(s) identified. Detailed information on the products/services should be provided in such a manner easily understood; this will be expanded upon in Section 3 if a technological product/service employs a new technology and also in the product section of the marketing plan. The mission statement of the company, as well as the business model, should be described — the entire picture of how the company does business — and whether this business model significantly differs from the way business is currently done in the industry should also be explained.

Description of industry

This section discusses the type and size of the industry, the industry trends for the last 3–5 years, future outlook and growth rate, and a thorough analysis of competition presently fulfilling the same need as the new idea. This is a large section with significant use of data from authoritative sources. Sometimes there is so much data that only part of it appears in the body of the plan and the rest appears in an appendix (exhibit) in Section 3. Graphs, charts, histograms, and other graphics should be used to thoroughly explain the industry, its growth projection, and the competitors. A graph showing the market growth is important and to understand related market trends to date. The market, the market segment, and target market for the first year will be further discussed in the first section of the marketing plan.

Technology plan

Following the description of the industry is the *Technology Plan*. Some business plans, where there is no significant technological advancement in the product/service being offered, will not have a technology plan. For example, one author founded a rainbow decal and sticker company with no significant new technology, so there was no technology plan in the business plan of the company. Whenever the product/service has a patent, there will always be a technology plan due to the added value to the venture. As a general rule, if uncertain whether to have a technology plan; then put one in because it is better to have a technology plan than not. The technology plan describes the state of the technology presently available and how the new technology revolutionizes the way things are done. The patent or patent filing should be discussed and the document itself put as an appendix (exhibit) in Section 3.

Marketing plan

The marketing plan begins with a discussion of the market segment and target market for the product/service (Lavinsky, 2013). It defines using one or more segmentation techniques to define the most appropriate market and market size. The many available segmentation techniques — demographic, geographic, psychological, benefit, the volume of use, and controllable market elements — are indicated for all three markets in Table 7, the two most widely used are the demographic and geographic techniques because of the way secondary data is published (Viselgaité and Vilys, 2011). If the venture is a business-to-consumer (B2C) venture, the most important market data are the demographics of the selected geographic market. The most widely demographic variables used to determine the size of the market and a typical customer profile are age, income, and gender. For a business-to-business (B2B) venture, the business market needs to be identified using the classification system of the country to determine the industrial (business) customers being targeted. The North American Industrial Classification System (NAICS) code in the United States, the Standard Industrial Classification (SIC) code in Korea, and the SIC code in China each uses a unique numbering system to classify each industry and specific products/services in that country. The sum of the final products/services produced is the gross national product of the country. This procedure provides the trends, size, and growth rate of the particular industry market which can be used to develop the typical customer profile.

Following the delineation of the target market, a marketing plan needs to be developed to successfully reach and sell to that target market. The marketing plan has four major areas — product or service, price, distribution, and promotion (see Figure 1). The product/service section describes the characteristics and quality of the offering, the assortment of items to be offered, the guarantee, any servicing provided, and the packaging. The latter can be very important in the B2C market because it can be a major area of distinctiveness as well as a sales tool in the distribution centers(s).

The second variable, price, is closely related to the product/service, particularly the quality level. The price, the worst executed of the marketing areas by entrepreneurs, needs to reflect the competitive prices, the

Table 7. Market segmentation by type of market.

Segmentation Criteria	Basis for type of market		
	Consumer	Industrial	Government
Demographic	Age, family size, education level, family life cycle, income, nationality, occupation, race, religion, residence, sex, social class.	Number of employees, size of sales, size of profit, the type of product lines.	Type of agency, size of the budget, amount of autonomy.
Geographic	The region of country, city size, market density, climate.	Region of country.	Federal, state, local.
Psychological	Personality traits, motives, life style.	Degree of industrial leadership.	Degree of forward thinking.
Benefits	Durability, dependability, economy, esteem enhancement, status from ownership, handiness.	Dependability, reliability of seller and support service, efficiency in operation or use, enhancement of firm's earning, durability.	Dependability, reliability of seller and support services.
Volume of Use	Heavy, medium, light.	Heavy, medium, light.	Heavy, medium, light.
Controllable Marketing Elements	Sales promotion, price, advertising, guarantee, warranty, retail store purchased service, product attributes, reputation of seller.	Price, service, warranty, reputation of seller.	Price, reputation of seller.

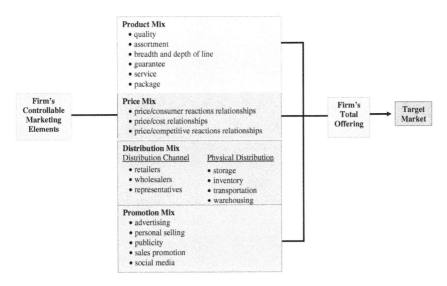

Figure 1.   Marketing mix.

cost, and the degree of consumer sensitivity to the price. If a distribution system is used, then there will be a chain of markups on the cost in the final price.

The distribution channels include entities handling the product such as retailers, wholesalers, or representatives. The physical distribution or logistics is becoming an increasingly important area and includes transportation, storage (warehousing), and inventory (Mac Naughton, 2012).

The final area of the marketing plan is the promotion area which is composed of advertising, personal selling, publicity, sales promotion, and social media. The latter three are particularly important for technology entrepreneurs because they can be used to produce multiple exposures cost effectively. Social media, including the website of the new venture, is a particularly useful part of the promotion area. A marketing budget needs to be prepared for the first year indicating where the money will be specifically allocated to promote the company and achieve the planned sales of the first year. This first-year sales figure concludes the marketing section of the business plan and is a good start for the next section — the financial plan.

Financial plan

The financial plan, the next part of Section 2, focuses on a discussion of the created statements indicated in Table 8. The financial information contained in the financial plan primarily consists of these 12 financial statements. All but one become actual statements after the business is launched. Although these statements have the same content, they are different from the actual statement in that they are forecasted — *pro forma* — statements which will, upon the end of the time period, become actual statements (Cassar, 2010). The first statement is the sources and uses of funds statement — which describes how much money is needed (uses) and where it will come from (sources). The "uses" part often includes money for renovations, inventory, working capital, and reserve for contingencies. Working capital is the money needed until the venture shows positive cash flows; the point in time when the revenues from operations exceed the cost of operations. Sources of money will always include the entrepreneur and usually friends and family. The other sources of financing include banks, private investors, venture capitalists, and grants.

Production (outsourcing) plan

Following the financial plan is the production or outsourcing plan highlighting how the offering will be developed and produced. Some ventures will not have this section in their business plan. Each individual cost needs to be specified to provide an understanding of the actual costs involved in the final offering and how much this can be reduced through economies of scale. Each supplier or outsourcing firm should be described in detail.

Organizational plan

The organizational plan discusses primarily two aspects of the venture: the form of ownership and lines of authority and responsibility. The selection of the general ownership form is country specific but needs to take into account several aspects: such as taxation; number and location of investors; liability issues; and number and type of employees' fringe benefits that will be paid.

Table 8. Financial statements.

- Sources and Uses of Funds Statement
- *Pro Forma* Income Statement: 5 year summary
- *Pro Forma* Income Statement: first year by month
- *Pro Forma* Income Statement: second year by quarter
- *Pro Forma* Income Statement: third year by quarter
- *Pro Forma* Cash Flow Statement: 5 year summary
- *Pro Forma* Cash Flow Statement: first year by month
- *Pro Forma* Cash Flow Statement: second year by quarter
- *Pro Forma* Cash Flow Statement: third year by quarter
- *Pro Forma* Balance Sheet: years 1, 2, 3, 4, and 5

Generally, the ownership form selected should have the lowest possible tax consequences and minimum liability. In some countries, there are also liability issues with hiring and firing employees and with the closing of the company.

In addition, a foreign (partner) may need to have a specific ownership position, which in some cases can be over 50%. The following are the overall organizational structures in the United States:

- **Individual legal entities:**
  - o Proprietorship
  - o Partnership
- **Organization legal entities:**
  - o LLC
  - o SC
  - o C-Corporation
  - o Professional Corporation
  - o Not-for-Profit Corporation
  - o Hybrid Corporation

Due to the organization becoming the legal entity in terms of liability, an entrepreneur should not establish his or her company as a proprietorship or partnership. Due to the tax laws, most entrepreneurial companies in the United States are started as an LLC or SC.

The second aspect — lines of authority — can be viewed in terms of an organizational chart. Although each functional area needs to be specified with a description of the duties and responsibilities, many of these will not have a specific person mentioned in the initial business plans. Sometimes, the chief financial officer or human resource managers will not be hired until years after the setting up of the startup. The new venture does need a CEO/president; someone responsible for the operation of the venture.

Operational plan

Following the organizational plan is a short section — the operational plan. This describes in detail how the company will operate, including the flow of goods and orders. An important aspect discussed here is the exit strategy by which investors will get their equity and return on equity hopefully in a 5- to 7-year period of time from the initial investment. There are three mechanisms by which the capital can provide this exit and the desired returns: (1) retaining earnings of the venture; (2) selling to another financial or non-financial institution or firm; or (3) going public and being a publically traded company. The most likely exit avenue is selling to another company, if this is the exit strategy, 3–4 exit companies need to be identified and discussed.

Section 2 concludes with a brief summary and completes this section of the business.

Section 3

Section 3 contains the backup material to support areas in Section 2. This includes secondary support data, any research data, contracts of leases, the patent documents, and most notably the resumes of the entrepreneur including any known members of the management team. Nothing new should be introduced in this section.

Summary

Every venture needs a business plan to set the direction for the firm and/or to obtain financial resources. The essential elements of a business plan are contained in three sections, with the main elements being in Section 2. The most important document in the plan is the executive summary since most business plans are not read beyond the summary by potential investors.

Each business plan needs to be well written and organized to address as many questions anticipated as possible. It needs to flow smoothly and consistently without errors so that the reader has a clear understanding of the details and future success of the new venture.

Selected Readings

(1) Gabler, C. B., Panagopoulos, N., Vlachos, P. A. and Rapp, A. (2017). "Developing an Environmentally Sustainable Business Plan: An International B2B Case Study". *Corporate Social Responsibility and Environmental Management*, 24(4), 261–272.

Business may be in the best position to address the world's environmental problems. However, firms are still struggling with the *how* and *when* of their sustainability strategies. The goal of this case study is to uncover bridges and barriers to incorporating environmental issues into a business strategy. We collected semi-structured depth interviews with upper-level executives at a global, B2B manufacturing firm. The analysis reveals six elements of an environmentally sustainable business plan: (1) unify the organizational vision, (2) create visible leadership, (3) address multiple stakeholders, (4) focus on innovation, (5) communicate the message, and (6) implement the strategy. We nest these components under the normative, strategic, and operational management framework of corporate sustainability and then present future research directions. Copyright © 2017 John Wiley & Sons, Ltd and ERP Environment.

(2) Hofer, C. (2016). "The Evolution of Business Plans in International Business Plan Competitions". In *Models of Start-up Thinking and Action: Theoretical, Empirical and Pedagogical Approaches*. Emerald Group Publishing Limited, pp. 145–211.

This chapter describes and analyzes the evolution of the structure, content, and other key parameters of business plans in international business plan competitions from the start of such competitions in 1991 to the current time. In particular, the chapter describes how these competitions have evolved over time, the standardization of the structure and content of the plans submitted to these competitions, and the changes that have occurred in their structure and content over time. Then it explains why these changes have occurred. Specifically, most of the changes that have occurred in these various areas are a direct or indirect result of pressures on the competitions from the major judges used in them — namely US venture capitalists. Appendices A and B describe the evaluation criteria used in two of the major competitions — Moot Corp/Venture Labs® and the Georgia Bowl® — in more detail, while Appendices C and D provide information on the Term Sheets and decision-making processes used by such venture capitalists. Appendix E contains four exhibits that provide additional insight into US venture capitalists' thought processes. The chapter concludes with a discussion of the additional changes that are likely to happen in the future.

(3) Hopp, C. and Greene, F. J. (2018). "In Pursuit of Time: Business Plan Sequencing, Duration and Intraentrainment Effects on New Venture Viability". *Journal of Management Studies*, 55(2), 320–351.

In this study, we examine three underexplored dimensions of the temporal relationship between formal written business plans and the achievement of new venture viability. First, we theorize and investigate the effects of plan sequencing, arguing that a business plan written early on in new venture development increases the prospects of venture viability. Second, we examine plan duration effects and argue that there is a curvilinear relationship between spending time on a plan and achieving venture viability. Finally, we investigate plan intraentrainment effects (synchronization with other gestation activities). We theorize that if plans are synchronized with other gestation activities, venture viability is more likely. Using longitudinal data and controlling for truncation and endogeneity issues, we find that it is beneficial to plan early but that this is contingent on how long a founder spent on a plan and whether or not a plan is intraentrained with other gestation activities.

References

Benson, B. W., Davidson, W. I., Wang, H. and Worrell, D. L. (2011). Deviations from expected stakeholder management, firm value, and corporate governance. *Financial Management*, 40(1), 39–81.

Boni, A. A. (2012). The pitch and business plan for investors and partners. *Journal of Commercial Biotechnology*, 18(2), 38–42. doi: 10.5912/jcb.509.

Cassar, G. (2010). Are individuals entering self-employment overly optimistic? An empirical test of plans and projections on nascent entrepreneur expectations. *Strategic Management Journal*, 8, 822. doi:10.1002/smj.833.

Cordeiro, W. P. (2013). Small businesses ignore strategic planning at their peril. *Academy of Business Research Journal*, 322–330.

Enman, C. (2013). Plan for growth; it won't happen by accident. *Security Distributing & Marketing*, 5, 42.

García-Martínez, Javier, Moniz, Ernest J. (2010). *Nanotechnology for the Energy Challenge*, Wiley.

García-Martínez, Javier, Serrano-Torregrosa, Elena (2011). *The Chemical Element: Chemistry's Contributions to Our Global Future*, Wiley.

García-Martínez, Javier, Moniz, Ernest J. (2013). *Nanotechnology for the Energy Challenge*, 2nd edition, Wiley.

Kwicien, J. (2012). *Put it in writing*. Retrieved September 30, 2016, from https://www.employeebenefitadviser.com/news/put-it-in-writing.

Lavinsky, D. (2013). Marketing plan template: Exactly what to include. Retrieved September 30, 2016, from https://www.forbes.com/sites/davelavinsky/2013/09/30/marketing-plan-template-exactly-what-to-include/#559e63e73503.

Mac Naughton, D. (2012). How to sell to the World's biggest company. *Harvard Business Review*, 90(7–8), 106–107.

Pollock, J., & Sumner, D. (2012). A close eye on business partners. *Internal Auditor*, 69(6), 43–46.

Rafael, F., Lorenzo, R. and Virginia, S. (2012). The business plan as a project: An evaluation of its predictive capability for business success. *The Service Industries Journal*, 15, 2399.

Trust & Estates. (2013). *A Look Inside the Estate Planning Industry: Key Findings from the 6th Annual Industry Trends Survey.* Retrieved September 30, 2016, from https://www.naepc.org/journal/issue14c.pdf.

Viselgaite, D. and Vilys, M. (2011). Peculiarities in construction of segmentation models: Theory and practice. *Business, Management & Education/Verslas, Vadyba Ir Studijos*, 9(2), 171–184.

Chapter 6

Funding Sources for University Startups

Learning Objectives

- To identify sources of funding for university startups.
- To understand Small Business Innovation grants.
- To understand Small Business Administrator loans.
- To understand the aspects of research and development in limited partnerships.

Opening Profile — Christopher Miller

Q1. Submitter Information

Name of Nominee	**Christopher Miller**
University the Nominee is representing	**University of Akron**
Email	cmm1@uakron.edu
Phone Number	330-972-5915

Q2. The nominee's position when they created the company. Describe the nominee's process with the university as they were creating the company. Be as detailed as possible.

University of Akron, Associate Professor of Civil Engineering, Christopher Miller spent more than a decade learning the technical details of how water quality is measured, tracked, and improved based on his sincere

145

belief that exceptional water quality is central to human health and safety. Based on this extensive background and years of university laboratory research around water quality issues, Chris launched Fontus Blue in 2011. Initially, the company focused its efforts on consulting with local municipalities to improve their water treatment practices, but over time, Chris recognized broader demand for the advanced algorithms he was developing as part of his consulting work. This customer feedback led to a pivot in the business model from a consulting company to a software as a service (SAAS) model. Fontus Blue launched a software product, Decision Blue A.I., which is customized to the data collection methods of individual water treatment municipalities. The software accepts human input and data from sensors, and learns over time how to optimize water quality — all based on Chris's algorithms.

Q3. Describe the nominee's experience working with the university in creating the company. What were the challenges? What support did they receive? Be as detailed as possible.

The University of Akron Research Foundation (UARF, a university-affiliated non-profit that assists with research commercialization) was critical in setting up Fontus Blue. UARF helped with initial incorporation and worked with Chris to provide a license to the knowledge developed at UA that underlies the software. UARF also provided day-to-day support including accounting services, credibility in approaching water municipalities, business coaching, and connections to the JumpStart Entrepreneurial Network. One of UARF's Project Managers, who sat on the Fontus Blue board of directors, was critical in the decision-making process of switching from a consulting to software business model. Fontus Blue faced challenges in bringing on and then losing CEO candidates who were expected to drive business growth.

Ultimately, Chris determined that he needed to grow professionally to fill the CEO role, and he did so. Further, two programs — UA's I-Corps Site and I-Corps@Ohio — provided extensive customer discovery training for Chris and the Fontus team. Messaging for sales and marketing strategy were shaped by things learned through this customer discovery.

Q4. What happened to the company the nominee created? Describe in detail where it is now and how is it doing. What is the history of the company? Be as detailed as possible.

Following the shift from a consulting to SAAS business model, Fontus Blue began to accelerate its growth. The Decision Blue A.I. software is used by water treatment plants in nine states and Canada, serving more than 3 million customers, with new municipalities being added to the system almost monthly. Fontus Blue's "exceptional water network" is developing brand awareness as an *imprimatur* of water quality through its work with municipalities that previously had water compliance issues and are now producing superior drinking water. Fontus Blue has received investment from Northeast Ohio's Innovation Fund, Northeast Ohio Student Venture Fund, and a private investor. It has added an experienced advisor, who previously exited a water technology startup. Chris Miller continues to serve as the company's CEO, managing a growing team that now stands at five employees.

Introduction

One of the biggest problems university startups face is financing the development of the idea and the new business venture created. This chapter will first introduce the overall concept of financing of both (debt versus equity capital and internal verse external financing) and then the overall general sources of capital for both by addressing the overall available sources of capital.

Debt or Equity Financing

There are two general types of financing available: debt financing and equity financing. *Debt Financing* is a financing method involving an interest-bearing instrument, usually a loan, the payment of which is only indirectly related to the sales and profits of the venture. Typically, debt financing (also called asset-based financing) requires that some asset (such as a patent, car, house, inventory, plant, machine, or land) be used as collateral.

Debt financing requires paying back the amount of fund borrowed as well as a fee usually expressed in terms of the interest rate. There can also be an additional fee, sometimes referred to as points, for using or being able to borrow the money. If the financing is short term (less than 1 year), the money borrowed is usually used to provide working capital to finance inventory, accounts receivable, or the operation of the business. The funds to repay the amount borrowed and interest are from the resulting sales and profits of the business during the year. Long-term debt (lasting more than 1 year) are frequently used to purchase some asset such as a piece of machinery, land, or a building, with part of the value of the asset (usual from 50% to 80% of the total value) being used as collateral for the long-term loan. Particularly when interest rates are low, debt (as opposed to equity) financing allows the entrepreneur to retain a larger ownership portion in the venture and have a greater return on equity. The entrepreneur needs to be careful that the debt is not so large that regular interest payments become difficult, if not impossible to make, a situation that will inhibit growth and development and possibly end in bankruptcy. Using debt as the financial instrument is called leveraging the firm. The higher the amount of leverage (debt/total assets), the greater the risk in the venture.

Equity financing does not require collateral and offers the investor some type of ownership position in the venture. The investor shares in the profits of the venture that are not reinvested, as well as any disposition of its assets on a *pro rata* based on the percentage of the business owned. Key factors favoring the use of one type of financing over another are the availability of funds, the assets of the venture, and the prevailing interest rates. Frequently, a combination of debt and equity financing needs to be used especially in venture financing.

All ventures have 100% ownership depending on how it is allocated. The individual with the idea starts with the 100% ownership, who is employed by the university and shares with the university. An owner may sometime not be directly involved in the day-to-day management of the venture. The amount of equity involved will vary the nature and size of the venture. In some cases, the equity may be entirely provided by the owner, such as in a small ice cream stand or pushcart in the mall or at a sporting event. Larger ventures may require multiple owners, including private investors or a venture capitalist. This equity funding combined with the debt funding make up the capital structure of the venture.

Internal or external funds

Financing can also come from both internal and external funds once a venture starts producing revenue. The funds most frequently employed are internally generated funds. Internally generated funds can come from several sources: profits, the sale of assets, reduction in working capital, extended payment terms, and accounts receivable. In every new venture, the start up years usually involve putting all, or at least most of the profits back into the venture; even outside equity investors do not expect any payback in these early years. Assets, whenever possible, should be on a rental basis (preferably on a lease with an option to buy), not an owner-ship basis, particularly when there is not a high level of inflation and the rental terms are favorable. Also, activities should be outsourced when-ever possible. This helps conserve cash, a practice that is particularly critical during the startup phase of the company's operation when cash is scarce.

Short-term, internal funds can also be in short-term assets: inventory, cash, and other working capital items. Sometimes an entrepreneur can generate the needed cash over a period of 30–60 days through extended payment terms from the supplier. While care must be taken to ensure good supplier relations and continuous sources of supply, taking a few extra days to pay can generate the much-needed short-term funds. A final method of internally generating funds is collecting payment due (accounts receivable) more quickly. Certain customers have established payment practices. Mass merchandisers, for example, pay supplying companies in 60–90 days, regardless of a supplying company's accounts receivable policy, the size of the company, or the discount offered for prompt pay-ment. If a company wants this mass merchandiser to carry its product, they will have to live with the established payment schedule.

One entrepreneur who is very successful at leveraging the discounts from vendors is home product distributor Jeff Schreiber. Schreiber always tries to take advantage of any discount for prompt payments, and he obtained over $15,000 in early payment savings in 1 year alone.

Table 1.   Guide for alternative sources of financing.

Source of financing	Length of time	Cost	Control
Self			
Family and friends			
The university			
Government grants and programs			
Suppliers and trade credit commercial banks			
R&D limited partnerships, crowdfunding			
Private equity funds, private investors (angels), venture capital			
Private equity placements			
Public equity offerings			

The other general source of funds is external to the venture. Alternative sources of external financing need to be evaluated based on three criteria: the length of time the funds are available, the cost involved, and the amount of company control lost. In selecting the best source of funds, each of the sources indicated in Table 1 need to be evaluated along these three dimensions. The more frequently used sources of funds (self, family and friends, the university, the government, commercial banks, private investors [angels], R&D limited partnerships, venture capital, and private placement) indicated in the table are discussed in the following pages.

Personal funds

Few, if any, new ventures are started without some personal funds of the entrepreneur and also the inventor. Not only are these the least expensive funds in terms of cost and control, but they are also needed to attract outside funding, particularly from banks, private investors, and venture capitalists. These invested personal funds are sometimes referred to as blood equity; the typical sources of personal funds include savings, life insurance, or a mortgage on a house or car. Outside providers of capital sometime feel that the individual is not sufficiently committed to the venture if he or she does not have money invested. As one venture capitalist succinctly said, "I want the individual whose venture I fund so financially committed that when the going gets tough, they will work through the problems and not throw the keys to the company on my desk."

This level of commitment is reflected in the percentage of total assets the entrepreneur has made available and committed to the venture but not necessarily the amount of money committed, particularly in countries like the United States. An outside investor wants an entrepreneur to have all available assets committed, an indication that he or she truly believes in the venture and will work the hours necessary to ensure success. Whether this is $1,000, $100,000, or $250,000 depends on the assets of the entrepreneur available. *Entrepreneurs should always remember that it is not the amount of the capital but rather the fact that all monies available are committed that makes outside investors feel comfortable with their commitment level and therefore more willing to invest, in most countries.*

Family and friends

After the entrepreneur, family and friends are the usual sources of capital for a new venture. They are most likely to invest due to their relationship with the entrepreneur. This helps overcome one portion of uncertainty felt by impersonal investors — they have knowledge of the entrepreneur. Family and friends usually provide a small amount of equity funding for new ventures, reflecting in part the small amount of capital needed for most new ventures at this time. Although it is relatively easy to obtain money from family and friends, like all sources of capital, there are positive and negative aspects of obtaining and using these funds. Although the amount of money provided may be small, if it is in the form of equity financing, the family members or friends then have an ownership position in the venture. This may make them feel that they have some say about the operations of the venture, which may have a negative effect on employees, facilities, or even on sales and profits. Frequently, family and friends are not a problem and in fact are more patient than other investors in their timing for a return on the investment. Generally, they cause more problems when the venture is not performing well and is about to fail or the venture is extremely successful.

One thing that helps minimize possible difficulties in the relationships is to keep the business arrangements strictly professional. Any loans or investments from family or friends should be treated in the same businesslike manner as if the financing were from an impersonal investor. Any loan should specify the rate of interest and the proposed repayment schedule of interest and principal. The timing of any future dividends must be disclosed in terms of an equity investment. If the family or friend is treated the same as an investor, potential future conflicts can be avoided. It is also beneficial to agree on everything upfront and in writing. It is amazing how short memories become when money is involved.

The impact of the investment on the family member or friend should be considered. Particular concern should be paid to any hardships that might result should the business fail. Each should receive unaudited income statements showing results on a regular basis — usually every 4 months or at least every 6 months, like any private investor.

Commercial Banks

Commercial banks are by far the source of short-term funds most frequently used by the entrepreneur when collateral is available. The funds provided are in the form of debt financing and, as such, require some tangible guaranty or collateral — some asset with value. This collateral can be in the form of business assets (land, equipment, or the building of the venture), personal assets (the entrepreneur's home, car, land, stock, or bonds), or the assets of the co-signer of the note.

Types of bank loans

There are many types of bank loans available. To help ensure repayment, these loans are based on the assets or the cash flow of the venture. The *asset base for loans* is usually accounts receivable, inventory, equipment, or real estate. Sometimes, the assets of the entrepreneur or an investor are used.

- **Accounts Receivable Loans:** Accounts receivable provides a good basis for a loan, especially if the customer base is well known and creditworthy. When strong creditworthy customers are involved, a factoring arrangement can be established whereby the factor (the bank) actually "buys" the accounts receivable at a value below the face value of the sale and collects the money directly from the account. In this case, if any of the receivables are not collectible, the factor (the bank) sustains the loss, not the business. The cost of factoring the accounts receivable is, of course, higher than the cost of securing a loan against the accounts receivable without factoring being involved, since the bank has more risk when factoring. The costs of factoring involve the interest charge on the amount of money advanced until the time the accounts receivable are collected, the commission covering the actual collection, and protection against possible uncollectible accounts.
- **Inventory Loans:** Inventory is another of the firm's assets that can often be the asset for a loan, particularly when the inventory is more liquid and can be easily sold. Usually, the finished good inventory can be financed for up to 50% of its value.
- **Equipment Loans:** Equipment can be used to secure longer term financing, usually on a 3- to 10-year basis. Equipment financing can fall into any of several categories: financing the purchase of new equipment, financing used equipment already owned by the company, sale–leaseback financing, or lease financing. When new equipment is being purchased or presently owned equipment is used as collateral, usually, 50–80% of the value of the equipment can be financed depending on its scalability. Given the tendency to rent rather than own, sale–leaseback or lease financing of equipment is more often used. In the sale–leaseback arrangement, the equipment is sold to a lender and then leased back for the life of the equipment. In lease financing, the company acquires the use of the equipment through a small down payment and guarantee to make a specified number of payments over a period of time. The total amount paid is the selling price plus the finance charge.

- **Real Estate Loans:** Real estate is also frequently used in asset-based financing. This mortgage financing is usually easily obtained to finance a company's land, plant, or another building, often up to 75% of its value.
- **Patent Loans:** Patents if very unique, protected, and in a very important area can be used to obtain financing.

Cash Flow Financing

The other type of debt financing frequently provided by commercial banks and other financial institutions is cash flow financing. These *conventional bank loans* include lines of credit, installment loans, straight commercial loans, long-term loans, and character loans. Lines of credit financing is perhaps the form of cash flow financing most frequently used. In arranging for a line of credit to be used, the company pays a "commitment fee" to ensure that the commercial bank will make the loan when requested and then pays interest on any outstanding funds borrowed from the bank. Frequently, the loan must be repaid or reduced to a certain agreed-upon level on a periodic basis.

- **Installment Loans:** These are short-term funds frequently used to cover working capital needs for a period of time, such as when seasonal financing is needed. These loans are usually for 30–40 days.
- **Straight Commercial Loans:** A hybrid of the installment loan is the straight commercial loan, by which funds are advanced for 30–90 days. These self-liquidating loans are often used for seasonal financing and for building up inventories.
- **Long-Term Loans:** When a long period for use of money is required, long-term loans are used. These loans (usually available only to strong, mature companies) can make funds available for up to 10 years. The debt incurred is usually repaid according to a fixed interest and principal schedule. The principal, however, can sometimes start being repaid in the second or third year of the loan, with only interest paid during the first year.
- **Character Loans:** When the assets to support a loan are not present, the individual may need a character (personal) loan. These loans frequently must have the assets of the individual seeking the loan or other

individual pledged as collateral or the loan cosigned by another individual. Assets that are frequently pledged include cars, homes, land, and securities. One father pledged a $50,000 certificate of deposit as collateral for his son's $40,000 loan.

Bank Lending Decisions

How do you successfully secure a loan from the bank? Banks are generally cautious in lending money, particularly to new ideas and ventures, since they do not want to have any bad loans. Regardless of geographic location, loan decisions are made only after the loan officer and loan committee conduct a careful review of the borrower and the financial track records. These decisions are based on both quantifiable information and subjective judgments. The bank's lending decisions are made according to the five Cs of lending: character, capacity, capital, collateral, and conditions. Any past financial statements (balance sheets and income statements) are reviewed in terms of key profitability and credit ratios, inventory turnover, aging of accounts receivable, and the entrepreneur's capital investment and commitment to the business. Future projections of market size, sales, and profitability are also evaluated to determine the ability to repay the loan. Although the analysis of this information allows the loan officer to assess the quantitative aspects of the loan decision, the intuitive factors, particularly the first two Cs — character and capacity — are also taken into account. This part of the loan decision — the gut feeling — is the most difficult part to assess. The inventor/entrepreneur must present his/her capabilities and the prospects for the idea or the company in a way that elicits a positive response from the lender. This intuitive part of the loan decision becomes even more important when there is little or no track record, limited experience in financial management, a nonproprietary product/service (one not protected by a patent or license), or few assets available.

Some of the concerns of the loan officer and the loan committee can be reduced through a good loan application. While the specific loan application format of each bank differs to some extent, generally the application format is a "mini" business plan that consists of an executive summary, business description, owner/manager profiles, business projections, financial statements, amount and use of the loan, and repayment schedule. This information provides the loan officer and loan committee with insight into the creditworthiness of the individual and the venture as well as the ability of the venture to make enough sales and profits to repay the loan and the interest. The entrepreneur should evaluate several alternative banks, select the one that has had a positive loan experience in the particular business area, call for an appointment, and then carefully present the case for the loan to the loan officer. Presenting a positive business image and following the established protocol is important in obtaining a loan from a commercial bank, particularly in conditions where the money is tight.

Generally, the entrepreneur should borrow the maximum amount that can possibly be repaid as long as the prevailing interest rates, the terms and conditions, and restrictions of the loan are satisfactory. It is essential that there is always enough cash to repay the interest and principal on the loan in a timely manner. The entrepreneur should evaluate the track record and lending procedures of several banks to secure the money needed on the most favorable terms available. This "bank shopping procedure" will provide the needed funds at the most favorable rates and in a timely manner.

Role of the SBA in Small-Business Financing

Frequently, an entrepreneur is missing the necessary track record, assets, or some other ingredient to obtain a commercial bank loan. When the entrepreneur is unable to secure a regular commercial bank loan, an alternative is obtaining a guaranty from the Small Business Administration (SBA). The SBA offers numerous loan programs to assist small businesses. In each of these, the SBA is primarily a guarantor of loans made by commercial banks and other institutions. The Basic 7(a) Loan Guaranty is the SBA's primary business loan program. This program helps qualified small businesses to obtain financing when they cannot obtain business loans through regular lending channels. The proceeds from such a loan can be used for a variety of business purposes, such as working capital; machinery and equipment; furniture and fixtures; land and building; leasehold improvements; and even, under some conditions, debt refinancing.

To get a 7(a) loan, repayment ability from the cash flow of the business is essential, other criteria include good character, management capability, collateral, and owner's equity contribution. Eligibility factors for all 7(a) loans include size, type of business, use of proceeds, and the availability of funds from other sources. All owners of 20% or more are required to personally guarantee SBA loans.

The SBA 7(a) loan program has a maximum loan amount of $5 million. In the case of a $5 million loan, the maximum guarantee to the lender by the SBA will be $3.75 million or 75%. Though the interest rates on the loan are negotiated between the borrower and the lender, they are subject to SBA maximums, which are pegged to the prime rate, the LIBOR rate, or an optional peg rate and may be fixed or variable. For example, a fixed-rate loan of $50,000 or more must not exceed the base rate plus 2.25% if the maturity is less than 7 years.

In addition to the 7(a) loan program, the SBA has several other programs. The 504 loan program provides fixed-rate financing to enable small businesses to acquire machinery, equipment, or even real estate in order to expand or modernize. The maximum cost of the program is $5 million and $5.5 million for manufacturing and energy companies, and the loan can take a variety of forms, including a loan from a Community Development Company (CDC) backed by a 100% SBA-guaranteed debenture.

Another SBA loan program that many entrepreneurs have used is the SBA Microloan, a 7(a) program. This program provides short-term loans of up to $50,000 to small businesses for working capital or the purchase of inventory, supplies, furniture, fixtures, machinery, or equipment. The loan cannot be used to pay an existing debt. The small business receives the loan from a bank or other organization, with the loan being guaranteed in full by the SBA. Other specific SBA loans include International Trade and Export Working Capital loans ($5 million maximum), Export Express loans ($500,000 maximum), and CDC/504 loans (1.5 million maximum when meeting job creation criteria or $20 million maximum when meeting a public policy goal). The entrepreneur should check with the SBA to see whether a loan program is available if a loan cannot be obtained without the SBA guarantee.

Private Financing

Another source of funds for the entrepreneur is private investors, also called angels, who may be family and friends or wealthy individuals. An investor usually takes an equity position in the company, can influence the nature and direction of the business to some extent, and may even be involved to some degree in the business operations. The degree of involvement in the day-to-day operations of the venture is an important point for the entrepreneur to consider in selecting an investor. Some investors want to be actively involved in the business while others desire at least an advisory role in the direction and operations of the venture. Still others are more passive in nature, desiring their investment plus a good rate of return.

Individuals who handle their own sizable investments frequently use advisors such as accountants, technical experts, financial planners, or lawyers in making their investment decision. This aspect of financing is covered in the next chapter.

Private Equity Market

The private equity market, which is better called the enterprise capital market, provides capital for privately held ventures. The market is composed of three verticals as indicated in Figure 1 — individuals, venture

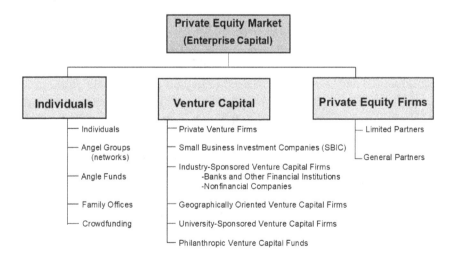

Figure 1. The enterprise capital market.

Funding Sources for University Startups 159

capital firms, and private equity funds. While the size of the investment increases from individual to private equity funds, the number of deals decreases. While the individual market is the least understood with limited information in the United States, the total amount invested in smaller amounts is about equal to the total amount invested by the venture capital market.

Individual investors make the largest number of investments in this market, often called angel investors. In the United States, these individuals have accredited investors, which means they have either $200,000 per year income and/or net worth of $1 million or more. Their individual investment usually occurs in the range of $10,000–500,000 with an average investment of $220,000. Sometimes, this individual gets other individuals involved so that the amount of capital per individual is reduced as well as the risk. These individuals, when not in groups, have no formal identification and are often found by referrals from accountants, bank officials, lawyers, and university professors teaching in the entrepreneurship/venture finance area.

Informal Risk-Capital Market

The informal risk-capital market is the most misunderstood type of risk capital. It consists mostly of a virtually invisible group of wealthy investors, often called *business angels*, who are looking for equity-type investment opportunities in a wide variety of entrepreneurial ventures. Typically investing anywhere from $10,000 to $500,000, these angels provide the funds needed in all stages of financing, but particularly in the startup stage (first stage). Firms funded from the informal risk-capital market frequently raise second- and third-round financing from professional venture capital firms in the public-equity market. While angel groups and angel funds will be discussed in Chapter 7, the final type of individual investing is crowdfunding. This has occurred in the United Kingdom and more recently in the United States. It is different from traditional funding models in that it is based on networks of individuals and sometimes companies. Crowdfunding can be used to actually pretest an idea for a product/service. Often the individuals involved in the crowdfunding idea are very interested in the idea and its potential for success. Sometimes, as in the case of LawBite, the idea is oversubscribed when listed on crowdfunding.

Crowdfunding

In 2010, the Jumpstart Our Business Startups (JOBS) Act became a law that relaxed rules over the General Solicitation of funds in equity offerings. This deregulatory measure effectively allowed companies to be more vocal about their intent to raise money in what is often referred to as *crowdfunding* (Sardar, 2016).

As a result of the passage of the JOBS Act, it was estimated in 2012 that there were 450 crowdfunding websites or platforms that help connect entrepreneurs and investors to facilitate deal flow (Fiez *et al.*, 2017). Some of the websites, noted in Table 2, provide a variety of services to inventors and small businesses seeking to raise capital including due diligence and online deal flow.

Given the proliferation, other sites have emerged to specialize in certain types of crowdfunding. For example, Kickstarter tends to focus on funding creative projects and does not offer equity or financial incentives for those to contribute.

Venture Capital

As indicated in the table, besides private individuals an important funding area in the private equity market is venture capital. This important area of

Table 2.   Crowdfunding websites.

- AngelList — https://angel.co/
- Appbackr — http://www.appbackr.com
- Crowdrise — http://www.crowdrise.com
- Crowdfunder — https://www.crowdfunder.com
- Indiegogo — http://indiegogo.com
- Investedin — www.investedin.com/
- Kickstarter — https://www.kickstarter.com
- Quirky — http://www.quirky.com
- RocketHub — http://www.rockethub.com

venture capital will be discussed in terms of its nature, the venture capital industry in the United States, and the venture capital process.

Nature of venture capital

Venture capital is another misunderstood area in the enterprise capital market. Some think that venture capitalists fund the early-stage financing of relatively small, rapidly growing technology companies. It is more accurate to view venture capital broadly as a professionally managed pool of equity capital. Frequently, the *equity pool* is formed from the resources of wealthy individuals or institutions who are limited partners. Other principal investors in venture capital limited partnerships are pension funds, endowment funds, and other institutions, including foreign investors. The pool is managed by a general partner — that is, the venture capital firm — in exchange for a percentage of the gain realized on the investment and a fee. The investments are made in early-stage deals as well as second- and third-stage deals and leveraged buyouts. In fact, venture capital can best be characterized as a long-term investment discipline, usually occurring over a 5-year period that is found in the creation of early-stage companies, the expansion, and revitalization of existing businesses, and the financing of leveraged buyouts of existing divisions of major corporations or privately owned businesses. In each investment, the venture capitalist takes an *equity participation* through stock, warrants, and/or convertible securities and has an active involvement in the monitoring of each portfolio company bringing investment, financial planning, and business skills to the firm. The venture capitalist will often incur debt along with the equity portion of the financing.

Overview of the venture capital industry

Although the role of venture capital was instrumental throughout the industrialization of the United States, it did not become institutionalized until after World War II. Before World War II, venture-capital investment activity was a monopoly led by wealthy individuals, investment banking syndicates, and a few family organizations with a professional manager.

The first step toward institutionalizing the venture capital industry took place in 1946 with the formation of the American Research and Development Corporation (ARD) in Boston. The ARD was a small pool of capital from individuals and institutions put together by General Georges Doriot to make active investments in selected emerging businesses.

The next major development, the Small Business Investment Act of 1958, married private capital with government funds to be used by professionally managed small-business investment companies (SBIC firms) to infuse capital into startups and growing small businesses. With their tax advantages, the government fund for leverage, and status as a private-capital company, SBICs were the start of the now-formal venture capital industry. The 1960s saw a significant expansion of SBICs with the approval of approximately 585 SBIC licenses that involved more than $205 million in private capital. Many of these early SBICs failed. There are approximately 360 SBICs operating today, of which 130 are minority enterprise small-business investment companies (MESBICs) funding minority enterprises.

During the late 1960s, small *private venture capital firms* emerged (Thodla and Kundu, 2017). These were usually formed as limited partnerships, with the venture capital company acting as the general partner that received a management fee and a percentage of the profits earned on a deal. The limited partners, who supplied the funding, were frequently institutional investors such as insurance companies, endowment funds, bank trust departments, pension funds, and wealthy individuals and families. There are over 900 of this type of venture capital establishment in the United States.

Another type of venture capital firm was also developed during this time — the venture capital division of major corporations. These firms, of which there are approximately 100, are usually associated with banks and insurance companies, although companies such as 3M, Monsanto, Xerox, Intel, and Unilever house such firms as well. Corporate venture capital firms are more prone to invest in technology or new market acquisition than are private venture-capital firms or SBICs. Some of these corporate venture capital firms have not had strong results.

In response to the need for economic development, the fourth type of venture capital firm has emerged in the form of the *state-sponsored venture capital fund.* These state-sponsored funds have a variety of formats. While the size, investment focus, and industry orientation vary from state to state, each fund typically is required to invest a certain percentage of its capital in a particular state. Generally, the funds that are professionally managed by the private sector, outside the state's bureaucracy and political processes, have performed better.

Besides the four types of funds previously discussed, there are now emerging university-sponsored venture capital funds as well as philanthropic venture funds. The university-sponsored funds, usually managed as separate entities, invest in the technology of the particular university. At schools such as Stanford, Columbia, and MIT, students assist professors and other students in creating business plans for funding as well as assisting the fund manager in his or her due diligence, thereby learning more about the venture-funding process.

The venture capital industry has not returned to the highest level of dollars invested in 1999 and 2000. While the total amount of venture capital dollars invested increased steadily from $7.8 billion in 1995 to a high of $104.7 billion in 2000 (see Table 3), the total dollars invested declined to $40.7 billion in 2001, $21.7 billion in 2002, and $19.6 billion in 2003. There was a slight increase to $21.6 billion in 2004 and $21.7 billion in 2005. The total amount invested increased again in 2006 ($26.7 billion) and 2007 ($30.9 billion) before declining with the economic downturn to $28.3 billion in 2008 and $19.7 billion in 2009. It has increased to $27.5 million in 2012, $29.9 billion in 2013, and $48.3 billion in 2014.

The total amount of venture capital dollars invested, disseminated across the number of deals, is indicated in column 3 of Table 3. The number of venture capital deals went from 1,773 in 1995 to a high of 7,809 in 2000. In 2003, 2004, and 2005, the number of deals stayed fairly steady, at 2,865, 2966, and 2,939, respectively. The number of deals increased in 2006 (3,675) and again in 2007 (3,952) before declining in 2008 to 3,808 deals and in 2009 to 3,056 deals. The number of deals increased to 3,496 in 2010 and 3,673 in 2011. The deals have steadily increased since then — 3,936 (2012), 4,193 (2013) and 4,356 (2014).

Table 3. Total venture dollars invested and number of deals.

Years	Total	Number of deals
1995	$7,879,331,900	1,773
1996	11,014,332,900	2,471
1997	14,621,026,900	3,084
1998	20,810,583,100	3,553
1999	54,475,711,500	5,396
2000	104,700,717,300	7,809
2001	49,703,455,300	4,456
2002	21,697,809,100	3,057
2003	19,585,475,700	2,865
2004	21,635,323,900	2,966
2005	23,173,465,300	3,155
2006	26,740,603,400	3,675
2007	30,885,861,100	3,952
2008	28,298,040,600	3,808
2009	19,667,943,200	3,056
2010	23,363,353,600	3,496
2011	29,119,041,600	3,752
2012	27,578,404,700	3,936
2013	29,964,019,900	4,193
2014	48,348,586,400	4,356

Source: 2014 Q4 Price water house Coopers LLP/National Venture Capital Association Money Tree™ Report, Data: Thomson Reuters.

These deals concentrated in three primary areas: software (39%), biotechnology (14%), and media and entertainment (10%). This investment has significantly impacted the growth and development of these three industry sectors. Other industry areas receiving venture capital investment include the following: computers and peripherals (7%), IT services (6%), medical devices and equipment (5%), and industrial energy (4%).

Venture capital process

To be in a position to secure the funds needed, the entrepreneur must understand the philosophy and objects of a venture capital firm, as well as the *venture capital process*. The objective of a venture capital firm is to generate long-term capital appreciation through debt and equity investments. To achieve this objective, the venture capitalist is willing to make any changes or modifications necessary in the business investment. Since the objective of the entrepreneur is the survival of the business, the objectives of the two are frequently at odds, particularly when problems occur such as the numbers not being met.

A typical portfolio objective of venture capital firms balances return criteria and risk involved. Since there is more risk involved in financing a business earlier in its development, more return is expected from early-stage financing (50% ROI) than from acquisition or leveraged buyouts (30% ROI), which are later stages of development. The significant risk involved and the pressure that venture capital firms feel from their investors (limited partners) to make safer investments with higher rates of return have caused these firms to invest even greater amounts of their funds in the later stages of financing. In these late-stage investments, there are lower risks, faster returns, less managerial assistance needed, and fewer deals to be evaluated.

The venture capitalist does not necessarily seek control of a company and actually would prefer the firm and the entrepreneur to have the most risk. The venture capitalist will require at least one seat on the board of directors. Once the decision to invest is made, the venture capitalist will do anything necessary to support the management team so that the business and the investment prosper. While the venture capitalist will provide guidance as a member of the board of directors, the management team is expected to direct and run the daily operations of the company. A venture capitalist supports the management team with investment, financial skills, planning, and expertise in any area needed.

Since the venture capitalist provides long-term investment (typically 5–7 years), it is important that there be mutual trust and understanding with the entrepreneur. There should be no surprises in the firm's performance. Both good and bad news needs to be shared with the objective of taking the necessary action to allow the company to grow and develop in the long run. The venture capitalist should be available to the entrepreneur to discuss problems and develop strategic plans.

A venture capitalist expects a company to satisfy three general criteria before he or she will commit to the venture. First, the company needs to have a strong management team composed of individuals with solid experience and background, a strong commitment to the company, capabilities in their specific areas of expertise, the ability to meet challenges, and the flexibility to scramble wherever necessary. A venture capitalist would rather invest in a first-rate management team and a second-rate product than the reverse. The management team's commitment needs to be reflected in dollars invested in the company. The amount varies by country. While the amount of the investment is important, more telling is the size of this investment relative to the management team's ability to invest. The commitment of the management team should be backed by the support of the family, particularly the spouse, of each key team player. A positive family environment and spousal support enables the entrepreneur and team members to spend the 60–70 hours per week necessary to start and grow the company. One successful venture capitalist makes it a point to have dinner with the entrepreneur and spouse, and even to visit the entrepreneur's home, before making an investment decision. According to the venture capitalist, "I find it difficult to believe an entrepreneur can successfully run and manage a business and put in the necessary time when the home environment is out of control."

The second criterion is that the product and/or market opportunity must be unique, having a differential advantage or three to five unique selling propositions in a growing market. Securing a unique market niche is essential since the product/service must be able to compete and grow during the investment period. This uniqueness needs to be carefully spelled out in the marketing promotion of the business plan and is even better when it is protected by a patent or a trade secret.

The final criterion for investment is that the business opportunity must have a *significant capital appreciation*. The exact amount of capital appreciation varies, depending on such factors as the size of the deal, the stage of development of the company, the upside potential, the downside risks, and the available exit. The venture capitalist typically expects a significant percent return on investment in most investment situations.

The venture capital process that implements these criteria is both an art and a science. The element of art is illustrated in the venture capitalist's intuition, gut feeling, and creative thinking that guides the process. The process is scientific due to the systematic approach and data-gathering techniques involved in the assessment.

The process starts with the venture capital firm establishing its philosophy and investment objectives. The firm must decide on the following: the composition of its portfolio mix (including the number of startups, expansion companies, and management buyouts); the types of industries; the geographic region for investment; and any product or industry specialization.

A venture capital process can be broken down into four primary stages: preliminary screening, agreement on principal terms, due diligence, and final approval. The *preliminary screening* begins with the receipt of the business plan. A good business plan is essential in the venture capital process. Most venture capitalists will not even talk to an entrepreneur who doesn't have one. As a starting point, the business plan must have a clearcut mission and clearly stated objectives that are supported by an in-depth industry and market analysis and *pro forma* income statements. The executive summary is an important part of this business plan, as it is used for initial screening in this preliminary evaluation. Many business plans are never evaluated beyond the executive summary. When evaluating the business, the venture capitalist first determines if the deals have been seen previously. The investor then determines if the proposal fits his or her long-term policy and short-term needs in developing a portfolio balance. In this preliminary screening, the venture capitalist investigates the economy of the industry and evaluates whether he or she has the appropriate knowledge and ability to invest in that industry. The investor reviews the numbers presented to determine whether the business can reasonably deliver the ROI required. In addition, the credentials and capability of the management team are evaluated to determine if they can carry out the plan presented.

The second stage is the agreement on general terms between the entrepreneur and the venture capitalist. The venture capitalist wants a basic understanding of the principal terms of the deal at this stage of the process before making the major commitment of time and effort involved in the formal due diligence process.

The third stage, detailed review and *due diligence*, is the longest stage, involving between 1 and 3 months. This includes a detailed review of the company's history, the business plan, the resumes of the individuals and their financial history, and target market customers. The upside potential and downside risks are assessed; there is a thorough evaluation of the markets, industry, finances, suppliers, customers, and management.

In the last stage, *final approval*, a comprehensive, internal investment memorandum is prepared. This document reviews the venture capitalist's findings and details the investment terms and conditions of the investment transaction. The information is used to prepare the formal legal documents that both the entrepreneur and venture capitalist will sign to finalize the deal.

Locating venture capitalists

One of the most important decisions for the entrepreneur lies in selecting the venture capital firm to approach. Since venture capitalists tend to specialize both geographically and by industry (manufacturing industrial products or consumer products, high technology, or service) and by the size and stage of investment, the entrepreneur should approach only those venture capitalists who may have an interest in their investment opportunity based on these criteria. Where do you find this venture capitalist?

Although venture capitalists are located throughout the United States, the traditional areas of concentration are found in Los Angeles, New York, Chicago, Boston, and San Francisco. Most venture capital firms belong to the National Venture Capital Association and are listed on its website (www.nvca.org). An entrepreneur should carefully research the names and addresses of prospective venture capital firms that might have an interest in their particular investment opportunity. There is also a regional and national venture capital association. For a nominal fee or none at all, these associations will frequently e-mail the entrepreneur a directory of their members, the types of businesses their members invest in, and any investment restrictions. Whenever possible, the entrepreneur should be introduced to the venture capitalist. Bankers, accountants, lawyers, and professors are good sources for these introductions.

Approaching a venture capitalist

The entrepreneur needs to approach a venture capitalist in a professional manner. Since a venture capitalist receives hundreds of enquiries and is frequently out of the office working with portfolio companies or investigating potential investment opportunities, it is important to begin the relationship positively. The entrepreneur should contact any potential venture capitalist to ensure that his/her business venture is in an area of investment interest. Then the business plan, or in some cases a two-stage executive summary, should be sent, accompanied by a short professional letter.

Since venture capitalists receive many more plans than they are capable of funding, many plans are screened out very quickly. A venture capitalist tends to focus and put more time and effort on those plans that are referred. In fact, one venture capital group said that 80% of its investments over the last 5 years were in referred companies. Consequently, it is well worth the entrepreneur's time to seek out an introduction to the venture capitalist. Typically, this is obtained from an executive of a portfolio company, an accountant, a lawyer, or a business school professor.

The entrepreneur needs to be aware of some basic rules of thumb before implementing the actual approach. First, care should be taken in selecting the right venture capitalist to approach. Venture capitalists tend to specialize in certain industries and will not invest in a business outside those areas, regardless of the merits of the business proposal and plan. Second, recognize that venture capitalists know each other, particularly in a specific region of the country. When a large amount of money is involved, they will invest in the deal together, with one venture capital firm taking the lead. Since this degree of familiarity is present, a venture capital firm will probably find out if others have seen your business plan. Do not shop among venture capitalists, as even a good business plan can quickly become "shopworn". Third, when meeting the venture capitalist, particularly for the first time, bring only one or two key members of the management team. A venture capitalist is investing primarily in you, the entrepreneur, and then your management team and its track, not in outside consultants and experts. Any consultant and/or experts can be called in when needed.

Finally, be sure to develop a succinct, well-thought-out oral presentation. This should cover the company's business, the uniqueness of the product/service, the prospects for growth, the major factors behind achieving the sales and profits indicated, the background and track records of the key managers, the amount of financing required, and the returns anticipated. This first presentation is critical, as is indicated in the comment of one venture capitalist: "I need to sense a competency, a capability, a chemistry within the first half hour of our initial meeting. The entrepreneur needs to look me in the eye and present his story clearly. If a chemistry does not start to develop, I start looking for reasons not to do the deal."

Following a favorable initial meeting, the venture capitalist will proceed with a preliminary investigation of the plan. If favorable, another meeting between the management team and the venture capitalist is scheduled so that both parties can assess the other and determine if a good working relationship can be established and if a feeling of trust and confidence is evolving. During the mutual evaluation, the entrepreneur should be careful not to be too inflexible about the amount of company equity he or she is willing to share. If the entrepreneur is too inflexible, the venture capitalist might end negotiations. During this meeting, initial agreement of terms is often established. If you are turned down by one venture capitalist, do not become discouraged. Instead, select several other venture capitalist candidates and repeat the procedure. A significant number of companies denied funding by one venture capitalist are able to obtain funds from other outside sources, including other venture capitalists.

Summary

This chapter, the first of two chapters on sources of funding for technological ideas in the ecosystem, focuses on overall sources and types of funding. Following a discussion of debt versus equity financing and using internal or external funds, various sources of funds such as personal funds, commercial banks, SBA financing, and private financing are presented. The chapter concludes with other specific sources of funds within the private equity market — the informal rush capital market, crowd funding, and venture capitalist.

Selected Readings

(1) Munari, F., Sobrero, M. and Toschi, L. (2018). "The University as a Venture Capitalist? Gap Funding Instruments for Technology Transfer". *Technological Forecasting and Social Change*, 127, 70–84.

The limited availability of private funding sources to support technology transfer activities represents a major barrier to the effective commercialization of university technologies. This article analyzes the key determinants of the activation of financial instruments by universities — such as seed funds and proof-of-concept programs — to address such funding gaps. Using data from a survey of technology transfer office managers in European universities, we detail the antecedents of the presence of such instruments at the university level and their perceived effectiveness. The findings, in turn, have notable policy implications.

(2) Koenig, J., Brenner, T. and Buenstorf, G. (2017). "Regional Effects of University Funding: Excellence at the Cost of Regional Disparity?" *Review of Regional Research*, 37(2), 111–133.

We investigate regional repercussions of the recent shift toward focusing academic excellence in German science policy. We find that the regional concentration of merit-based public research funding has increased since the late 1990s. However, it is challenging to identify the characteristics of winning and losing regions. There is some evidence indicative of advantages for regions with larger overall university size. In contrast, our results do not suggest that more urbanized regions, or regions with stronger private sector R&D activity, benefit disproportionately from the policy shift.

(3) Herber, D. L., Mendez-Hinds, J., Miner, J., Sedam, M. C., Wozniak, K., McDevitt, V. L. and Sanberg, P. R. (2017). "University Seed Capital Programs: Benefits beyond the Loan". *Technology & Innovation*, 18(4), 305–314.

While seed funding for startup companies certainly provides crucial cash necessary to conduct business, the advantages of these initial infusions go well beyond the actual monies received, particularly for university-based technology startup companies. Additional benefits for the institution and community can be realized when the seed funding comes from the academic institution where the technology was invented. These benefits include expanded funding opportunities, hiring and retention of top entrepreneurial faculty, goal setting, entrepreneur development, economic development, and university engagement. Examples of seed loan programs at both the regional and university level are numerous, and several case studies are presented to highlight the variety of benefits. We end with a consideration of the metrics that can be used to measure the success of these programs, including revenue generation as well as more traditional technology transfer aims, such as development of industry partnerships and realizing public good from the commercialization of academic research.

References

Fiez, T. S., Hershenson, M., Sanders, L. and Ashcraft, C. (2017). Innovation, startups, and funding in the age of accelerations: A survey of the evolving landscape. *IEEE Solid-State Circuits Magazine*, 9(4), 66–72.

Sardar, R. (2016). Bolstering startups and incubators centers through industry-academia partnership. *CLEAR International Journal of Research in Commerce & Management*, 7(10).

Thodla, R. and Kundu, S. G. (2017). A study on equity crowd funding as a viable option to pre-seed capital in IT startups. *Ushus-Journal of Business Management*, 16(1), 77–85.

Chapter 7

Frequently Used Funding Sources: Government Grants and University Angel Groups

Learning Objectives

- To understand funding at various levels.
- To know the various government funding programs available.
- To know how to apply for an SBIR grant.
- To understand private investors.
- To understand angel funds and groups.

Opening Profile — Alex Reed

Q1. Submitter Information

Name of Nominee	**Alex Reed**
University the Nominee is representing	**Tulane University**
Email	alex.reed@fluenceanalytics.com
Phone Number	5047772804

Q2. The nominee's position when they created the company. Describe the nominee's process with the university as they were creating the company. Be as detailed as possible.

When Alex founded the company, he was the Associate Director for Operations and Strategy at Tulane-PolyRMC, an R&D center which is active in fundamental and applied polymer research. He has also received a BA in Economics and Latin American Studies and a minor in Business Administration from Tulane University in 2008, and worked during college at PolyRMC with his dad, who is a Tulane Professor and Director of PolyRMC. While working at PolyRMC, Alex realized that his dad's research could have a real impact on the polymer industry and began seeking advice from Tulane's Office of Technology Transfer & Intellectual Property Development. Through Tulane, Alex was also connected to his mentor, Dr. William Bottoms, a former Tulane Professor and experienced CEO and investor.

Q3. Describe the nominee's experience working with the university in creating the company. What were the challenges? What support did they receive? Be as detailed as possible.

After his company, Applied Polymer Monitoring Technologies (APMT), obtained a license for the technologies his dad invented at Tulane, Alex set up shop at Tulane (through a negotiated lease agreement with the university) to continue commercial development along with his dad and another PolyRMC researcher.

Federal commercialization grants applied for in partnership with Tulane helped APMT continue operations in conjunction with research performed at PolyRMC until a dilutive funding round was raised through connections made with the help of Tulane.

Q4. What happened to the company the nominee created? Describe in detail where it is now and how is it doing. What is the history of the company? Be as detailed as possible.

Fluence Analytics, formerly APMT, was founded in 2012 to commercialize technologies developed at Tulane University's PolyRMC, an R&D center active in fundamental and applied polymer research. The company was rebranded as Fluence Analytics in 2017 to emphasize its focus on continuous process analytics and to better reflect its vision for the future of polymer and biopharmaceutical manufacturing.

Fluence Analytics is a privately held company headquartered in New Orleans, LA, only a couple of miles from Tulane's main campus.

Fluence Analytics is a manufacturer of industrial and laboratory monitoring solutions that produce continuous data streams. The company has two product lines on the market, ACOMP and ARGEN. Combined with powerful, proprietary analytical tools, the confluence of data from measurements enables real-time optimization leading to improved process control and faster R&D for polymer and biopharmaceutical manufacturers. They currently have approximately 20 employees, and have hired over 40 employees and interns from Tulane through the years.

Introduction

In evaluating the appropriateness of financing alternatives; the amount and the timing of funds required must be determined as does the projected company sales and growth. Some funding milestones for technical and business companies are indicated in Table 1. As is indicated, the first four phases are usually funded by the founder, family, and friends (discussed in the previous chapter) and government grants, particularly SBIR/STTR grants. In stage 4, there is the possibility of securing funding from university mentoring angels. Beginning at stage 5, private investors (angels) and venture capitalists, discussed in Chapter 6, become the primary funding source until stage 10 where an exit can occur through sales to a large corporation or private equity firm or by going public through issuing an initial public offering (IPO).

The types of funding provided as the business develops are indicated in Table 2. The funding problems and the cost of the funds differ for each type. Early-stage financing is usually the most difficult and costly to obtain. Two types of financing are available during this stage: seed capital and startup capital. Of the two, seed capital is the most difficult funding to obtain from outside funds and is usually a relatively small amount of capital that is needed to prove concepts and finance feasibility studies. Since venture capitalists usually have a minimum funding level of above $500,000, they are rarely involved in this type of funding, except in the

Table 1.   Commercialization readiness levels.

CRL	Technical milestones	Business milestones	Funding milestones
0	Research validated	Opportunity validated; corp. license if applicable	Public Research Grants
1	Startup and technology development plan	Startup created, management team. IP licenses, legal issues settled.	Public/Private
2	Market and technical feasibility established	Business plan validated at level 1 (accelerator) and level 2 (CCC).	Public; SBIR/STTR PH 1; other public sources/ University Mentor-Angels.
3	"Works-like" laboratory proof of concept	Key corporate advisors in hand; pharma target validated.	Public; PH 2 SBIR/STTR; other/ University Mentor-Angels.
4	"Works-like" operational prototype	Commercialization plan updated including competitive update; tech landscape; preclinical validation and safety profile.	Public; PH 2 SBIR/STTR; other/University Mentor-Angels.
5	Operational product development and launch	Funding for manufacturing/organizational development; human clinical validation.	Public; PH 2 SBIR/STTR; other; Angel. Pharma: Corp./VC/Angel.
6	Sale/Service and Support/Scaling	SSGNA in place $0–1 million revenues	Angel/VC/Corp.
7	Sale/Service and Support/Scaling	$1–5 million revenues	Angel/VC/Corp.
8	Sale/Service and Support/Scaling	$5–10 million revenues	VC/Corp.
9	Sale/Service and Support/Scaling	$10–100 million revenues	VC/Corp.
10	Sale/Service and Support/Scaling	>$100 million revenues	Exit/IPO

Source: National Council of Entrepreneurial Tech. Transfer (NCET2).

Table 2. Stages of business development funding.

Early-Stage Financing	
• Seed capital	Relatively small amounts to prove concepts and financial feasibility studies.
• Startup	Product development and initial marketing, but with no commercial sales yet; funding to get company operations started.
Expansion of Development Financing	
• Second stage	Working capital for initial growth phase, but no clear profitability or cash flow yet.
• Third stage	Major expansion for a company with rapid sales growth; company is at breakeven or positive profit levels but is still private.
• Fourth stage	Bridge financing to prepare the company for a public offering.
Acquisition and Leveraged Buyout Financing	
• Traditional acquisitions	Assuming ownership and control of another company.
• Leveraged buyouts (LBOs)	Management of a company acquiring company control by buying out the present owners.
• Going private	Some of the owners/managers of a company buying all the outstanding stock, making the company privately held again.

case of high-technology ventures of entrepreneurs who have a successful track record and need a significant amount of capital. The second type of funding is startup financing. As the name implies, startup financing is involved in developing and selling some initial products to determine if commercial sales are feasible. These funds are also difficult to obtain. Angel investors are the most active in these two types of financing.

Expansion of developing financing (the second basic financing type) is easier to obtain than early-stage financing. Venture capitalist plays an active role in providing funds at this stage. As the firm develops, the funds for expansion are less expensive. Generally, funds in the second stage are used as working capital to support initial growth. In the third stage, the company is at breakeven or a positive profit level and uses the funds for major sales expansion. Funds in the fourth stage are usually used as bridge financing in the interim period as the company prepares to go public.

Acquisition financing or leveraged buyout financing (the third type) is more specific in nature. It is issued for such activities as traditional acquisitions, leveraged buyouts (management buying out the present owners), and going private (a publicly held firm buying out existing stockholders, thereby becoming a private company).

Government Grants

One of the best sources of money for entrepreneurs and scientists in the first six stages of commercialization come from the SBIR and STTR Programs overseen by the Small Business Administration (SBA). These programs, affiliated with government agencies involving research and development in specified areas, now have a 2.2 billion dollar base to support the financing of cutting-edge technologies.

These programs started in 1977 in the National Science Foundation due to the efforts of Roland Tibbetts (often labeled as the father of the SBIR Program), Senator Edward Kennedy (whose recognized the vital role small businesses play in the US economy), and other legislators including Judith and Arthur Obermeyer (who called for every government agency with a budget of over $100 million to establish a program in their agency modeled after the original Tibbetts' NSF SBIR Program).

The SBIR Program is highly competitive and encourages the engagement in Federal Research and Development projects that have the potential for commercialization. The mission of the program is to support scientific excellence and technological innovation; to accomplish this, the SBIR Program has the following specific goals:

- stimulate technological innovation;
- fulfill the research and development needs of federal agencies;
- foster and encourage participation and entrepreneurship by socially and economically disadvantaged individuals;
- increase private sector commercialization of innovations derived from federal research and development funding.

Each year, federal agencies with research and development budgets over $100 million are required to allocate 3.2% of these budgets to their own

Table 3. SBIR participating agencies.

- Department of Agriculture
  https://www.usa.gov/federal-agencies/u-s-department-of-agriculture
- Department of Commerce — National Institute of Standard and Technology
  https://www.nist.gov/
- Department of Commerce — National Oceanic and Atmospheric Administration
  www.noaa.gov/
- Department of Defense*
  https://www.defense.gov/
- Department of Education
  https://www.ed.gov/
- Department of Energy*
  https://energy.gov/
- Department of Health and Human Services*
  https://www.hhs.gov/
- Department of Homeland Security
  https://www.dhs.gov/
- Department of Transportation
  https://www.transportation.gov/
- Environmental Protection Agency
  https://www.epa.gov/
- National Aeronautics and Space Administration*
  https://www.nasa.gov/
- National Science Foundation*
  https://www.nsf.gov/

Note: *This agency also participates in the STTR Program.
Source: SBIR Information Report, Office of the Small Business Administration

SBIR Program. Each of the agencies involved, indicated in Table 3, administers its own individual program under general guidelines. Each agency determines its own R&D topics, solicits proposals, and makes awards based on stringent proposal evaluation.

The SBIR Program is structured into three phases as follows:

- **Phase I:** The objectives of Phase I is to establish the technical merit, feasibility, and commercial potential of the proposed research and development effort as well as the quality of the submitting organization. Phase I awards usually do not exceed $150,000 for a 6 month period.

- **Phase II:** The objectives of Phase II awards, based on the results of Phase I efforts, are to continue the merited research and development efforts initiated in Phase I. These Phase II awards usually do not exceed $1 million in 2 years.
- **Phase III:** The objective of Phase III is to support the commercialization of the research and development efforts occurring in Phases I and II. This phase is not funded by the SBIR Program. Some agencies can sign R&D or procurement contracts for products, services, or processes for use by the United States Government.

Added after the SBIR Program, the Small Business Technology Transfer Program (STTR) was established to facilitate the transfer of technology developed by a research institution through the entrepreneurship of a small business concern. The firm has to be organized for profit and have a place of business located in the United States, with at least 51% of its ownership by one or more individuals who are citizens or permanent resident aliens of the United States. The organization can have no more than 500 employees. The nonprofit research institute which must be located in the United States and also be a nonprofit college or university, a domestic nonprofit research organization, or a federally funded research and development center.

The STTR differs from the SBIR in several ways. First, in the STTR Program, the SBC and its participating institutions are required to establish an intellectual property agreement. Second, the STTR requires the SBC to perform at least 40% and the research partner institution to perform at least 30% of the research and development contract. Third, with STTR the principal investigator of the project does not have to be employed by the SBC.

To date, the SBIR and STTR Programs have resulted in over 70,000 issued patents, about 700 public companies, and venture capital (VC) investments worth about $41 billion. The breakdown of the 2015 fiscal year of SBIR and STTR budgets by the agency is indicated in Table 4. A guide to SBIR/STTR Programs can be obtained from the SBA of the United States Government. Many countries have adopted these programs for their own use.

Table 4. SBIR/STTR budgets by agency, FY2015.

Agencies with SBIR and STTR Programs	Budget ($)
Department of Defense (DOD)	1.070 B
Department of Health and Human Services (HHS), including the National Institutes of Health (NIH)	797.0 M
Department of Energy (DOE), including Advance Research Projects Agency-Energy (ARPA-E)	206.1 M
National Aeronautics and Space Administration (NASA)	180.1 M
National Science Foundation (NSF)	176.0 M
Agencies with SBIR Programs	**Budget**
US Department of Agriculture (USDA)	20.3 M
Department of Homeland Security (DHS): Science and Technology Directorate (S&T) and Domestic Nuclear Detection Office (DNDO)	17.7 M
Department of Commerce: National Oceanic and Atmospheric Administration (NOAA) and National Institute of Standard and Technology (NIST)	8.4 M
Department of Transportation (DOT)	7.9 M
Department of Education (ED)	7.5 M
Environment Protection Agency (EPA)	4.2 M

Source: Office of the Small Business Administration.

Federal and state technology partnership program

Another less known government program is the Federal and State Technology Partnership Program (FAST). FAST provides about $100,000 per accepted proposal. The annual funding for the program is approximately $2 million with only one applicant funded per state. The proposal needs to have a letter of support from the Governor of the State. The funding is provided to support a community in the state to increase SBIR and STTR awareness and/or to provide support to science and technology-driven small businesses. Proposals that focus on helping socially and economically disadvantaged firms competing in the SBIR and STTR programs are particularly encouraged.

Other government grants

There are other grants available to the entrepreneur at the federal, state, and local levels. These take many different forms and vary greatly depending on the objectives of the level of government involved and the geographic area. Sometimes the federal and some state governments provide training grants to companies, particularly to those located in and/or hiring in what has been determined to be a labor-surplus area. These training grants often take the form of paying 50% of the salary of the employee for the first year only, at which time the employee should be fully productive. Companies often get some tax reductions at the state and federal levels for a period of time.

Research and Development Limited Partnerships

Research and development limited partnerships are another possible source of funds for entrepreneurs in high-technology areas. This method of financing provides funds from investors looking for tax shelters. A typical R&D partnership arrangement involves a sponsoring company developing the technology with funds being provided by a limited partnership of individual investor(s). R&D limited partnerships are particularly good when the project involves a high degree of risk and significant expense in conducting the basic research and development, since the risks, as well as the ensuing rewards, are shared.

Major elements

The three major components of any R&D limited partnership are the contract, the sponsoring company, and the limited partnership. The contract specifies the agreement between the sponsoring company and the limited partnership, whereby the sponsoring company agrees to use the funds provided to conduct the proposed research and development that hopefully will result in a marketable technology for the partnership. The sponsoring company does not guarantee results but rather performs the work on a best-effort basis, being compensated by the limited partners on either a fixed-fee or a cost-plus arrangement. The typical contract has several key features. The first is that the liability for any loss incurred is borne by the limited partners. Second, there are some tax advantages to both the limited partnership and the sponsoring company.

The second component involved in this contract is the limited partners. Similar to the stockholders of a corporation, the *limited partners* have limited liability and are not a total taxable entity. Consequently, any tax benefits of the losses in the early stages of the R&D limited partnership are passed directly to the limited partners, offsetting other income and reducing the partners' total taxable income. When the technology is successfully developed in later years, the partners share in the profits. In some instances, these profits for tax purposes are at the lower capital gains tax rate as opposed to the ordinary income tax rate.

The final component, the sponsoring company, acts as the *general partner* developing the technology. The sponsoring company usually has the base technology but needs funds to further develop and modify it for commercial success. It is the base technology that the company is offering to the partnership in exchange for money. The sponsoring company usually retains the right to use this base technology to develop other products and to use the developed technology in the future for a license fee. Sometimes, a cross-licensing agreement is established whereby the partnership allows the company to use the technology for developing other products.

Procedure

An R&D limited partnership generally progresses through three stages: the funding stage, the development stage, and the exit stage. In the funding stage, a contract is established between the sponsoring company and its limited partners, and the money is invested for the proposed R&D effort. All the terms and conditions of ownership, as well as the scope of the research, are carefully documented.

In the development stage, the sponsoring company performs the actual research using the funds from the limited partners. If the technology is subsequently successfully developed, the exit stage commences, in which the sponsoring company and the limited partners commercially reap the benefits of the efforts. There are three basic types of arrangement: equity partnerships, royalty partnerships, and joint ventures.

In the typical equity partnership arrangement, the sponsoring company and the limited partner form a new, jointly owned corporation. On the basis of the formula established in the original agreement, the limited partners' interest can be transferred to equity in the new corporation on a tax-free basis. An alternative is to incorporate the R&D limited partnership itself and then either merge it into the sponsoring company or continue as a new entity.

A possible alternative to the equity partnership arrangement is a royalty partnership. In this situation, a royalty based on the sale of the products developed from the technology is paid by the sponsoring company to the R&D limited partnership. The royalty rates typically range from 6% to 10% of gross sales and often decrease at certain established sales levels. Frequently, an upper limit, or cap, is placed on the cumulative royalties paid.

A final exit arrangement can be through a joint venture. Here, the sponsoring company and the partners form a joint venture to manufacture and market the products developed from the technology. Usually, the agreement allows the company to buy out the partnership interest in the joint venture at a specified time or when a specified volume of sales and profits has been reached.

Benefits and costs

As with any financing arrangement, the entrepreneur needs to assess the appropriateness of establishing an R&D limited partnership in terms of the benefits and costs involved. Among the several benefits is an R&D limited partnership provides the funds needed with a minimum amount of equity dilution while reducing the risks involved. In addition, the sponsoring company's financial statements are strengthened through the attraction of outside capital.

There are costs involved in this financial arrangement. Typically, it is more expensive to establish a limited partnership than conventional financing. First, time and money are expended. An R&D limited partnership frequently takes a minimum of 6 months to establish and well over $50,000 in professional fees. The time and money estimates can increase to a year and cost up to $400,000 for a major effort. The track record for R&D partnerships is not good, as most are unsuccessful. Second, the restriction placed on the technology can be substantial. To give up the technology developed as a by-product of the primary effort may be too high a price to pay for the funds. Third, the exit from the partnership may be very complex and involve too much fiduciary responsibility. These costs and benefits need to be evaluated in light of other financing alternatives available before an R&D limited partnership is chosen as the funding vehicle.

Example

In spite of the many costs involved, there are numerous examples of successful R&D limited partnerships. Syntex Corporation initially raised $23.5 million in an R&D limited partnership to develop five medical diagnostic products. Genetech was so successful in developing human growth hormone and gamma interferon products from its first $55 million R&D limited partnership that it raised $32 million through a second partnership 6 months later to develop a tissue-type plasminogen activator. Trilogy Limited raised $55 million to develop a high-performance computer. As the many cases illustrate, R&D limited partnerships can be good financial alternatives to developing high-cost technology.

Private Investor Market

Private investors are a significant part of the Enterprise Capital Market and Informal Risk Capital Market discussed in the Chapter 6. Private investors such as individuals, angel networks, and angel funds provide one of the largest pool of risk capital in the United States. Although there is no verification of the size of this pool or the total amount of financing provided by private investors often called angels, related statistics provide some indication. A 1980 survey of a sample of issuers of private placements by corporations, reported to the Securities and Exchange Commission under Rule 146, found that 87% of those buying these issues were individual investors or personal trusts, investing an average of $74,000.[1] Private placements filed under Rule 145 averaged over

---

[1] *Report of the Use of the Rule 146 Exemption in Capital Formation* (Washington, DC: Directorate of Economic Policy Analysis, Security and Exchange Commission, 1983).

$1 billion per year. Another indication is apparent on examination of the filings under Regulation D — the regulation exempting certain private and limited offerings from the registration requirements of the Securities Act of 1933. In its first year, over 7,200 filings, worth $15.5 billion, were made under Regulation D. Corporations accounted for 43% of the value ($6.7 billion) or 32% of the total number of offerings (2,304). Corporations filing limited offerings (under $500,000) raised $220 million, an average of $200,000 per firm. The typical corporate issuers tended to be small, with fewer than 10 stockholders, revenues and assets less than $500,000, stockholders' equity of $50,000 or less, and five or fewer employees.[2]

Similar results were found in an examination of the funds raised by small technology-based firms prior to their initial public offerings. The study revealed that unaffiliated individuals (the informal investment market) accounted for 15% of these funds, while venture capitalists accounted for only 12–15%. During the startup year, unaffiliated individuals provided 17% of the external capital.[3]

A study of angels in New England again yielded similar results. The 133 individual investors studied reported risk-capital investments totaling over $16 million in 320 ventures between 1976 and 1980. These investors averaged one deal every 2 years, with an average size of $50,000. Although 36% of these investments averaged less than $10,000, 24% averaged over $50,000. While 40% of these investments were startups, 80% involved ventures less than 5 years old (Wetzel, 1986).

The size and number of these investors have increased dramatically, due in part to the rapid accumulation of wealth in various sectors of the economy. One study of consumer finances found that the net worth of 1.3 million US families was over $1 million (Avery and Elliehausen, 1986). These families, representing about 2% of the population, accumulated most of their wealth from earnings, not inheritance, and invested over $151 billion in nonpublic businesses in which they have no management interest. Each year, over 100,000 individual investors finance between

---

[2]*An Analysis of Regulation D* (Directorate of Economic Policy Analysis, Security and Exchange Commission, 1984).

[3]Charles River Associates, Inc., *An Analysis of Capital Market Imperfections* (Washington, DC, National Bureau of Standards, February 1976).

30,000 and 50,000 firms, with a total dollar investment of between $7 billion and $10 billion. Given their investment capability, it is important to know the characteristics of these angels.

One article determined the angel money available for investment each year was about $20 billion (Gannon, 1999). This amount was confirmed by another study indicating that there are about 250,000 angel investors who invest an amount of $10–20 billion annually in about 30,000 firms (Prowse, 1998). A recent study found that only about 20% of the angel investors surveyed tended to specialize in a particular industry, with the typical investment in the first round being between $29,000 and over $100,000.

The characteristics of these informal investors, or angels, are indicated in Table 5. They tend to be well educated; many have graduate degrees. Although they will finance firms anywhere in the United States (and a few in other parts of the world), most of the firms that receive funding are within one day's travel. The location preference for angel investors can be found in Figure 1. Business angels will make one to two deals each year, with individual firm investments ranging from $100,000 to $500,000 with the average being $340,000. If the opportunity is right, angels might invest from $500,000 to $1 million. In some cases, angels will join with other angels, usually from a common circle of friends, to finance larger deals.

Is there a preference for the type of ventures in which they invest? While angels invest in every type of investment opportunity, from small retail stores to large oil exploration operations, some prefer manufacturing of both industrial and consumer products, energy, services, and the retail/wholesale trade. A decrease in return is expected as the number of years the firm has been in business increases, from a median 5-year capital gain of 10 times for startups to three times for established firms over 5 years old. These investing angels are more patient in their investment horizons and do not have a problem waiting for a period of 7–10 years before cashing out. This is in contrast to the more predominant 5-year time frame in the Venture Capital industry. Investment opportunities are rejected when there is an inadequate risk/return ratio, a subpar management team, a lack of interest in the business area, or insufficient commitment to the venture from the principals.

The angel investor market averages about $20 billion each year, which is about the same level of yearly investments as the Venture Capital

Table 5.   Characteristics of informal investors.

- **Demographic Patterns and Relationships**
  - Well educated with many having graduate degrees.
  - Will finance firms anywhere in the United States.
  - Financing provided to most firms that are within a distance of one day's travel.
  - The majority expect to play an active role in ventures financed.
  - Have clusters of 9–12 other investors.
- **Investment Record**
  - Range of investment: $10,000–500,000
  - Average investment: $225,000
  - One to two deals each year
  - Venture preference
  - Most financings in startups or ventures less than 5 years
  - Most interested in financing:
    - Manufacturing–industrial/commercial products
    - Manufacturing–consumer product
    - Energy/natural resources
    - Services
    - Retail/wholesale trade
- **Risk/Reward Expectations**
  - Median 5-year capital gains of 10 times for startups.
  - Median 5-year capital gains of 6 times for firm less than a year old.
  - Median 5-year capital gains of 5 times for firms 1–5 years old.
  - Median 5-year capital gains of 3 times for established firms over 5 years old.
- **Reason for Rejecting Proposals**
  - Risk/return ratio not adequate;
  - Inadequate management team;
  - Not interested in the proposed business area;
  - Unable to agree on the price;
  - Principals not sufficiently committed;
  - Unfamiliar with the area of business.

---

industry. The angel investment is about eight times the number of companies. Under normal economic conditions, the number of active investors is around 250,000 individuals in the United States, with five or six investors typically being involved in an investment. The deal structure preference is found in Table 6.

Where do these angel investors generally find their deals? Deals are found through referrals by business associates, friends, active personal

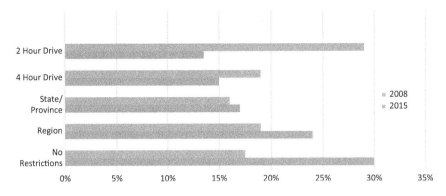

Figure 1. Where angel groups invest.

Notes:

• In 2008 (represented by a top bar), 63% preferred closer to home.
• In 2015 (represented by a bottom bar), 54% invest in the region or have no geographic restrictions.

Source: Angel Capital Association, Member Group Survey, March 2015 — 106 groups reporting.

Table 6. Deal structure preferences.

• Strong preference for priced rounds and preferred stock.
• Some will prefer convertible debt.
• Most sectors: products developed and have customer traction.
• Valuation not only for the sector but for the location as well (not unlike real estate).
• Board seat for significant investments.
• Most groups stay away from generally solicited offerings.

Source: Angel Capital Association.

research, investment bankers, and business brokers. However, even though these *referral sources* provide some deals, most angel investors are not satisfied with the number and type of investment referrals. Around 51% of the investors surveyed were either partially or totally dissatisfied with their referral systems and indicated that at least moderate improvement is needed.

Angel groups

To be able to get more and to have better deal flow, a phenomenon that is increasing in numbers each year is the foundation of organized angel groups. This is particularly true in countries such as Austria, China, Germany, Ireland, United Kingdom, and the United States. Each Angel group or club has a meeting for about 2–3 hours about 6–10 times each year. Some groups co-invest with other groups. The group as a whole does not have any money but serves as a convening and screening device for the presentations. The individual members of the group make the investment either individually or with parties interested in any of the investments available.

The typical club process is to send the required form to the designated club member. Following initial screening, if the entrepreneur is chosen, follow-up meetings with several club members occur. If the entrepreneur is selected to present at a future meeting, then the entrepreneur is provided guidance in terms of business plan refinement and the presentation. Usually, 12–30 min is allocated for a presentation and questions, and then any interested club members meet with the entrepreneur to discuss further steps in the investment decision process. Approximately 300 organized angel investor groups were identified by the Kauffman Foundation (www.kauffman.org/).

Each angel group has a somewhat different format and meeting times. For example, TAN meets five times each year and looks at three to four deals per meeting, screened from 75 to 100 applicants. Each invited firm has 12 min to present their idea, market, financials, and management team followed by a 10-min question-and-answer period and then by a 5-min initial due diligence done by Thunderbird School of Global Management students. Those ventures of interest by the investors then receive further evaluation (due diligence) to determine the investment potential and valuation. The hosting group itself has no investment money but charges a small annual fee for hosting the meeting and securing the possible investment deals.

When the private individual investors put money into a fund, which usually has a manager, this becomes an angel fund. An angel fund operates much like a small VC fund except the private investor or their designated representatives make the investment decision. Since most private investors prefer to invest on a deal-by-deal basis without this upfront commitment in angel groups or networks, there are very few angel funds that are operational.

Similar to many individual private investors, angel groups are having fewer restrictions regarding the geography of the deal they are willing to invest in. As indicated in Figure 1, a survey of angel groups indicated that 63% preferred to invest within a 2–4 hours drive while in 2015, 54% had no geographic restrictions regarding the area for investment. Some such as the Thunderbird Angel Network will invest anywhere in the world using alumni and contacts to do at least the initial due diligence.

The preferences for the structure of the deal for angel groups are indicated in Table 6. Similar to individual investors, angel groups prefer either preferred stock or convertible debt.

Angel networks versus angel funds

There are two types of angel groups: angel networks and angel funds. The majority of angel groups are angel networks. In an angel network, each high-net worth individual makes a decision to invest on a deal-by-deal basis. The network is managed by an individual who, usually with a board of other members in the venture, screens the deal, is the communication line with the companies seeking investment (receives the request for funding and communicates with the company until the due diligence committee is established), and creates and manages the agenda for each meeting. Since each individual makes the investment decision on a deal-by-deal basis, the network itself is not a funds provider, so there is no legal liability and minimal legal documentation is required. The Security and Exchange Commission (SEC) views a network as an information provider, not as a funds provider which can occur depending on the structure of an angel fund.

An angel fund is established to make investment decisions usually through a vote of its members present at the meeting. In an angel fund, each individual with a specific net worth contributes a specified amount of money most often ranging from $25,000 to 100,000. The angel net worth individual receives a proportional share of every deal voted on for investment by the group. He/she cannot opt out of an investment as the angel fund is making the decision, not the individual. The angel fund is similar to a small VC fund discussed in Chapter 6 and almost always requires at least one full-time manager as deals that are brought before the angel fund are at least thought of as being recommended by the fund manager for approval by the majority vote of members present at the meeting.

High-net worth individuals who like to make their own individual investment decisions prefer an angel network over an angel fund. Except for the higher costs of operation due in part to the employment of one or more manager(s), angel networks and angel funds meet several times each year and look at the number of deals in each meeting as specified in the bylaws of the group. Generally, once the individual seeking investment is screened for a presentation, he/she has a higher probability of receiving funds from an angel fund versus an angel network.

University angel network

A university angel network is an angel group tied closely to a university. It is similar to an angel network in its concept — any net worth individual who either makes $200,000 or more per year or has assets over $1 million. They differ in that they are at least closely connected, if not housed, at a university and tend to invest frequently in the technology at every stage in the ecosystem of the university — mainly in dental school, engineering school, medical school, or other sciences in the university. The benefits of a university angel network to a university include the following: (1) providing education to students and faculty on investing and business start-ups; (2) providing student training and expenditure education through student teams taking an initial due diligence of the presenting companies; (3) helping to evaluate, develop, and fund the technology and the ensuing startups at the university; (4) providing mentors at all stages of the commercialization process; (5) bringing high-net worth individuals to the campus of the community and increasing their engagement in other university activities; (6) assisting the university in engaging in one of its missions — encourage community development in the region; and (7) creating jobs and interest in other local companies in the broader region of the university. Two successful examples of university angel networks are the Baylor University Angel Group and the Thunderbird Angel Network (TAW) of the Thunderbird Graduate School of Management.

Summary

This is the second of the two chapters (the other is Chapter 6) on sources of funding process. The two most important providers of finance for technological ideas in a university are government grants and angel financing. Government grants particularly SBIR and STTR are presented as potential sources of funding as well as other government grants available on the federal, state, and community levels. Following the discussion of research and development partnerships is a discussion on angel funding in terms of angel groups and funds' aspects of the private investor market. This chapter concludes with a discussion on establishing a university angel fund.

Selected Readings

(1) Munari, F., Rasmussen, E., Toschi, L. and Villani, E. (2016). "Determinants of the University Technology Transfer Policy-Mix: A Cross-National Analysis of Gap-Funding Instruments". *The Journal of Technology Transfer*, 41(6), 1377–1405.

University–industry technology transfer (TT) has become increasingly institutionalized and is supported by numerous reforms and initiatives at the national, regional, and university levels. Most countries have implemented a policy mix involving a range of instruments to support the commercialization of research. Still, there is no systematic evidence indicating why the mix of policy instruments differs between countries. This study offers a novel cross-national investigation of the policy mix emphasizing the level of centralization and decentralization of policy instruments. We map and analyze two specific types of public instruments aimed at addressing the so-called funding gap in TT: proof of concept programs (POCs) and university-oriented seed funds (USFs). Based on a survey across 21 European countries, we find that such instruments are widely used but are organized differently depending on the level of implementation of TT practices in the country and the specific type of instrument considered. More precisely, we find a U-shaped relationship between the use of centralized gap-funding instruments and the country's implementation of TT practices.

Moreover, the type of gap-funding instrument (POC or USF) moderates this relationship. We discuss the implications of our findings and suggest that the policy mix of gap-funding instruments evolves with the maturity of the national TT infrastructure.

(2) Munari, F., Sobrero, M. and Toschi, L. (2017). "Financing Technology Transfer: Assessment of University-Oriented Proof-of-Concept Programmes". *Technology Analysis & Strategic Management*, 29(2), 233–246.

This study analyses the characteristics of the proof-of-concept (POC) programs initiated by university and public research organizations in Europe, as a mechanism to address funding gaps and improve the transfer of research-based inventions to markets. We contribute to the literature on investment readiness of new ventures and on financing technology transfer by assessing the structure of such funding instruments and identifying critical success factors for their design and implementation. The analyses rely on seven in-depth case studies of university-oriented POCs in Europe.

(3) Islam, M., Fremeth, A. and Marcus, A. (2018). "Signaling by Early-Stage Startups: US Government Research Grants and Venture Capital Funding". *Journal of Business Venturing*, 33(1), 35–51.

Entrepreneurship researchers have documented that early-stage startups rely on signals to demonstrate the transitions in their identities that they must make when they cross organizational life cycle thresholds. However, early-stage startups in emerging industry contexts tend to have few good signals to rely upon. Public agencies can play a valuable role in this process, but prior research has not sufficiently examined how startups effectively leverage this support. In this chapter, therefore, we develop a framework to investigate the role that signals can play for early-stage startups when they win prestigious government research grants. We test this framework in the setting up of the emerging US clean energy sector and find that in comparison to a matched sample of clean-energy startups that have not won prestigious research grants, startups with these grants were 12% more likely to acquire subsequent VC funding. Another significant result is that the value of this signaling is greater for startups that have fewer patents. The important contribution of this finding is that it shows signaling has the potential to *redistribute* benefits rather than just provide an additional accrual of advantages to the already high-status actors. Together, these results highlight the advantages for startups in emerging industries of pursuing signaling strategies with public agencies when they attempt to make important transitions through the stages of their organizational life cycles.

References

Avery, R. B. and Elliehausen, G. E. (1986). *Financial Characteristic of High-Income Families*. Federal Reserve Bulletin. Washington, DC.

Gannon, M. (1999 May). Financing purgatory: An emerging class of investors is beginning to fill the Nether regions of start-up financing — The Murkey World between the angels and the venture capitalist. *Venture Capital Journal*, 40–42.

Prowse, S. (1998). Angel investors and the market for angel investments. *Journal of Banking and Finance*, 23, 785–792.

Wetzel, W. E. Jr. (1983). Angels and Informal Risk Capital. *Sloan Management Review*, 24, 23–24.

Wetzel, W. E. Jr. (1986). Entrepreneurs, angels, and economic renaissance. In Hisrich, R. D. (ed.), *Entrepreneurship, Intrapreneurship, and Venture Capital*. Lexington, MA: Lexington Books, pp. 119–140.

Wetzel, W. E. Jr. (1987 Fall). The informal venture capital market: Aspects of scale and market efficiency. *Journal of Business Venturing*, 299–314.

Chapter 8

The Role of Incubators and Accelerators

Learning Objectives

- To understand the history of incubators and accelerators.
- To be able to identify the differences between incubators and accelerators.
- To understand how university incubators/accelerators can help academic entrepreneurs with research commercialization.
- To be able to benefit from industry insights to provide market pull for research commercialization.

Opening Profile — David Giljohann

Q1. Submitter Information

Name of Nominee	**David Giljohann**
University the Nominee is representing	**Northwestern University**
Email	davidg@exicuretx.com
Phone Number	847 7087907

Dr. Giljohann has served as CEO of Exicure since 2013. Dr. Giljohann obtained his PhD in 2009 from Northwestern University under the direction of Dr. Chad A. Mirkin, where he developed oligonucleotide-modified nanoparticles, including NanoFlare™ and Spherical Nucleic Acid (SNA™) constructs. Dr. Giljohann has been recognized for his work with a Materials Research Society Gold Award, Baxter Innovation Award, Rappaport Award for Research Excellence, and National Security Engineering Center (NSEC) Outstanding Research Award and as a finalist in the National Inventors Hall of Fame Collegiate Inventors Competition. He was also named to the Analytical Scientist's "Top 40 Under 40 Power List" in 2014. Dr. Giljohann has contributed to over 25 manuscripts and over 100 patents and applications.

Q2. The nominee's position when they created the company. Describe the nominee's process with the university as they were creating the company. Be as detailed as possible.

David Giljohann was a graduate student at Prof Chad Mirkin's lab, and they co-founded the company based on the technology he researched, discovered, and patented at Northwestern. Being the first graduate biology student in Dr. Mirkin's lab, he made a unique discovery that helped him build a patent portfolio for several years. After graduating in 2009, Giljohann along with Mirkin worked with the Tech Transfer Office to begin the process of translating the technology. This involved writing a business plan, seeking outside investors, building infrastructure, and hiring a team. Northwestern provided assistance and advice on all critical steps along the way.

Q3. Describe the nominee's experience working with the university in creating the company. What were the challenges? What support did they receive? Be as detailed as possible.

The student was working with a serial faculty entrepreneur who had previous knowledge on founding companies but not in the therapeutics space. The University TTO supported him as much as possible but the IP portfolio of the prolific faculty founder was very complex to navigate at times. David received financial support as a postdoctoral fellow, which helped to bridge the gap between graduate work and the funding of the company. Northwestern University also provided assistance with facilities access, rent in an incubator site, and mentorship with the university faculty. Finally, a business plan was developed with help provided by connections and through conversations with the Kellogg Business School.

Q4. What happened to the company the nominee created? Describe in detail where it is now and how is it doing. What is the history of the company? Be as detailed as possible.

The company is now public following a reverse merger and has three assets in clinical trials. Two of the trials are now in Phase 1b/2. Exicure has successfully completed multiple fundraising rounds (over 100 million raised to date) and several strategic partnerships. They have 10,000 square feet of laboratory and office space in Boston and Chicago and 37 employees. They have attracted notable attention for how rapidly and cost-effectively they have been able to translate research-stage drugs into clinical use. The company plans to have four drugs in clinical trials by the end of 2019, all based on the IP generated initially while David was a student at the Northwestern University.

Introduction

In recent years, accelerators have captured the imagination of startup entrepreneurs, eclipsing the traditional business incubators as the place to receive advice, mentoring, and access to both funders and service providers. With Y Combinator as the premier accelerator creating multiple unicorns (i.e., companies with billion dollar valuations) within the first decade of its existence, it became a media darling, and therefore raised the profile of the accelerator model beyond that of incubators. But what are the differences between incubators and accelerators?

Incubators and accelerators both have the mission of helping early-stage entrepreneurs create and build startup companies, but their structures, business models, and goals differ in significant ways.

Incubators have the older pedigree, tracing the formal concept to 1959 with the Batavia Industrial Center in Batavia, New York (Zehner *et al.*, 2014). In 1957, a large manufacturer closed their plant leaving behind a large empty space and 18% local unemployment.[1] Finding it difficult to interest a suitable tenant for the space, the landlord decided to cater to "small businesses needing short-term leases, shared office supplies and equipment, business advice, and secretarial services".[2] To a local reporter, the landlord analogized his new business to the special care in incubating young chicks and told him, "I guess we're incubating businesses,"[3] creating the nomenclature.

The number of incubators grew slowly in the 1980s when industrial plants started closing in large numbers in the Northeast. Regional economic development strategies that previously focused on attracting large corporations turned to "creating and expanding new businesses to sustain [the] local economy."[4] With the new focus on supporting new businesses, resources and services supporting these new businesses became more important, and the US Small Business Administration (SBA) promoted the development of incubators by holding a series of regional conferences during the decade.[5] In 2011, the National Business Incubator Association (NBIA)[6] estimated that approximately 1,400 business incubation programs were operating in North America in 2011 (Zehner *et al.*, 2014).

In "Innovation Accelerators: Defining Characteristics Among Startup Assistance Organizations", the US SBA in comparing incubators to accelerators listed the common characteristics for incubators, which are shown in Table 1.[7]

---

[1] https://www.wired.com/story/how-a-1950s-egg-farm-hatched-the-modern-startup-incubator/.

[2] *Ibid.*

[3] *Ibid.*

[4] http://www.svbic.com/node/20.

[5] *Ibid.*

[6] The National Business Incubator Association is now InBIA International Business Incubator Association https://inbia.org/.

[7] Innovation Accelerators: Defining Characteristics Among Startup Assistance Organizations By C. Scott Dempwolf, Jennifer Auer, and Michelle D'Ippolito Optimal Solutions Group, LLC College Park, MD 20740 https://www.sba.gov/sites/default/files/rs425-Innovation-Accelerators-Report-FINAL.pdf.

Table 1.   Incubators.

Characteristics	Incubators
Clients	All kinds, including science-based businesses (biotech, medical devices, nanotechnology, clean energy, etc.) and nontechnology; all ages and genders; includes those with previous experience in an industry or sector.
Selection Process	Competitive selection, mostly from the local community.
Terms of Assistance	Generally, 1–5 or more years (33 months on average).
Services	Offers access to management and other consulting, specialized intellectual property and networks of experienced entrepreneurs; helps businesses mature to self-sustaining or high-growth stage; helps entrepreneurs round out skills and develop a management team; and, often, to obtain external financing.
Investment	Usually does not have funds to invest directly in the company; more frequently than not, does not take equity.

Startup Accelerators

In 2005, Y Combinator originally based in Massachusetts (now located in Silicon Valley) created a new model to support startup companies that was substantially different from the traditional incubator model. Y Combinator describes itself this way[8]:

> Y Combinator created a new model for funding early stage startups. Twice a year we invest a small amount of money in a large number of startups. The startups move to Silicon Valley for 3 months, during which we work intensively with them to get the company into the best possible shape and refine their pitch to investors. Each cycle culminates in Demo Day, when the startups present their companies to a carefully selected, invite-only audience. But YC doesn't end on Demo Day. We and the YC alumni network continue to help founders for the life of their company, and beyond.

---

[8] https://www.ycombinator.com/.

Table 2.   Accelerators.

Characteristics	Accelerators
Clients	Web-based, mobile apps, social networking, gaming, cloud-based, software, etc.; firms that do not require significant immediate investment or proof of concept; primarily youthful, often male technology enthusiasts, gamers, and hackers.
Selection Process	Competitive selection of firms from wide regions or even nationally (or globally).
Terms of Assistance	Generally, 1- to 3-month boot camps.
Services	"Fast-test" validation of ideas; opportunities to create a functioning beta and find initial customers; linkage of entrepreneurs to business consulting and experienced entrepreneurs in the Web or mobile apps space; assistance in preparing pitches to try to obtain follow-up investment.
Investment	Invests $18,000–25,000 in teams of co-founders; takes equity in every investee (usually 4–8%).

As of 2017, Y Combinator had invested in approximately 2,000 companies including very successful companies, like Dropbox, Airbnb, Stripe, and Reddit, with a combined value of over $100 billion.[9]

In "Innovation Accelerators: Defining Characteristics Among Startup Assistance Organizations", the US SBA listed the characteristics for accelerators, which are provided in Table 2.[10]

In 2016, the Global Accelerator Report found that there were over 579 accelerator programs around the world with over $206,740,005 worth of total investments in 11,305 startups.[11] Seed-DB publishes an online list of 188 accelerator programs worldwide.[12]

---

[9] *Ibid.*

[10] Innovation Accelerators: Defining Characteristics Among Startup Assistance Organizations By C. Scott Dempwolf, Jennifer Auer, and Michelle D'Ippolito Optimal Solutions Group, LLC College Park, MD 20740 https://www.sba.gov/sites/default/files/rs425-Innovation-Accelerators-Report-FINAL.pdf.

[11] http://gust.com/accelerator_reports/2016/global/.

[12] http://seed-DB.com.

Differences between incubators and accelerators in structures, business models, and goals

Incubators and accelerators have significantly varying attributes and attempts have been made to distinguish them. Isabelle (2013), Adkins (2011), and Hoffman and Radojevich-Kelley (2012) distilled several distinguishing characteristics between them. For incubators, they found that the typical characteristics include the following:

- They are nonprofit organizations, frequently associated with universities.
- They provide office space at reasonable rates for the startups they support.
- They target local startups.
- They do not invest in the startups.

For accelerators, they found the following characteristics:

- They are for-profit organizations that receive equity in exchange for the provision of funding to the startups.
- They do not necessarily provide office space for the startups they support, but typically provide meeting space.
- They target regional, national, or even global startups.

The SBA's Innovation Accelerator report[13] distinguishes the two models along a nonprofit/for-profit axis finding "blurred identities of incubators and accelerators", because generally incubators have been an economic development tool for the public sector, while accelerators were popularized for the benefit and enrichment of players in the private sector. As a result, accelerators generally only support high-growth, venture-backable startups working in a limited number of technology areas with success defined by outsized returns on investment for the 4–8% equity they receive from the startups to participate in their programs. Incubators, on

---

[13] SBA report, infra.

the contrary, more patiently support a diverse group of companies in many technology areas and stages of development, with less concern on how quickly the companies grow, because they are "a business-support process that helps launch startup and fledgling companies ... [whose] main goal is to produce successful firms that will be financially viable and free-standing when they leave the program. These incubator graduates have the potential to create jobs, revitalize neighborhoods, commercialize new technologies, and strengthen regional economies."

Office and lab space are also a common, defining difference. Accelerators typically provide free short-term space for 3–6 months for company development and educational and networking events. Incubators, on the contrary, typically charge monthly rents for space while the company resides in the incubator for 1–3 years before graduating to a larger outside space.

University Incubators and Accelerators

Historically, universities have focused on two missions: education and research. However, because of state and federal pressure over the last few decades to commercialize federally funded research and development, some universities have added programs to aid regional economic development to their missions. The "entrepreneurial university" (Etzkowitz, 2008; Mowery *et al.*, 2001) focuses on technology licensing and business creation as the key ways to commercialize academic research. While licensing is still the most common way to bring R&D to market, more recently, startup creation has become more important (Kenney and Patton, 2011; Siegel *et al.*, 2007).

The Bayh–Dole Act[14] assigned intellectual property rights of federally funded R&D to universities, to which universities responded by creating technology transfer offices to manage invention disclosure, patenting, licensing, and, more recently, startups. The results have been impressive

---

[14]The Bayh–Dole Act or Patent and Trademark Law Amendments Act (Pub. L. 96-517, December 12, 1980) is United States legislation dealing with intellectual property arising from federal government-funded research.

with the Association of University Technology Managers (AUTM)[15] reporting in its 2017 annual member survey that invention disclosure reached 24,998 for the year, that there were 7,459 US patents issued to universities and research institutions (the most ever reported), that licensing revenue was $3 billion, and that 7,849 licenses and options were executed. AUTM members also reported that 755 new products and 1,080 university startups formed, with 72.4% headquartered within the home state of the institution.

With universities creating so many startups, it is not surprising that over half of the incubation members of the International Business Incubator Association have some association with universities and colleges.[16] In recent years, the creation of startups has become "one of the most effective forms of exploration and commercialization of new knowledge and technologies, and is different from licensing models or joint ventures."[17]

Along with space, shared facilities, equipment, advisers, and networking that traditional incubators provide, university incubators also provide companies with access to university faculty, staff, and students. This greatly benefits the startups, which are constantly in search of finding the best people.

The relationship also benefits the universities because they can use the startups for student employment and training, faculty consulting, sponsored research, and for fulfilling economic development responsibilities to state and federal government officials.

A study of 152 US-based university incubators and 7,651 companies found that company outcomes from university incubators were superior to traditional incubators (Vernet *et al.*, 2015):

"University incubated firms have greater employment and sales than the non-incubated firms. Further, we observe that university incubated firms grew faster (in number of jobs and sales) than the non-incubated firms above and beyond the incubation period" (Vernet *et al.*, 2015).

---

[15] AUTM 2017 Licensing Activity Survey.

[16] https://inbia.org/blog/university-incubation/.

[17] The role of university incubators in stimulating academic entrepreneurship Eva Stal, Tales Andreassi, Asa Fujino.

Table 3. Top 25 university business incubators.

Rank	Country	Incubators
Number 1	United States	Rice Alliance for Entrepreneurship
Number 2	United Kingdom	SETsquared
Number 3	China	National Science Park at the South China University of Technology
Number 4	Australia	Cicada Innovations
Number 5	Canada	The DMZ at Ryerson University
Number 6	Chile	IncubaUC
Number 7	Taiwan	Center of Industry Accelerator and Patent Strategy
Number 8	Sweden	Encubator
Number 9	Brazil	Instituto Genesis PUC-Rio
Number 10	Canada	TEC Edmonton
Number 11	Austria	INiTS Universitäres Gründerservice Wien GMBH
Number 12	Denmark	DTU Symbion Innovation
Number 13	Australia	Melbourne Accelerator Program
Number 14	China	Huazhong University of Science and Technology National Science
Number 15	Italy	Incubatore di Imprese Innovative del Politecnico di Torino (13P)
Number 16	China	Hefei National University Science Park
Number 17	United States	VentureLab
Number 18	Sweden	Uppsala Innovation Centre
Number 19	Ireland	NDRC
Number 20	United States	Portland State University Business Accelerator
Number 21	United States	Dean L. Hubbard Center for Innovation and Entrepreneurship
Number 22	Canada	Western Research Parks
Number 23	Chile	Chrysalis
Number 24	Taiwan	Center for Entrepreneurship and Incubation
Number 25	Belgium	iMinds

Sources: http://ubi-global.com/2014-2/my-category/ranking-2/ or https://www.youtube.com/watch?v=iXW5mSA-czE.

According to Forbes, the following are the five best university incubators: (1) Berkeley SkyDeck, (2) Venture Incubation Program (VIP) at Harvard, (3) delta V at MIT, (4) StartX at Stanford, and (5) StartUP at UPenn,[18] whereas UBI Global had a different list of the top US university incubators in their global rankings of the Top 25 University Business Incubators (Table 3).[19]

The NCET2 Model for Academic Entrepreneurs Working with Industry

The attraction between industry and universities has been going on for a long time through multiple mutually beneficial activities for both the industry and the university.

University–Industry Relations	
Research partnerships	Inter-organizational arrangements for conducting collaborative R&D.
Research services	Activities commissioned by companies, including contract research and consulting.
Academic entrepreneurship	Development and commercial exploitation of technologies by academic scientists through the creation of firms (alone or with partners).
Human resources transfer	Multi-context learning mechanisms such as training of companies' employees at the university; postgraduate activities in firms; graduate trainees; and temporary transfer of scientists to companies.

(Continued)

[18] https://www.forbes.com/sites/avivalegatt/2019/01/07/launch-your-startup-at-these-five-college-incubators/#231352004a77.
[19] UNI Global Sources: http://ubi-global.com/2014-2/my-category/ranking-2/ or https://www.youtube.com/watch?v=iXW5mSA-czE.

	(Continued)
Informal interaction	Formation of social relationships and networks at conferences, etc.
Commercialization of property rights	Licensing of university-generated intellectual property (patents) to firms.
Scientific publications	Use of codified scientific knowledge within industry.

Source: Perkmann and Walsh (2007).

But in the early 2000s, Henry Chesbrough, adjunct Professor and Faculty Director of the Center for Open Innovation of the Haas School of Business at the University of California, provided a new impetus for multinational companies to work with universities with the book, *Open Innovation: The New Imperative for Creating and Profiting from Technology* (Chesbrough, 2003). In the book, Chesbrough argued that because disruptive innovations tend to be created by outside researchers, inventors, and founders (rather than by the multinationals themselves), companies cannot rely solely on their own research, but need to procure innovation from the outside.

Multinational corporations quickly learned that university startups are an effective and resource-efficient method for R&D commercialization because academic entrepreneurs and outside investors provide the funding and talent to de-risk outside innovations. Successful entrepreneurs reap outsized rewards as well, since they capture wealth creation produced by their innovation as it is brought to market.

In 2016, NCET2 created the Corporate-Startup Development Program,[20] a national virtual corporate accelerator for university startups. It provides a means for academic entrepreneurs to work together with multinational corporations to commercialize federally funded R&D with corporate involvement and milestones.

The program has the following three main parts:

1. Discovery — A review of startups is done by NCET2 Corporate Members and Startup Development Officers (SDOs) through Virtual

---

[20] http://ncet2.org.

Startup Pitches to find potentially market-aligned startups and technologies.

2. Development — Startups with corporate and SDO interests are considered for development with corporates providing milestones and SDOs providing guidance.

3. Funding — Startups in the Development Program are presented for funding through a National Angels funding network and an Investment Banker Fund.

NCET2 Corporate Startup Development program provides help to the academic entrepreneurs in the following ways:

- incorporation and post-corporation set-up, including a stock option plan,
- IP development,
- science team development,
- management team development,
- milestone development,
- product development,
- sales projections,
- gross margins and price/earnings gross ups,
- total global potential market,
- general counsel services,
- legal compliance work, and
- startup funding.

Summary

As academic entrepreneurs increasingly endeavor to commercialize their research, this trend over several decades has dovetailed with a separate trend by state governments and for-profit organizations to fund and create incubators and accelerators that provide essential support and services to entrepreneurs to help them succeed. In many cases, universities have worked with these outside parties to provide their resources to academic entrepreneurs or in some cases have created their own incubator and accelerator programs on campus tailored specifically to the needs of their faculty, students, and staff. Some programs such as NCET2's Startup-Corporate Development program have been specifically developed to support academic entrepreneurs to commercialize their research with corporate open innovation programs, providing strategic industry alignment and funding.

Selected Readings

(1) Mian, S. (1994). US University-Sponsored Technology Incubators: An Overview of Management, Policies and Performance". *Technovation*, 14(8), 515–528.

Despite the increased worldwide interest in the university-sponsored technology incubator (USTI) as a mechanism for supporting the development of new technology-based firms (NTBFs), there is a dearth of empirical evidence on determinants of their best organization and management, and policy practices. This article presents results from a national survey of more than 30 American USTIs that are 5 or more years old. The study focused on a sample comprising three state university-sponsored and three private university-sponsored facilities, generally viewed as being successful. The USTI practices and performances are explored using several key dimensions: organizational design, tenant performance review, funding sources, targeted technologies, strategic operational policies, services and their value-added components, and growth of the client firms.

(2) Lasrado, V., Sivo, S., Ford, C., O'Neal, T. and Garibay, I. (2015). "Do Graduated University Incubator Firms Benefit from their Relationship with University Incubators?" *The Journal of Technology Transfer*, 41(2), 205–219.

Business incubators have become a popular policy option and economic development intervention tool. However, recent research shows that incubated firms may not benefit significantly from their incubator relationships and may even be more vulnerable to failure postdeparture (graduation) from an incubator. These findings suggest that the impact of business incubation on new venture viability may be contingent on the type of support offered by an incubator and attributes of business environments within which incubation services are provided. Incubation services that protect and isolate ventures from key resource dependencies may hinder venture development and increase subsequent vulnerability to environmental demands. Alternatively, incubation services that help ventures connect and align with key resource dependencies are likely to promote firm survival. We propose that incubators vary in the services and resources they offer and that university incubators typically provide greater connectivity and legitimacy with respect to important contingencies associated with key industry and community stakeholders. This leads us to propose that university affiliation is an important contingency that affects the relationship between firms' participation in incubators and their subsequent performance. The purpose of this study is to evaluate this contingency by examining whether firms graduating from university incubators attain higher levels of post-incubation performance than firms participating in non-university affiliated incubators. We test this by evaluating the performance of a sample of graduated firms associated with the population of university-based incubators in the US contrasted against the performance of a matched cohort of non-incubated firms. The analysis uses an enhanced dataset that tracks the number of employees, sales, and the entry and graduation (departure) points of incubated firms from a university incubation program, so as to delineate the scope of influence of the incubator.

(3) Soetanto, D. and Jack, S. (2016). "The Impact of University-Based Incubation Support on the Innovation Strategy of Academic Spin-Offs". *Technovation*, 50–51, 25–40.

This article develops an understanding on how incubation support and innovation strategy can determine the performance of academic spin-offs. Using a sample of spin-offs from the United Kingdom, the Netherlands, and Norway, we analyze the potential moderating effect of incubation support (networking and entrepreneurial support) on innovation strategy effectiveness. The empirical results demonstrate that (1) a technology and market exploitation strategy has a stronger and more positive effect on the performance of spin-offs than a technology and market exploration strategy. In relation to an ambidextrous technology and market exploration and exploitation strategy, a market growth strategy (combining technology exploitation and market exploration) has a positive effect on performance while a product development strategy (combining technology exploration and market exploitation) has little effect on performance; (2) incubation support in the form of networking and entrepreneurial support has a positive effect on the performance of spin-offs; (3) networking support moderates the relationship between an exploitation strategy and spin-off performance while entrepreneurial support moderates the relationship between a market growth strategy and spin-off performance. By examining the interactions between types of innovation strategies and incubation support, this study provides a more refined understanding of the strategy selected by spin-offs. In doing so, it offers new insights about the role of incubator support in enhancing the effect of strategy on performance.

(4) McAdam, M. and McAdam R. (2008). "High Tech Start-Ups in University Science Park Incubators: The Relationship between the Start-Up's Lifecycle Progression and Use of the Incubator's Resources". *Technovation*, 28(5), 277–290.

University Science Park incubators (USIs) have emerged as a means by which government, academia, and business can develop high-technology business firms (spin-out HTBFs) from initial conception through to becoming established small firms, which are ready to move beyond the Science Park confines. Although there is considerable literature on how USIs can be improved and developed, there is a paucity of studies, which explore how life cycle development within HTBFs in USIs can affect how they use the unique resources and opportunities of the USI. Moreover, there is a focus on a single point in time studies, which do not adequately investigate the longitudinal dynamics of HTBF life cycle development within USIs. Therefore, the aim of this article is to explore the longitudinal use of the unique resources of the USI by HTBFs at different life cycle stages. The research methodology involved 18 HTBFs within two separate USIs. A series of longitudinal interviews and focus groups were conducted with HTBFs and USI staff over a 36-month period. NUD*IST software was used in developing the coding and analysis of transcripts. The results show that a HTBF's propensity to make effective use of the

USI's resources and support increases as the life cycle stage of the company increases and the small-firm searches for independence and autonomy. Therefore, further research is required to investigate the following two outstanding questions; first, which usage pattern is associated with the HTBF's ultimate success or failure in the marketplace? And second, are there any services missing from the observed array that the USI could provide to enhance the HTBF's degree of ultimate success?

References

Adkins, D. (2011). What are the new seed or venture accelerators? *NBIA Review*. Retrieved June 5, 2014 from http://www.nbia.org/resource_library/review_archive/0611_01.php.

Chesbrough, H. W. (2003). *Open Innovation: The New Imperative for Creating and Profiting from Technology*. Boston: Harvard Business School Press, ISBN 978-1578518371.

Etzkowitz, H. (2008) *The Triple Helix: University-Industry-Government Innovation in Action*. London and New York: Routledge, 15.

Hoffman, D. L. and Radojevich-Kelley, N. (2012). Analysis of accelerator companies: An exploratory case study of their programs, processes, and early results. *Small Business Institute Journal*, 8(2), 54–70.

Isabelle, D. (2013). Key factors affecting a technology entrepreneur's choice of incubator or accelerator. *Technology Innovation Management Review*. Retrieved August 11, 2014 from http://timreview.ca/article/656.

Kenney, M. and Patton, D. (2011). Does inventor ownership encourage university research-derived entrepreneurship? A six-university comparison. *Research Policy*, 40, 1100–1112. 10.2139/ssrn.1847184.

Mowery, D., Nelson, R., Sampat, B. and Ziedonis, A. (2004). Ivory tower and industrial innovation: University-industry technology transfer before and after the Bayh-Dole Act.

Perkmann, M. and Walsh, K. (2007). University–industry relationships and open innovation: Towards a research agenda. *International Journal of Management Review*, 9(4), 259–280.

Siegel, D., Wright, M. and Lockett, A. (2007). The rise of entrepreneurial activity at universities: Organizational and societal implications. *Industrial and Corporate Change*, 16(4), 489–504.

Vernet, L., Stephen, S., Cameron, F., O'Neal, T. and Garibay, I. (2015). *Do Graduated University Incubator Firms Benefit from their Relationship with*

University Incubators? New York: Springer Science+Business Media, Published online: 18 April 2015.

Zehner, W., Trzmielak, D., Gwarda-Gruszczyńska, E. and Jacquelyn, A. Z. (2014). *Business incubation in the USA.* https://www.researchgate.net/ publication/282668212_BUSINESS_INCUBATION_IN_THE_USA.

Chapter 9

Creating a Business Venture and Technology Transfer

Learning Objectives

- To understand that technology transfer is the end result of the commercialization process.
- To understand the legal issues involved.
- To determine the best alternative for the academic entrepreneur.

Opening Profile — Amit Dhingra

Q1. Submitter Information

Name of Nominee	**Amit Dhingra**
University the Nominee is representing	**Washington State University (WSU)**
Email	adhingra@wsu.edu
Phone number	509 432-3683

Amit Dhingra worked for his Ph.D. at the University of Delhi, India and at Rutgers University, New Jersey supported by fellowships from the University Grants Commission and The Rockefeller Foundation, USA.

After his postdoctoral training at Rutgers University, the University of Central Florida, and the University of Florida; he joined Washington State University in 2006 where he is currently a Full Professor of Genomics and Biotechnology. Dhingra also serves as the Chair of the Entrepreneurial Faculty Ambassadors Program, a presidential-level task force.

The Dhingra research program investigates important biological processes in agriculture plants pertaining to the industry's current and future needs. The knowledge results crop improvement through various agricultural approaches. He has published more than 50 papers in high-impact peer-reviewed refereed journals. He serves on the editorial board of four internationally reputed plant science journals, and has been awarded two US patents and one NZ patent on regulating ripening fruits to reduce post-harvest wastage. Dr. Dhingra's research has been featured in the *New York Times*, *The Atlantic*, *BBC*, *The Times of London*, and several other news sources.

Amit is the Founder of Phytelligence Inc. (www.phytelligence.com), an agricultural biotechnology spin-off at Washington State University. Phytelligence is an agricultural biotechnology company that is revolutionizing the way food crops are grown by developing and commercializing innovative solutions for growers. Phytelligence is headquartered in Seattle, WA with locations in Pullman, WA and Portland, OR.

Additional information about Dr. Dhingra's research activities at WSU can be obtained by visiting https://genomics.wsu.edu/category/news/.

Q2: The nominee's position when they created the company. Describe the nominee's process with the university as they were creating the company. Be as detailed as possible.
Amit Dhingra was an Assistant Professor of Genomics and Biotechnology in the Department of Horticulture, Washington State University when he founded Phytelligence. The founding of Phytelligence is an interesting story as it did not follow a prescribed path out of the university. Amit and his team had developed methods to produce trees of high-value commodities such as apple, pear, and cherry. He first approached the Commodity Commissions to set up a cooperative. That idea was turned down by the commission since there was no known construct around such an approach.

The industry members continued to consider Amit's program to produce hundreds to thousands of fruit trees.

The demand and need were also noticed by two undergraduate students who were conducting research in the program. One of them had been conducting hands-on research to understand the benefits of the new, improved process over the traditional process of producing trees in the nursery. This undergraduate student represented the largest apple producer in Latin America and was convinced that the new method could shorten the time to production as well as hard-to-get plant material. He pushed Amit to consider starting a company. The father of the second undergraduate student was a Senior Principal Consultant at Spokane Intercollegiate Research and Technology Institute (SIRTI), a Washington State organization that scouts technologies at state organizations worthy of commercialization. The consultant arranged for her father to meet with Amit and evaluate the market readiness of the solution that had been developed in the lab. Mr. Mike Urso from SIRTI facilitated interactions with Gonzaga Law School, where a student-based group helped Amit register his company.

After that, a Washington state-sponsored program enabled an Entrepreneur-in-Residence to work with Amit to prepare the business plan, the equity plan, and the licensing agreement with WSU.

Q3: Describe the nominee's experience working with the university in creating the company. What were the challenges? What support did they receive? Be as detailed as possible.

At the time Phytelligence was established, there were not many examples at the institution to follow. The university staff did their best given the lack of experience in supporting the formation of a company such as Phytelligence. Some of the challenges included negotiations regarding the licensing agreement, but the negotiator provisioned for a delayed payment of royalties. Since the formation happened via a unique route, there was not much financial assistance at the initial stages. The challenges came when the company had been formed. While the university's president's office lauded the formation of the spin-off, the support was missing at the college level and to a greater extent the department chair level. The former chair refused to acknowledge the formation of the spin-off was a form of community engagement emerging out of Amit's research.

In time, with the change in departmental leadership and impact of the newly elected president's futuristic vision, the activities leading to tangible socioeconomic impact were highly encouraged. Amit, now a Full Professor and Chair of the WSU Entrepreneurial Faculty Ambassador program, a presidential-level task force. He serves as faculty in two interdisciplinary graduate programs. Amit has also been participating in WSU Entrepreneurship Skills and Knowledge Accelerator (WESKA) — a summer accelerator program organized by the School of Business — where he shares his experiences, both internal and external, with aspiring entrepreneurs. As the leader of the EFA program, Dhingra provides experience-based advice regarding various forms of intellectual property and safeguard strategies; pathways to the commercialization of a concept in an academic institution; building entrepreneurial teams; and the pitfalls to avoid when taking a concept to market. He has also gained experience in the business world during the last 8 years, which is very useful in his role as a mentor to WSU community members.

Q4: What happened to the company the nominee created? Describe in detail where it is now and how it is doing. What is the history of the company? Be as detailed as possible.

Amit founded Phytelligence Inc. in 2011 with four of his graduate students and one lab technician. Phytelligence turned out to be the first agricultural biotechnology spin-off out of WSU. In 2012, he hired a startup-stage CEO to run and grow the company. The company had support from the tree fruit industry. However, Angel Investors were hard to come by, and in 2014, Amit took over as the interim CEO to raise capital and also deliver the products to the market place. He enlisted the help of several executive consultants to run the day-to-day business efficiently while saving capital for operations. His former graduate students, who were the key founders, were the first key employees who worked to develop the product. The company experienced a setback when 80% of the trees grown in the greenhouse died. The customers were very supportive and continued to support Amit. The business began being featured on the national scale. Phytelligence won the

Regional Sustainability award in the National Cleantech Open competition and got to participate in an intensive accelerator program in California. The company was also featured at the WSU TEDx event, where Amit presented the history of his interactions with the tree fruit industry, as well as his position at WSU which resulted in the formation of Phytelligence.

Amit was engaged in his research, teaching, and outreach activities while running Phytelligence. A capital investment bank took notice and helped Amit develop a refined business plans as well as introduced him to a seasoned CEO. In 2015, as Amit delivered the first set of orders — which performed very well — he handed off leadership to an external CEO. Amit continued to serve as the Chief Science Officer and Board member. He worked with the CEO to raise investments and developed collaborations with various entities, both national and international. He also established a team for the R&D development for Phytelligence. The company grew to over 200 employees and had its operations in Pullman, Seattle, Burien, and Tigard. A strategic collaboration was also established with Mahyco Group in India.

As is often the case with companies during their growth, Phytelligence had to do a course correction and undergo reorganization in early 2019. The company now has about 150 employees and is focusing on its original mission to serve the tree fruit industry with its exceptional quality products. In his role as the CSO, Amit continues to work to ensure that the technological concepts, which are the foundation of the company, continue to support the operations as Phytelligence serves its stakeholders.

Introduction

As stated in the profile of Amit Dhingra, as well as in the profiles of other academic entrepreneurs featured in other chapter profiles, there is a general process that occurs in commercializing technology in a university environment. This process is impacted by the ownership and policies of the university as well as its royalty and income-sharing policies. The commercialization usually occurs through technology transfer or new venture (business) creation.

Invention/Commercialization Process

The invention/commercialization process of the academic entrepreneurs is presented in Figure 1. As indicated, the steps in the process include the following: inventing and reporting, technological assessment by the university, filing for a patent, and commercialization.

Inventing and reporting

When the inventing process is nearing completion, the academic researcher, feeling a sense of personal satisfaction and adding to the state of knowledge of a particular discipline, should look-up to determine if the research already has a patent application from the general public (companies, consumers, or the government). It is important to know at the inventing stage whether the research output (1) can be advanced through a corporate partnership or an accelerator program (discussed in Chapter 8), (2) can have its intellectual property protected, and (3) is ready for the development of a commercialization strategy that can result in a licensing agreement or a new venture being created.

Collaboration with an industry partner can often significantly enhance intellectual exchange, help foster better recognition of the research efforts and abilities of the academic researchers, and perhaps attract financial sponsorship for the research. Any licensing and royalty fees obtained in return for the transfer of the commercial rights of the invention are shared by the researcher, his/her department and college, and the university. The amounts vary by universities which are discussed in Chapter 10.

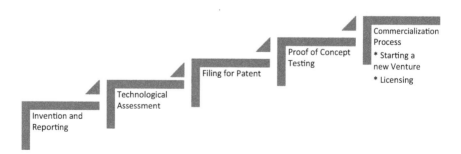

Figure 1. Invention/commercialization process.

What is intellectual property? Intellectual property, the focus of Chapter 3, refers to the idea, process, or invention that are the output of the intellectual endeavors. It can be protected from an unauthorized use by filing the appropriate documents — copyrights, patent, or trademarks. For example, a company wants to market Pabst beer and purchase the name, trademark, and brewing formula from the company who owned the intellectual property after the previous producers of the beer went bankrupt. The intellectual property policies vary by universities which will be discussed in Chapter 10.

When an academic researcher (faculty, staff, or student) has a scientific/technological discovery that has the possibility for commercial development or partnership, the individual should contact the Technology Transfer Office (TTO) at the university before publicly disclosing the information and/or publishing the manuscript about the discovery to protect the information or manuscript. Once the information or the manuscript is publicly disclosed in any form, the intellectual property is in the public domain and cannot be protected.

Technological assessment

Assessing technology is the next critical step in the process. This assessment will include the degree of patentability of the invention; the protectability of the technology; the operationality and scalability of the technology; the marketability of the technology including the potential markets of the technology; the size and growth potential of the market; the amount of money required for any further development of the technology; and the level of present and future competition. Concept testing confirms the technology works and is discussed in the next section. In addition, it is important to know if there is a market for the technology which can be done through the market evaluation checklist, need and value assessment, and/or the market opportunity assessment plan.

The market evaluation checklist expresses each new idea in terms of its chief values, merits, and benefits. The test involves the presentation of consumer clusters with new product/service values to determine which consumer cluster, if any, should be pursued. Many potential new ideas can be evaluated with this method, but only the promising ideas will receive further development when they are compatible with the market values. Both the need for the new technological idea as well as its value needs to be determined. If there are no present or near-future needs, the developments should not be continued. Similarly, the product/service idea should not be developed if it does not add any benefit or value to the academic entrepreneur and the university. To accurately determine the need for new ideas: define the potential factors of the market in terms of timing, satisfaction, alternatives, benefits and risks, future expectations, price versus product/service performance features, market structure and size, and economic conditions. A form that helps in the need determining process for a new technological consumer product/service is indicated in Table 1. The factors should also be evaluated not only in terms of the characteristics of the potential new product/service but also in terms of the new product's/ service's competitive strength in relation to each factor. This competitive evaluation of a product/service will indicate the proposed idea's strengths and weaknesses.

The need determination should focus on the type of need, its timing, the users of the product/service, the importance of controllable marketing variables, the overall market size and structure, and the characteristics of the market. Each of these factors should be evaluated in terms of the characteristics, aspects, and capabilities of present products/services available for satisfying the need. This analysis will indicate the extent of the opportunities available.

In determining the value of the new technological product/service idea, the financial scheduling — such as cash outflow, cash inflow, contribution to profit, and return on investment — needs to be evaluated based on investment alternatives. Using the form in Table 2, the dollar equivalent for each of the cost corresponding to the new technological idea is evaluated and should initially be determined at a lower level of accuracy.

Another method for determining the potential need and value of a new technology idea is by creating an opportunity assessment plan. An opportunity assessment plan is not a business plan as discussed in Chapter 5. It replaces the lengthier more time-consuming business plan to determine if the opportunity is worth pursuing. Compared to a business plan, the opportunity analysis plan is shorter, focuses on opportunity and not the venture, and has no *pro forma* financial statements. It is the basis for

Table 1.   Determining the need for a new product/service idea.

Factor	Aspects	Competitive capabilities	New product idea capability
Type of Need			
Continuing need			
Declining need			
Emerging need			
Future need			
Timing need			
Duration need			
Frequency of need			
Demand cycle			
Position in life cycle			
Competing ways to satisfy need			
Doing without using			
Present way modifying			
Present way			
Perceived benefits/risks			
Utility to customer			
Appeal characteristics			
Customer tastes and preferences			
Buying motivations			
Consumption habits			
Price versus performance features			
Price–quantity relationship			
Demand elasticity			
Stability of price			
Stability of market			
Market size and potential			
Market growth			
Market trends			
Market development requirements threats to market			

(Continued)

Table 1. (*Continued*).

Factor	Aspects	Competitive capabilities	New product idea capability
Availability of customer funds			
General economic conditions			
Economic trends			
Customer income			
Financing opportunities			

Source: Hisrich *et al.* (2020).

making the decision to either act on an opportunity or wait until another better opportunity emerges.

An opportunity assessment plan has four sections — two major sections and two minor sections.

The first major section discusses and develops the product/service technological idea, analyzes the competitive products and companies, and identifies the individuality of the idea in terms of its unique selling propositions (the four or five items that make this idea different from any product/service presently available in the market filling this need). This section includes the following:

- the market's need for the product/service;
- the description of the product/service;
- the specific aspects of the product/service;
- the competitive products presently available filling this need including their features and pricing;
- the companies in this product/service market space;
- the unique selling propositions of this product/service.

The second major section of the opportunity assessment plan focuses on the market — its size, trends, characteristics, and growth rate. This section includes the following:

- the market needing to be filled;
- the social condition underlining this market need;
- any data available to describe this market need;

Table 2. Determining the value of a new technology.

Value consideration	Cost (in $)
Cash Outflow	
R&D costs	
Marketing costs	
Capital equipment costs	
Other costs	
Cash Inflow	
Sales of new product	
Effect on additional sales of existing products	
Salvageable value	
Net Cash Flow	
Maximum exposure	
Time to maximum exposure	
Duration of exposure	
Total investment	
Maximum net cash in a single year	
Profit	
Profit from new products	
Profit affecting additional sales of existing products	
Fraction of total company profit	
Relative return	
Return on shareholders' equity (ROE)	
Return on investment (ROI)	
Cost of capital	
Present value (PV)	
Discounted cash flow (DCF)	
Return on sales	
Compared to Other Investment	
Compared to other product opportunities	
Compared to other investment opportunities	

Source: Hisrich *et al.* (2020).

- the size, trends, and characteristics of the domestic and/or international market(s);
- the growth rate of the market.

The third section (a minor one) focuses on the team's need based on their background, education, skills, and experience. It should include answers to the following questions:

- How does the product/service idea fit into the background and experience of the team?
- What business skills and experience are needed?
- Who in the team has these needed skills and experience?

The final section of the opportunity assessment plan develops a timeline indicating the steps needed to be taken to successfully launch the venture by translating the idea into a viable business entity. This minor section should focus on the following:

- identifying each step of the launching process;
- determining the critical steps and the sequence order of activities;
- identifying what will be accomplished in each step;
- determining the time and money required at each step;
- determining the total amount of time and money needed;
- identifying the sources of funding for the launch.

An example of a timeline is presented in Table 3.

Filing the patent

Safeguarding the intellectual property with protection through patents and copyrights is a very important part of the innovation/commercialization process. The importance and process of determining when and how to file a patent and copyright have been discussed in Chapter 3.

Proof of concept

Proof of concept (POC) is used to test the functionality and/or design of a technological idea to determine if the technology works according to what

Table 3.   Example: Timeline.

OA Plan	Stage 1	Stage 2	Stage 3	Stage 4
			Launch Venture	
(a) (b) (c)	• Accomplish • Cost • Time	• Accomplish • Cost • Time	• Accomplish • Cost • Time	• Accomplish • Cost • Time
(a)	• Create Business Plan	• Form Company • Find Potential Investors	• Find an Outsource Provider • Develop Packaging • Develop Marketing Plan	• Develop Launch Plan • Sign Agreements
(b)	0	$9,000	$40,000	$20,000
(c)	30 days	60 days	30 days	15 days

Note: Total time = 135 days/total cost = $69,000.

it is supposed to do. The main purpose of the POC is to demonstrate the functionality of the technology and to verify that the concept and/or theory can be achieved through further development of the idea. This step is frequently needed and should be performed before approaching a funding source such as an investor (particularly when the goal is to license the technology for development and sales).

The method of concept testing usually follows a similar process as outlined in what follows (see DeLuna and Malik, 2014):

- **Step 1: Define**
  - ○ Organize an initiative team, owners, and any key stakeholders.
  - ○ Collectively define goals, inputs, objectives, scope, and success criteria.
  - ○ Establish resource commitments and finalize a POC schedule.
  - ○ Deliverables in the "Define" phase should include detailed POC scope and plan documentation, successful criteria and POC schedule.
- **Step 2: Develop**
  - ○ Create POC-specific use cases for minimal but necessary functionalities within the POC scope (for proof of capability initiatives). Align use cases to each capability in scope.
  - ○ Work with stakeholders to prioritize functionalities across the use cases.
  - ○ Deliverables in the "Develop" phase should include use cases and success criteria (revised based on preliminary findings throughout this process step).
- **Step 3: Engineer**
  - ○ Configure and test the required infrastructure and software in a replication of the operational environment.
  - ○ Define solution steps for use cases and implement the POC solution build.
  - ○ Deliverables in the "Engineer" phase should include solution design, implementation plan, and success criteria (revised again based on the latest findings).
- **Step 4: Execute**
  - ○ Create test design for use cases and define positive/negative scenarios.

- Design and execute test scripts. Record results and information on failed or skipped tests or test case steps.
- Deliverables in the "Execute" phase should include test cases, test scripts, and test results.
- **Step 5: Evaluate**
  - Review and validate the POC results with all stakeholders.
  - Compare outcomes to success criteria in order to develop a summary of findings and present the lessons learned.
  - Gain agreement for a "Move Forward" decision and develop a full execution plan.
  - Deliverables in the "Evaluate" phase should include an evaluation model, summary of findings (with lessons learned), and an execution plan (if applicable).

If the results of the POC are positive, they are frequently followed by prototyping where the innovative technology becomes a functional entity.

Commercialization

The final step in the invention/commercialization process (Figure 1) is usually to decide how to commercialize innovative technology. In the past, this was done by transferring the technology to an outside entity, usually a corporation. The process of obtaining a licensing agreement between the university and the corporation is often called technology transfer and is done by the TTO.

The source of the original funding of the research for technological innovations may impact the commercialization activity. For example, if the research was funded by a federally funded research grant, the university can or cannot choose to take an ownership position. If the university chooses not to take an ownership position, then the researcher can circumvent the university's process and pursue commercialization on his/her own.

The environment of the university is not always favorable to commercialization. The intuitional logic of academics may conflict with any attempts to commercialize scientific discovery. Academic scientists tend to focus on basic science that is difficult to commercialize into any useful inventions. The usefulness of the scientific discoveries varies significantly across disciplines and the industries. The presence of professional schools such as business, medicine, dentistry, and engineering tends to enhance the number of useful discoveries that occur at a university.

As previously stated, TTOs mainly focus on licensing (the process by which the technology is transferred to a third party) in which the university grants its right in the technology to a third party (the licensee) for a period of years. Since most of the technology of a university is at a very early stage and is licensed at a large discount, a substantial payoff to the university is not frequent. Very few startups are being created directly as a result of the efforts of the TTO. Today, startups are created more frequently due to the availability of capital and grants as discussed in Chapters 5 and 6 and due to the increasing interest by faculty, the presence of entrepreneurs and entrepreneurship as an academic discipline, and the de-risking of startups through the innovation/commercialization process. In fact, in some universities, the development of the startup company as the means of commercialization has surpassed licensing in terms of both frequency of occurrence as well as economic return.

University Model of the Process

While the innovation/commercialization process varies from university to university, one model developed and used by Harvard University is indicated in Figure 2. The first step in the Harvard model is for the inventor to contact the Office of Technology Development before any public disclosure as previously discussed in the role of patents (Chapter 3). To reiterate, once an invention has been publicly disclosed, any protection of the invention is not enforceable as the invention in the public domain. Following the reporting, the technology is assessed and evaluated, and a decision regarding whether to file for a patent is made as well as the path for commercialization — creating the startups or licensing. The commercialization by company formation results in a useful product/service on the market, economic development, and job creation (the third dimension of the university discussed in the Chapter 10), money to both the university, the inventor, the academic entrepreneur team and the financial providers, and university reinvestment in research and education.

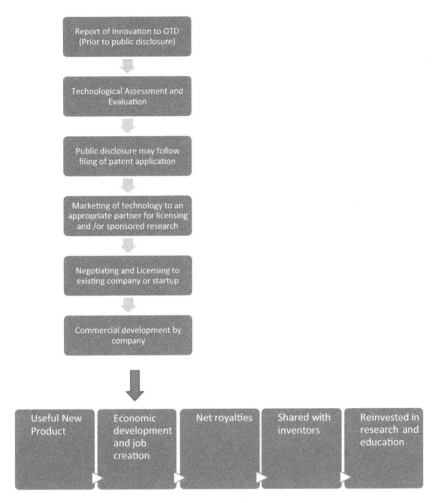

Figure 2. Technology development at Harvard University.

Source: Harvard University (2016), *The Inventors Handbook*.

Summary

This chapter focused on the steps in the general commercialization process used to commercialize technological ideas — inventing and reporting, technological assessment, filing the patent, POC, and commercialization. Three ways of technology assessment are presented: market evaluation checklist, need and value determination, and the market opportunity assessment plan. The chapter concludes with a presentation of one university model of the process.

References

DeLuna, J. and Malik, A. (2014). *Core Fundamentals in any Proof of Concept/ Capability*. Tuexin Consulting, LLC, pp. 1–3.

Harvard University (2016). *The Inventors Handbook*. Harvard University, Office of Technology and Development.

Hisrich, R. D., Peters, M. P. and Shepherd, D. A. (2020). *Entrepreneurship*, 11th edition. Dubugae, IA: McGraw-Hill Education, pp. 105–106.

Chapter 10

Managing and Increasing the Results of the Ecosystem

Learning Objectives

- To understand the overall process of academic entrepreneurship and its ecosystem.
- To understand the impact of various ownership and royalty policies at different universities.
- To know how to manage and measure the results of the ecosystem for academic entrepreneurship.
- To learn of ways to start and improve the academic entrepreneurship ecosystem.

Opening Profile — Michael J. Voor

Q1. Submitter Information

Name of Nominee	**Michael J. Voor**
University the Nominee is representing	**University of Louisville**
Email	mike.voor@louisville.edu
Phone number	502 2958667

Associate Professor Michael Voor has joint appointments in the Department of Orthopaedic Surgery and the Bioengineering Department.

Dr. Voor earned his Bachelor's degree in Mechanical Engineering from Tulane University in 1988 and his Master's and PhD in Biomedical Engineering from Tulane University in 1990 and 1992, respectively. He was appointed as an Assistant Professor in the Department of Orthopaedic Surgery from the University of Louisville in 1992 and founded the Orthopaedic Bioengineering Laboratory. Since that time, he has had several associate appointments in other departments of the university and in 2012 he was jointly appointed to Bioengineering. He is a member of Pi Tau Sigma, Tau Beta Pi, the American Society of Biomechanics, the Orthopaedic Research Society, and the North American Spine Society. His research has focused on bone mechanics and orthopedic implant design and performance. His research has received funding of over $4 million from various agencies including NIH, NSF, DoD, KSEF, KSGC, Whitaker, Coulter, Fischer-Owen, and various industry partners.

Lab. The Orthopaedic Bioengineering Laboratory was designed to evaluate the biomechanical performance of orthopedic devices and procedures in animal models, cadaver specimens, and synthetic bone surrogates using biomechanical testing, computational finite element analysis, and micro-CT scanning. Recent projects include the development of a new intramedullary reamer for placement of fracture fixation devices; evaluating the bone quality in mice and the role of homocysteine; and exercise therapies for improved bone quality during spaceflight. Dr. Voor has also developed a novel bone graft substitute product that led to the formation of a successful orthopedic company, Vivorte, Inc.

Students. Dr. Voor has mentored 10 Master's degree students and 6 PhD students, had 10 full-time orthopedic research residents, numerous medical students, and other students involved in his research over the past 25 years. Current projects include computational simulation of the strain patterns in a human femur during targeted exercise to prevent bone loss at the hip during aging; experimental validation of a predictive model for the mechanical properties of a healing bone graft; the development of a surgical assistive computational and three-dimensional printing process to create custom bending templates for plate fixation of complex pelvic fractures; and experimental and computational evaluation of the effects of site-specific bone quality parameters on osteoporotic hip fracture strength with a fall to the side of the body.

Q2: The nominee's position when they created the company. Describe the nominee's process with the university as they were creating the company. Be as detailed as possible.

Dr. Voor remains a full-time faculty member of the Department of Orthopaedic Surgery at the University of Louisville School of Medicine. Currently, he is jointly appointed in the Department of Bioengineering of the Speed School of Engineering. Initially, the company was simply founded as an LLC with Dr. Voor as one of two co-founders. The company, Vivorte, immediately began negotiating with the university for licensing rights to two of the technologies that Dr. Voor had developed in his laboratory. The university was very supportive of this process as Dr. Voor had previously submitted the technology for patent submission to the university's Office of Technology Transfer. The nature and maturity of the technology suggested that the best commercialization route would be through a startup company that could further develop, rather than attempting to immediately out-license to a large orthopedic device company. Thus, the university encouraged the formation of the LLC.

Q3: Describe the nominee's experience working with the university in creating the company. What were the challenges? What support did they receive? Be as detailed as possible.

As the LLC was attempting to raise capital to get the company started and to commercialize (prepare for FDA clearance application), the university helped by introducing Vivorte to potential investors, including the group known as MetaCyte, a technology incubator affiliated with U of FL. In turn, other potential investors, including a lead investor with experience working with the university, were brought on and the initial capital was raised. After consideration, the University of Louisville Research Foundation, decided not to invest.

Q4: What happened to the company the nominee created? Describe in detail where it is now and how is it doing. What is the history of the company? Be as detailed as possible.

The company raised to date over $7 million through mostly private equity investment. In 2013, Vivorte received FDA clearance for two products sold in the bone graft substitute market for space in the US. The first use of the products in humans occurred in 2015 and sales continue. The company has grown to include additional products, some of which were licenses from third parties. Negotiations continue for partnership deals with other larger or similar sized companies to grow distribution, which currently represents approximately 10 states. Vivorte employs five people full-time and two people part-time and continues to develop new orthopedic implant technology while supporting the existing product lines. The company website is at www.Vivorte.com.

Introduction

Since to date, there has not been a universally accepted definition of academic entrepreneurship, the research results have not built a solid theoretical base. When first conceptualized, the term was an extension of regular entrepreneurship except the funding company was based on academic knowledge. Some viewed academic entrepreneurship as university spin-offs (Shane, 2004; Wright *et al.*, 2009). This view was further refined by separating academic entrepreneurship into general academic entrepreneurship and research-based academic entrepreneurship (Goel and Grimpe, 2011). Others viewed academic entrepreneurship as any commercialization of intellectual property of a university regardless of whether the entrepreneur involved in the project was an employee of the university (Hayter, 2011).

Another view of academic entrepreneurship is all contacts made by individual academics with business entities who had activities that gave more tangible results and soft activities which result in academic publication, grants, or cohort research (Philpott *et al.*, 2011). A final view of academic entrepreneurship is of an activity done to transfer knowledge for the university to an external environment to produce social value for the parties involved (Cantanagu, 2017). In this book, the definition of academic entrepreneurship used is the formation of a new non-profit or profit venture by a member of the academic community (professor, staff, and/or student). By using this definition of academic entrepreneurship, the technology transfer activity is clearly separated into licensing or into a new venture creation. This concluding chapter will illuminate this activity by looking at the impact of academic entrepreneurship and technology transfer, the aspects of each and the difference in ownership, and revenue-sharing policies of universities. The chapter and book closes with a discussion on managing the ecosystem and provide suggestions for building a new or improving existing ecosystem.

Technology Transfer

Since the Bayh–Dole Act of 1980, university technology transfer has increased each year and has accelerated in recent years. The various aspects of the output of technology transfer are indicated in Table 1. Between 1996 and 2015, the gross industrial output in US by technology transfer was 1.3 trillion. Measuring 2016 only, the amount of research expenditures related to technology transfer was 66.9 billion. The number of inventors in the 1996–2015 time period was 380,000 with 25,825 investors in 2016. Similar increases occurred in US patents issued and startups formed as a result of technology transfer. The number of US patents was 16,845 and the number of startups formed were 1,024 in 2016 (see Table 1).

Table 1.   Impact of technology transfer.

	1996–2015	2016
Contribution to US gross industrial output	$1.3 trillion	
Research expenditures		$66.9 billion
Inventions disclosed	380,000	25,825
US patents Issued	80,000	16,847
Startups Formed	11,000	1024

Source: Association of US Technology Transfer Managers (AUTM), www.autm.net/STATT.

Of the three categories of individuals in a university — administration faculty, staff, and students — the faculty and students are the most heavily involved at least in the earliest phases of the technology transfer process. The following are the usual ways by which these occur:

- Faculty, principle investigator, and PhD/postdoctoral students.
- Faculty, principle investigator, and experienced entrepreneurs.
- Faculty, principle investigator PhD, postdoctoral students, and business school students.
- Total student effort that includes at least one of the several categories of students such as Master/PhD students and/or business school students.

The ideal and most successful arrangement is the faculty principle investigator and the entrepreneur who results in more technology commercialization (company formation) than the technology transfer method. This combination allows the faculty to complement their technological expertise with the small experience and network of a successful business person in either a large corporation or an entrepreneur.

The earlier this occurs, the easier and better the transition from the lab to technology or technology commercialization, as this business experience helps in guiding the research into a more marketable product/service and also in determining the partner distribution system and funding sources available.

The most common arrangement is faculty and PhD/postdoctoral students. While the students involved are highly motivated in the creation of the technology and the creation of the technological product/service, they often lack business knowledge and experience. This can result in a strong technological idea that has no market. Sometimes, this can result in a technological idea that is ahead of the market. Adding a business student significantly increases the probability to successfully transfer or commercialize the idea as well as shorten the time of process. Student-only technological transfer and commercialization usually results from more structured programs such as the BioDesign program of Stanford University or the Master of Science in entrepreneurship or the Master of Engineering in entrepreneurship at Case Western Reserve University. These types of programs facilitate student collaboration.

The usual sequence in the technology transfer process is as follows: academic research, idea and invention, report and evaluation, strategy for commercialization, patent filing, obtaining a partner/institution (usually a company), negotiations, and commercialization. Oftentimes, the stages are not easily identifiable but the activities do occur regardless of the exact process of the university.

Technology Commercialization

Technology commercialization resulting in company formation is a main output of academic entrepreneurship. There are several stages in this process: research and idea generation, commercialization discussion, prototype generation, establishing the technology and commercialization feasibility, patent filing, forming a founding team, determining the process of strategizing and commercialization, obtaining funding sources, and launching the venture. These stages are the focus of the previous chapters. This result of the ecosystem is very appealing to the university, particularly one that has some ownership in the resulting company and results in a larger financial return and impact on the external ecosystem, in close proximity to the university. Technology transfer usually occurs with the company outside the immediate region and sometimes outside the country of the university. This process is greatly facilitated by the university being in close proximity to the incubator/accelerator, the focus of Chapter 8. This allows students and faculty to meet, develop teams, and discuss the processes and problems in forming a company to take the new technological product/service to the market. Another factor that assists and accelerates the process is having a university venture fund or an university associated angel group or funds to provide the needed capital for the startup and growth of the new venture (see Chapters 6 and 7).

What Every Academic Entrepreneur Needs to Know about Creating a Startup

Once the academic entrepreneur has decided to create a startup, the following question arises: "What needs to be done?".

Incorporation

It is important to create a legal entity that is separate from the people managing and owning the company. By formally registering a company in a state, the company itself becomes a "person" in law, with many of the rights and obligations of individuals (i.e., the right to own property, contract, right to sue, right to be sued). Even though the company needs human agents to do everything, incorporation is seen as a completely separate legal person from those owning individuals.

There are many legal entities[1] recognized by law to accomplish this process; the two most common for entrepreneurs are (1) limited liability companies (LLCs) and (2) corporations. These two have many similar characteristics but differ significantly in key areas that are crucial for successful university startups.

LLCs are used if the entrepreneur is not looking to raise investor funding, since most sophisticated investors will only invest in a corporation.[2] LLCs are usually used for closely held businesses managed and funded by a small number of people. They are flow-through entities, which allow losses and profits to be taxed at the owners' personal, rather than the business, rate. Since most startups have losses in the early years, if those losses flow to the personal accounts of the owners, they can offset other personal income, so owners pay lower personal income taxes on their 1040s.

LLCs generally have lower setup and maintenance costs because they do not need to have the more complicated governance structure in place for outside investors. But for startups envisioning high growth and involving outside investors, the LLC is generally not appropriate and most entrepreneurs with larger visions use a corporation.[3]

---

[1] LLPs, LLCs, corporations, benefit companies; technically, sole proprietorships and partnerships are not legally separate from the people managing and owning them.

[2] Specifically, investors take equity in a C-Corporation, not an S-Corporation.

[3] In early days, setting up a business as an LLC did not seem to cause too many problems, but as more employees, advisers, and investors are involved, the LLC structure begins to strain for a high-growth company and the LLC needs to be converted into a corporation. The downside in converting an LLC to a corporation is the business can incur a lot of legal costs and can create unnecessary tax issues requiring an expensive valuation of the LLC

Corporations are used because of their limited liability,[4] their governance structure, and their ease for issuing stock. Limited liability refers to the fact that managers, directors, and shareholders of the corporation are not liable for the debts incurred by the corporation. The general governance structure for corporations of managers, board of directors, and stockholders has been used for hundreds of years by some of the world's most successful companies, so it is widely understood. In fact, the State of Delaware[5] has one of the most fully developed corporate statutes, and most startups incorporate there, governed by Delaware laws, because investors and corporate/securities attorneys are well versed in its rules.

The ability to easily issue stock is one of the corporation's most important features. Because the rights and obligations of stockholders in corporations are well defined, investors prefer becoming shareholders in corporations over all other ownership interests.

> Another reason corporations are preferred by entrepreneurs is because stock option plans can be easily put in place. Successful startups create a lot of value very quickly, mostly because of the efforts of the people working for the startups, so stock option plans allow team members to benefit from the increased value of the company. Because startups seldom have the cash to pay market rates to employees, stock option plans allow the startups to attract people based on the ability to share some of the wealth creation. In some cases, the value of the stock options can be life-changing, which is one of the key benefits of working at a risky startup (along with bringing some amazing useful technologies to the world).

---

so that it is converted at fair market value. The other main reason to use a corporation is creating a stock plan that can be used as currency to hire employees and advisers before the company has money to do so. The catch 22 for startups is that they need funding to attract talent and they need talent to attract the funding. How to break that vicious circle is using stock options to attract the talent first without funding, but with the promise that they will share in the value created by the startup. Corporations are allowed to have stock option plans while LLCs does not.

[4]Limited liability companies (LLCs) as their name implies also provide the same protections.

[5]A corporate can be governed by the laws of the incorporating state, while doing business anywhere in the country.

Corporate governance

Corporations have shareholders, directors, officers, and employees with defined rights and obligations stipulated in the state corporate statute or in the company bylaws. While this provides a maximum amount of flexibility in corporate governance with well-established boundaries, it also establishes certain legal and maintenance requirements.

Board of directors

The board of directors is the main governing body of the corporation. The incorporator can choose the number of directors it likes to sit on the board.[6] For actions of the board, there must be a quorum[7] present, and by default, decisions are made by the majority votes of the directors present at the meeting. Board decisions in Delaware can be done by meeting or in writing. If decisions are done in writing, they must be consented to by all directors.

Officers

Officers manage the company on a day-to-day basis. They are appointed and removed by the board of directors. Typical officers are CEO/President, CFO/Treasurer, and Secretary. Because the corporation must have people perform its actions, the CEO is given the authority by the board of directors to execute agreements on behalf of the corporation. The CEO can then delegate authority to others to sign as a duly authorized person to bind the corporation and fill the ranks of employees needed to execute all business functions.

Stockholders

Stockholders are the people who own the shares of the corporation, but they do not control the company directly. They elect the directors, who

---

[6]Delaware allows even just one director; usually there is an odd number of directors, so that there will be no tie decisions.

[7]A quorum is the minimum number of directors needed to be present at a meeting according to the corporate bylaws.

control the corporation, who in turn appoint the officers, and they work with employees to run the day-to-day activities of the company.

Startups issue either common or preferred stocks. Common stock generally goes to founders, employees, advisers, and consultants. Preferred stock is usually sold to investors. Preferred stocks have additional rights and privileges beyond what common stocks have.

The number of authorized shares is defined in the certificate of incorporation but can be amended by filing an amendment to the certificate of incorporation, both to be filed with the Secretary of State.

When forming the corporation, the founders decide how the equity of the company should be allocated, which usually includes allocations to current team members[8] and a stock option plan to reserve shares for future team members.

Building the startup team

The most important job for the academic entrepreneur is to build the startup team: employees, officers, directors, advisers, and consultants who will work with him or her to build the company essentially from ground up. Officers and employees are generally full-time, and directors, advisers, and consultants are part-time and *ad hoc*.

Another useful functional categorization for university startups is founder(s)/entrepreneurs, science team, and management team. Usually, the academic entrepreneur is the founder(s), who has the vision and creates the startup to actuate that vision. Because academic startups are commercializing R&D, the science/engineering team takes the technology and turns it into a product. The management team are the people who will sell the product and scale the operations, along with taking care of other administrative and operational activities. On an exit, most industry buyers want the science team, but may not need the management team. The corporate buyer usually already has the people to sell, market, and scale the business across the world and so has a limited need for the startup management team beyond a transitional period after the acquisition.

---

[8]Vesting terms are generally included, so that the equity vests as the team member performs to ensure that equity is tied to effort.

What the corporate buyer usually is looking for is the innovation de-risked into a working and saleable product with the science team that created the technology and commercialized it.

This distinction between the science and management team is important because your employee contracts need to facilitate the employees who will need to go with the startup to the buyer and those who most likely will not, so as to properly manage employee expectations.[9]

Directors,[10] advisers,[11] and consultants are generally people who will not generally transition with the startup and the corporate buyer. There are outside people who should bring the "3 Ws: work, wisdom, or wealth".[12] Their main functions are to supplement corporate governance, the science team, and the management team members and find customers and investors using their skills, expertise, experience, and networks.

Confidentiality/Non-disclosure Agreements[13]

Team members have access to the company's competitive proprietary information, so terms are required in agreements to be protected from disclosure to outside parties. Such intellectual property may include anything that the company wants to keep as a business secret, such as formulas, processes, production methods, customer lists, business plans, strategies, salary structure, contract terms, reports, data, know-how, works-in-progress, designs, development tools, and specifications. The non-disclosure agreement will place a legal duty on the key employees to refrain from disclosing the information to non-authorized recipients.

---

[9]Common problems are faculty entrepreneurs and foreign students who take central strategic roles, e.g., CSO or CEO, and have no plans to continue in the corporation acquiring the startup.

[10]Some directors may be full-time employees who may go to the corporate buyer as a science or management team member.

[11]Directors have formal responsibilities under corporate law. Advisers, on the contrary, are informal.

[12]The startup checklist, p. 108.

[13]These agreements can be called different names: non-disclosure agreement (NDA), confidentiality agreement (CA), confidential disclosure agreement (CDA), proprietary information agreement (PIA) or secrecy agreement (SA).

All proprietary information in the possession of the key employee's must be returned to the company upon termination of the employee relationship but is typical for the non-disclosure provisions to survive and continue after termination.

Intellectual property assignment

As part of employment agreements with the company, key employees agree to assign intellectual property developed within the scope of employment to the company.[14] Prior inventions by the employee are listed in the agreement to highlight that that property is retained by the employee and will not be assigned to the company, though care should be taken to not commingle those ideas and inventions with those that the employee will be working on for the company.[15] The agreement also provides for duties of the employee to maintain proper records of any new intellectual property developed and to assist the company to properly protect and secure the IP as the company deem appropriate, most typically by assisting the company with filing appropriate patents resulting from the employee's work as an inventor.

Non-competition

A non-competition agreement provides protection to the startup that team members will not start a separate company to compete with the company or work for a competitor for a specified time after voluntary or involuntary termination. The fear is key employees will learn confidential information about the startup and then leave and use it to the detriment of the startup. Because non-competes can prevent employees from earning a living in

---

[14] Founders typically assign key intellectual property developed before founding the company to the company on incorporation.

[15] If the employee incorporates elements of the prior invention into a company product, process, or machine; it is the typical term of the agreement to grant a nonexclusive, royalty-free, irrevocable, perpetual, worldwide license to make, have made, modify, use, and sell such prior invention as part of or in connection with such product, process, or machine.

their field, they are restricted or even prohibited from depending on the state.[16] Generally, non-competes' provisions are delimited by geography and time, which if properly executed will increase the likelihood of enforcement in those states that permit them.

Stock option plans

A properly executed stock option plan is one of the most important features of a high-growth startup because it facilitates in attracting the team members that will make the company successful. Since startups usually cannot pay market rates and do not have the stability of more established companies, startups provide a way to participate in the success of the company through partial ownership in the company. These key team members[17] help make the company successful and therefore are given partial ownership in the startup, i.e., key employees, officers, directors, advisers, and consultants.

Properly used, stock options are powerful incentives for people to work to ensure the startup's long-term success. Well-advised startups setup stock plans when they form the corporation since it's easiest to be done at that time. It also signals to future team members and investors that the founders are sophisticated entrepreneurs who have the understanding to execute an ambitious plan.[18]

A stock plan reserves a fixed number of authorized shares (usually around 10–30%) for a number of years (traditionally for 10 years) to give to key team members. The shares can be given when they are hired or through advisory agreements.

To be properly issued, stock plans need to be legally documented, adopted by the board of directors, and usually approved by the

---

[16]Except for specific situations like when the company is being sold, California effectively voids all non-compete provisions.

[17]We will refer to team members as the key people who help make the startup a success: founders, employees, officers, directors, advisers, and consultants.

[18]A properly executed stock plan is a key indicator that the entrepreneurs have hired a startup attorney to form the corporation, because non-startup lawyers generally wouldn't form the corporate with a stock option plan.

stockholders. Also, there are tax benefits for the startup and the team members eligible for the stock plan, if structured appropriately with the tax rules.[19]

Vesting

Startups provide stock to team members in exchange for helping develop the company, so it is important that if the team member leaves or is terminated, further stock should no longer be given to that team member. Startups achieve this goal by "vesting", which schedules when the options are formally earned. The most common vesting schedule for high-growth startups is "4-year vesting with a 1-year cliff". This means that ¼ of the options will vest in 1 year from the vesting commencement date for that team member, and 1/36 of the total shares will be earned each month for the next 3 years.

Impact of Ownership and Royalty-Sharing Policies

Another factor that impacts the interest and frequency of occurrence for both technology transfer and technology commercialization are the ownership and income-sharing policies of the university. The various ownership and revenue-sharing policies of selected universities are indicated in Tables 2 and 3, respectively.

Most university ownership policies delineate between ideas created within the scope of university employment, whether university resources are used, and ideas not involving either. The policies also vary between the three categories of staff, students, and faculty with students generally having the most favorable ownership policy of the three groups (see Table 3).

The royalty and income-sharing policies from intellectual property created by the three groups also vary among universities. Again, students usually have the most favorable policy.

---

[19]There are technical rules to follow including the exercise price of the options that needs to be at fair market value (FMV) preferably supported by a "409a valuation".

Table 2.   Ownership policy at different universities.

University of Utah

Works created by university staff, student-employees, students, and faculty within the scope of their university employment are considered to be works made for hire, and thus, are works to which the university is the owner and controls all legal rights of the work. In contrast, works created by university staff and student-employees outside the scope of their university employment are not covered by this policy and are considered to be owned by the creators, unless such works are created through "substantial use of University resources".

Source: https://regulations.utah.edu/research/7-003.php.

Columbia University

The university asserts copyright ownership in any work of authorship that is (i) created with substantial use of university resources, financial support or non-faculty university personnel beyond the level of common resources provided to faculty; (ii) created or commissioned for use by the university; or (iii) created under the terms of a sponsored project where the terms of the sponsored project require copyright be in the name of the university. Additionally, any work created by an officer of administration (including a faculty member or officer of research only when acting in his or her capacity as an officer of administration) or by a support staff member acting within the scope of his or her employment generally constitutes a "work made for hire" as defined by federal law.

Source: http://www.columbia.edu/cu/provost/docs/copyright.html.

University of Florida

An invention that is made in the field or discipline in which the creator is engaged by the university or made with the use of university support is the property of the university. The creator shall share in the proceeds therefrom subject to preexisting commitments to outside sponsoring agencies. An invention made outside the field or discipline in which the creator is engaged by the university and for which no university support has been used is the property of the creator. In the latter case, however, the creator and OTL may agree that the invention be pursued by the university and the proceeds shared pursuant to this Intellectual Property Policy. A work that is made in the course of independent efforts is the property of the creator. A university-supported work is the property of the university. The creator shall share in the proceeds from a university-supported work subject to preexisting commitments to outside sponsoring agencies.

Source: http://generalcounsel.ufl.edu/media/generalcounselufledu/documents/Intellectual-Property-Policy.pdf.

Brigham Young University

Pursuant to law and university policy, and without an express agreement specifying otherwise, any work (whether a technical work or a creative work) prepared by university personnel within the scope of their employment is work for hire owned by the university.

(*Continued*)

Table 2. *(Continued)*

When works are commissioned to an individual who is not an employee of the university or when the commissioned individual is an employee but the work to be created falls outside that person's scope of employment, the university will proceed with a written agreement, signed by the university and the individual, stating that the resulting intellectual property is owned by the university and assigning to the university all intellectual property rights to the work held by the individual.

The university retains ownership rights to all technical works but relinquishes ownership rights to the developer(s) of creative works when "nominal" use of university resources are involved in the production of the intellectual property. When "substantial" university resources are used in the production of creative works, however, the university will retain its ownership position, and income from the project will be shared with the developers. The conditions that differentiate between nominal and substantial use of university resources can be found in the link provided below (in Sections IV.A and IV.B). Decisions based upon the extent of the utilization of university resources are to be negotiated with the developers by the deans, in consultation with the appropriate Intellectual Property Services support office and within these general guidelines prior to approval by the academic Vice President's office.

Source: http://creativeworks.byu.edu/infocenter/ippolicy.htm#_IV.A._Substantial_Use.

University of Washington

Employees engaged in sponsored research are bound by the provisions of the agreement between the university and the sponsor. Title to any inventions conceived or first reduced to practice in the course of research supported by federal agencies, industry, or other sponsors shall generally be vested with the university.

As a condition of employment, and even if a specific patent agreement is not signed, university employees agree to assign all inventions in which the university has an interest to the university, to an invention management agency designated by the university, or to the sponsor if required under agreements governing the research.

Source: http://www.washington.edu/admin/rules/policies/PO/EO36.html.

Managing the ecosystem

Managing the ecosystem for academic entrepreneurship has been a problem at most universities. This reflects the character of the individuals involved (professors, staff, and students), the focus of the university (liberal arts, science, and professional schools), and the mission of the university. The growth of the third mission activities in universities throughout the world, particularly in the English-speaking world, is reflected in the rise of policies promoting this "third mission or third stream" orientation.

Table 3. Royalty and income from intellectual property-sharing policy at different universities.

Universities	Royalty sharing		
1. University of Utah	The creator's share of income shall be based on a percentage of such income or revenue remaining after reimbursement of all the university's direct costs of copyright registration, licensing, and other legal protection of the work ("net revenue").		
	The creator's share (which, in the case of co-creators, shall be divided between them equally or as they shall agree in their sole discretion) shall normally be 40% of the first $20,000 of net revenue, 35% of the next $20,000 of net revenue, and 30% of any additional net revenue received by the university from the work.		
2. Columbia University	Conditions: 20% of gross income is used for pooled legal and administrative expenses and internally reinvested funds. Net income is 80% of the gross income.		
	Revenue distribution:		
		Cum Net Income < 100k	Cum Net Income > 100k
	Developer/Creator	50%	25%
	Developer's research and innovation account	25%	25%
	Central university	25%	33%
	Department	0%	8.5%
	School	0%	8.5%

3. University of Florida

Conditions: Net income less than any foreseeable development expenses the university or UFRF deems necessary to defend or maintain the work or invention, Net Adjusted Income, will be distributed.

Revenue Distribution:

	NI < 500k	NI > 500k
Creator(s)	40%	25%
Programs(s)	10%	10%
Department(s) of creator(s)	7.5%	10%
College(s) of creator(s)	7.5%	10%
University or research foundation:	35%	45%

4. Brigham Young University

Conditions: Costs incurred in the process of perfecting, transferring, and protecting university rights to the property or works will be paid by the university and, together with interest costs, will first be deducted from the gross income available for distribution. An accurate accounting of all such costs shall be made available to the developer(s) upon request. The net income (gross income minus university expenses) from university-owned intellectual properties will be distributed to academic developers and to developers in support areas.

Revenue Distribution:

Developer(s)	45%
College(s) of the developer(s)	27.5%
Technology Transfer or Creative Works Office:	27.5%

(Continued)

Table 3. (*Continued*)

Universities		Royalty sharing
5. Stanford University	Inventors	33.33%
	Inventor's department	33.33%
	Inventor's school	33.33%
6. University of Pennsylvania	Inventor's personal share	30%
	Inventor's research activity share	12.5%
	Departments of inventors	12.5%
	School of inventor's share	15%
	University research share	30%
7. University of Washington	Direct costs incurred by the university in the protection and licensing of intellectual property must be recovered before distribution of income begins. The vice provost for innovation may also retain amounts necessary to recover reasonably anticipated direct costs.	
	CoMotion shall retain licensee-paid cost recoveries and shall deduct an administrative fee of 20% from adjusted gross revenue. From the remainder, CoMotion and the Treasure Office (in cases of distribution of equity or equity proceeds) shall deduct amounts necessary to cover incurred and reasonably anticipated direct costs.	
	Inventors 33.33%	
	Inventor's department 33.33%	
	University research fund 33.33%	

8.	Massachusetts Institute of Technology	1. Deduct 15% administrative fee from Gross Royalty Income.
		2. Then, deduct out-of-pocket costs not reimbursed by licensees and, in some cases, a reserve to arrive at Adjusted Royalty Income.
		Inventor's Share — 33.33% of Adjusted Royalty.
		A total of 50% of Total Program Contribution is distributed among departments and centers proportional to their department/center case contribution.
		Remaining net income from Total Program Contribution and from the Administrative Fees are first used to cover TLO office and patent expenses, with the remainder going to the General Fund at the end of the fiscal year.
		Notes:
		Calculate: "Case Contribution" for each case = Gross Case Royalties less Administrative Fee and Inventors' Share. Also subtract share of royalties owed to third-party joint owners or other third parties, if any Sum: Case Contributions for each department or center = "Department/Center Case Contribution" Sum: All Case Contributions for all departments and centers = "Total Case Contribution" calculate "Total Net Patent Expenses" = Total TLO patent expenses for the fiscal year minus all patent reimbursement payments received from licenses. Calculate "Total Program Contribution" = Total Case Contribution minus Total Net Patent Expense.
9.	California Institute of Technology	Inventors 25% University 75%
10.	Carnegie Mellon University	

(Continued)

Table 3. *(Continued)*

Universities	Royalty sharing

11. New York University	When NYU owns the rights to an invention, each inventor has the right to share in the Net Proceeds received by NYU from commercializing the invention except as otherwise provided in this policy. Specifically, Net Proceeds ordinarily are distributed as follows:
	
	(1) Fifteen percent (15%) of the Net Proceeds for the general support of the OIL and to cover any other expenses associated with the commercialization of NYU's inventions.
	(2) The remaining Net Proceeds (85%) are distributed as follows:
	
	    Inventors 50% of the Net Proceeds
	    NYC 50% of the Net Proceeds
	
	    Of the 50% allocated to NYC,
	    Inventor's school 66.67%
	    NYC 33.33%

12. Purdue University	A total of 25% of the fee is retained to cover costs of processing contracts with special IP terms and conditions. Net proceeds are distributed among different parties as follows: Office of technology transfer 1/3rd University research unit 1/3rd Investigator 1/3rd
13 University of Texas System	In those instances where the U.T. System or any U.T. System institution licenses rights in intellectual property to third parties, the costs of licensing, including, but not limited to, the costs to operate and support a technology transfer office and the costs of obtaining a patent or other protection for the property on behalf of the Board of Regents must first be recaptured from any royalties or other

license payments received by the U.T. System or any U.T. System institution. The remainder of any such income (including, but not limited to, license fees, prepaid royalties, minimum royalties, running royalties, milestone payments, and sublicense payments) shall be divided as follows:

30–50% to creator(s) and 50–70% to U.T. System institutions. To be specific, royalties and incomes are divided to the following parties:

Inventors	50%
University	35%
College	5%
Department	5%
Faculty	5%

14. University of Minnesota — The university shall share with inventors the net income from the commercialization of technology as follows:

Inventors	33.33%
Department	25.33%
Collegiate Unit	8%
Office of the Vice President for Research	33.33%

15. University of California, Los Angeles

UCLA general fund	50%
Department	15%
Inventors	35%

16. University of Michigan — After recovery of university expenses, aggregate revenues resulting from royalties and sale of equity interests shall be shared as follows. The division of revenues is subject to change through appropriate university procedures.

(*Continued*)

Table 3.   (*Continued*)

Universities	Royalty sharing
	Up to $200,000: 50% to the inventor(s), 17% to the inventor's department, 18% to the inventor's school or college, 15% to the central university administration.
	Over $200,000 (and up to $2,000,000): 30% to the inventor(s), 20% to the inventor's department, 25% to the inventor's school or college, 25% to the central university administration.
	Over $2,000,000: 30% to the inventor(s), 35% to the inventor's school or college, 35% to the central university administration.
17. Cornell University	Inventors: 33.33%
	Inventor's research Unit: 33.33%
	• Inventor's research unit: 40%
	• University research support: 60%
	Centre for Technology Licensing: 33.33%
18. University of Illinois, Chicago	When revenue is received by the university, all out-of-pocket payments or obligations (and in some cases, a reasonable reserve for anticipated future expenses) attributable to protecting (including defense against infringement or enforcement actions), marketing, licensing, or administering the property may be deducted from such income. The income remaining after such deductions is defined as net revenue. In the case of multiple intellectual properties licensed under a single licensing agreement, the university shall determine and designate the share of net income to be assigned to each intellectual property.
	Inventors: 40%
	Inventors unit: 20%
	University: 40%

19. University of South Florida

The need for fair and consistent sharing of revenue with inventors/authors and the prudent exercise of the public trust requires clear guidelines and procedures for the conduct of the negotiations between the USF System and the inventor or author to determine the allocation of revenue derived from the commercial application of inventions or works. Therefore, the USF System policy is to initiate the negotiations by offering terms that are at least as favorable to the inventor or author as the following:

A. To the inventor or author: A share to be specified by the inventor or author but not exceeding forty-five percent (45%) of net revenue.

B. To the inventor's or author's research support: A share to be specified by the inventor or author but not exceeding the difference between fifty-five percent (55%) of net revenue and the share allocated to the inventor or author.

C. To the USF System: Forty-five percent (45%) of net revenue.

20. Northwestern University

A deduction of 15% to cover operating expenses incurred by INVO will be taken annually from the gross license revenue, with funds exceeding the annual INVO budget moving into a quasi-endowment earmarked for INVO operations, entrepreneurial activities, and research operations as determined by the Provost and Vice-President for Research. Income then remaining is the net income, which is distributed as set forth below.

To limit administrative costs, if the net income in any year is less than $10,000, then no distribution will be made in that year to the schools, departments, or centers; rather, such net income will be tracked until either (1) the dispersible net income (i.e., the net income summed over several years) exceeds $10,000 or (2) 5 years passes, at which time a distribution will be made as set forth below.

(Continued)

258   *Academic Entrepreneurship*

Table 3. *(Continued)*

Universities	Royalty sharing		

21. Arizona State University

	NI ≤ 50 M	50 M ≤ NI ≤ 500 M	500 M ≤ NI
Inventors:	33%	33%	33%
Department:	17%	10%	N/A
School:	17%	10%	5%
University:	33%	47%	62%

For this policy, "Net Income" is defined as gross revenues, received by the university or its nominee, resulting from any given intellectual property, less an administrative fee of 15%, then less all unreimbursed costs incurred by ASU or its nominee in protecting, licensing, maintaining, and litigating rights in the intellectual property or any agreements thereon as described under "Administrative Responsibilities" above, including, for the sake of clarity, any legal fees and other costs and expenses associated with intellectual property protection and litigation.

	NI < $10,000	NI > $10,000
Inventors:	50%	40%
Lab:	16.67%	26.67%
University:	33.33%	33.33%

22. University of Central Florida

Distribution of royalties follows the standard policy in place at UCF. Cumulative net income (gross royalties minus direct costs of patenting, copyright registration, trademark registration, licensing, legal, and other related expenses) resulting from inventions and works (excluding books) to which UCF takes title is currently divided according to the following distribution:

	$1K–100K	$101K–199K	>$200K
Inventor/Creator:	50%	40%	30%
Dean of inventor's College:	20%	24%	28%
Inventor's department:	20%	24%	28%
UCF research foundation:	10%	12%	14%

23. University of Pittsburgh

First, income from each particular license or other transfer will reimburse the "Patent Rights Fund" for legal, professional, and government fees paid for outside services incurred for that licensed or transferred patent or portfolio of patents.

Second, if a particular patent was facilitated by financial support from a University Development Fund (see below), then the income attributable to that patent must reimburse the fund if the support was categorized as a reimbursable expense at the time of the award. The balance of proceeds from any license, sale, or other amounts derived from the transfer of patent rights or unpatented intellectual property (excluding copyrights) will then be distributed as follows:

Inventors	30%
Patent rights fund	30%
University development fund	10%
Department	15%
Office of Technology Transfer	15%

24. North Carolina State University

Inventors:	40%
College:	5%
Department/Unit:	5%
Patent trust fund:	50%

Note: Includes universities only listed on "Best Universities for Technology Transfer" https://www.prnewswire.com/news-releases/the-milken-institute-ranks-the-best-us-universities-for-technology-transfer-300442457.html.

Source: From their websites.

This has resulted in many more activities, particularly in knowledge transfer, thereby forging links with the surrounding community and country and commercializing technology through academic entrepreneurship. While some universities have been concerned about and involved in these activities for some time, what is new and more pronounced is the extent to which these activities have been promoted and even in some cases institutionalized through the direct involvement of the university itself. This trend has been driven in part by circumstances such as changes in the political economy of higher education, decreasing funding of the university at the state level, and the view that university education is a personal private investment and not an investment for public good (Robertson and Kitigawa, 2009; Thrift, 2010; Vernon, 2010; Viale and Etzkowitz, 2010). Similar to academic entrepreneurship, there is no accepted definition on what constitutes a third mission activity. It generally refers to activities such as the linking of research to commercialization outcomes, establishment of incubators and accelerators, starting up companies, academic business relationship (consulting and contract research), students/industry projects, professional education and certificate programs, policymaking, employment, and overall well-being of the region and country. These third mission activities are becoming a core of some universities along with their traditional core activities of teaching and research.

This new university ecosystem requires a new framework for majoring, analyzing, and understanding the effects of both the internal system of the university as well as its external constituencies. In turn, this requires implementing an additional set of measurement and management frameworks such as balance scorecard, activity-based costing (ABC), quality management, and customer relationship management which are derived from various disciplines and used in many business situations. Each of these are discussed in the following:

Of these measurements and management framework, the most widely used by universities are customer relationship management and the balance scorecard. The balance scorecard originally focused on reporting the leading indicators of the organization's health to supplement traditional accounting measures and was refocused to also measure anything related the organization's mission statement and strategy; in the case of universities, this would include the three-core mission areas (Kaplan and Lamotte,

2001; Kaplan and Norton, 2001; Frigo and Krumwiede, 2000; Lingle and Schiemann, 1996). The balance scorecard normally focuses on four perspectives: the financial perspective (the strategy for growth, the financial well-being, and stability); the customer perspective (the quality of the students' education and placement); the internal business perspective (the efficiency of the internal processes and programs and employee well-being); and the learning and growth perspective (the overall climate supporting change and innovation in the organization). It will be interesting to see how various universities implement the balance scorecard method in measuring their performance and output.

The second most widely used by universities is customer relationship management (CRM). This provides a university with better data integration and measurement regarding their customers (students, alumni, employees, and members of the external community) (Gale, 1994; Kellen, 2002). CRM focuses on addressing the university stakeholder's perception of value and the stakeholder's subjective appraisal of value in the relationship that creates retention and commitment of each of the stakeholders.

ABC is a method for better understanding the actual costs including overhead costs involved in technology transfer and technology commercialization (academic entrepreneurship). The method links all expenses to resources supplied to each activity in transferring a particular technology as well as in each new venture created. This is very supportive information in fund-raising and resource allocation as it provides the cost side of each of the two and these can be compared to the revenue obtained, thereby giving a return on investment by each separate activity.

Increasing university academic entrepreneurship

Academic entrepreneurs as well as technology transfer is increasing at universities all over the world reflecting various micro- and macrolevel aspects of both the university and the society in which it operates. Aspects of each of these include the allocation of resources and the capabilities of firms, funding sources of resources and their accumulation to provide a return on investment, and the temporal special, social, and institutional dimensions of the macrolevel (Kaplan, 2001; Meyer, 2002).

This importance of knowledge creation provides the opportunity for universities to play a pivotal role in partnering with both the government and business to impact economic development and the well-being of a society. Some believe that the university is best suited to do this due to their very nature of being driving by innovation, being impartial, having a long-term perspective, and having minimal disruption and low turnover. A university can, in fact, become a "business incubator" bringing technology to the market. This third dimension of the university along with performing research will continue to become an increasingly important part of the university and its mission. This can be done through implementing all or at least some of the suggestions below:

- Develop and implement project-based classes in technology transfer. These project-based classes should bring together an interdisciplinary team to create road maps and business plans to further develop and de-risk the technologies of the university.
- Recognize and engage innovation as a reiterative process where basic and applied research, proof of concept testing, and prototype development stimulate and enhance each other in a cooperative process rather than a linear process.
- Establish a mentorship program particularly with students having an interest for starting a business and the CEOs of companies in the incubator/accelerator by using alumni and entrepreneurs in the industry of interest.
- Adopt a policy of open innovation for those technologies that are appropriate. Open innovation can help overcome some of the problems of increasing complexity of the technology and accelerate the innovation cycle by including external partners even in the core technology development process.
- Establish a formal university-wide business pitch competition in the Fall semester and a business plan competition in the Spring semester with prize money for the first three winners of each. The judges should be entrepreneurs and individuals from the venture-funding community. These events provide a platform for team formation, development of business plans, presentation skills of the plan, and involvement of alumni, entrepreneurs, capital providers, and members of the regional community.

- Establish an alignment between the university and the operating regional development strategy. This will provide a basis for accessing regional strengths, positively impacting the region, and increasing the number of student jobs in the region.
- Establish a formal accelerator/incubator program to assist startup companies over a period of time and provide mentoring, office space, funding, oversight and management, as well as credibility to the new venture.
- Establish a culture of interdisciplinary research, thinking, and competencies based on individuals with significant command of their discipline and the research methodology of the discipline.
- Broaden the definition of innovation to include technological, social, economic innovation; increasing the breadth and depth of the research and the education agenda of the university. Providing a systematic approach for individuals from business, government, and the university allows for joint innovations that address the challenges that are prioritized by all the partners involved. By focusing on having innovation between independent individuals from the three sectors, this new innovation framework can be developed over a period of time as experience, working together, and trust that allows co-creation-based innovation to be the norm rather than the exchange-based innovation.
- Provide entrepreneurship education to faculty and students to stimulate interest and impart the knowledge of a startup development.
- Implement and service an overall university academic entrepreneurship ecosystem that should have most of the following elements: senior leadership sponsorship and support; a vision for academic entrepreneurship; entrepreneurship courses and workshops for students, faculty, and staff in all academic disciplines; endowed chaired professors in entrepreneurship and innovation; strong relationships between entrepreneurship, science, and engineering; entrepreneurship concentration and minor; an entrepreneurship research program or center; an innovation center; entrepreneurship student clubs; business pitch and business plan competitions; a student venture investment fund; accelerators and incubators; networking events; and a university venture fund or angle group or links to these and other funding sources.

The presence and nature of these elements in the academic entrepreneur ecosystem will vary and reflect the local conditions. It is important to engage and sustain as many of these elements as possible, thereby enabling the academic entrepreneurship ecosystem to develop new ventures; resulting in a three-dimensional university engaged in teaching, research, and economic development — the university of the future. This requires senior leadership vision and sponsorship, strong faculty interest and leadership, commitment of substantial financial resources, sustained commitment over a period of time, and commitment to continuous innovation in educational programs and organizational structure.

Summary

This final chapter appropriately focuses on the topics every academic entrepreneur needs to know while creating a startup company: incorporation, corporate governance, officers, stockholders, building the startup team, confidentiality non-disclosure agreements, intellectual property assignment, non-competition agreements, and stock option plans. Following a discussion of ownership and royalty-sharing policies for academic entrepreneurs in various universities, the chapter concludes with managing the ecosystem and various ways to increase the level of academic entrepreneurship at a university.

References

Cantanagu, R. (2017). "Towards a Conceptual Definition of Academic Entrepreneurship". In *5th Annual Euro Med Conference of the Euro Med Academy of Business*, pp. 255–264.

Frigo, M. L. and Krumwiede, K. R. (2000). The balanced scorecard. *Strategic Finance*, 81(7), 50–54.

Gale, B. T. (1994). *Managing Customer Value*. The Free Press.

Goel, R. K. and Grimpe, C. (2011). "Are All Academic Entrepreneurs Created Alike? Evidence from Germany". In *Fourth Annual Conference on Entrepreneurship and Innovation*, Northwestern University School of Law, Chicago, June 16–17.

Hayter, C. S. (2011). "What Drives an Academic Entrepreneurs: New Research Seeks to Understand a Startup's Definition of Success". *The New York Academy of Science*, https://www.nyas.org/magazines/spring-2011/what-drives-an-academic-entrepreneur/. Accessed 4 June 2019.

Kaplan, R. (2001). *Integrating shareholder value and activity-based costing with the balanced scorecard*. Balanced Scorecard Report. January 15, 2001.

Kaplan, R. and Lamotte, G. (2001). *The Balanced Scorecard and Quality Programs*. Balanced Scorecard Report, March 15.

Kaplan, R. S. and Norton, D. P. (2001). *The Strategy-Focused Organization*. Harvard Business School Press.

Kellen, V. (2002). *CRM Measurement Frameworks*. http://www.crm-forum.com.

Lingle, J. H. and Schiemann, W. A. (1996). From balanced scorecard to strategic gauges: Is measurement worth it?, *Management Review*, 85(3), 56–61.

Meyer, M. W. (2002). Finding performance: The new discipline of management. In Neely, A. (ed.), *Business Performance Measurement: Theory and Practice*. Cambridge University Press.

Philpott, K., Dooley, L., O'Reilly, C. and Lupton, G. (2011). The entrepreneurial university: Examining the underlying academic tensions. *Technovation*, 31, 161–170.

Robertson, S. and Kitigawa, F. (2009). *Understanding knowledge mediation strategies in university incubators: From policy to practice, and back again*. Unpublished research paper. LLAKES. University of Bristol.

Shane, S. (2004). Encouraging university entrepreneurship: The effect of the Bayh–Dole act on university patenting in the United States. *Journal of Business Venturing*, 19(1), 127–151.

Thrift, N. (2010). Across the world: The privatization of higher education. *The Chronicle of Higher Education*, https://www.chronicle.com/blogs/worldwise/across-the-world-the-privatization-of-higher- education/25189.

Vernon, J. (2010). The end of the public university in England. *GlobalHigherEd*, https://globalhighered.wordpress.com/2010/10/26/the-end-of-the-public-university-in-england/.

Viale, R. and Etzkowitz, H. (2010). *The Capitalization of Knowledge: A Triple Helix of University–Industry–Government*. Dheltenham: Edward Elgar.

Wright, M., Piva, E., Mosey, S. and Lockett, A. (2009). Academic entrepreneurship and business schools. *The Journal of Technology Transfer*, 34(6), 560–587.

Appendix

1. Alexandre Albuquerque
2. Anna Knapinska
3. Cedric Francois
4. Dean Sicking
5. Derek Sakata
6. Heloise Anne Pereira
7. Kavun Nuggihalli
8. Laurence Hurley
9. Marija Gajdardziska-Josifovska and Carol Hirschmugl
10. Matt Bilsky
11. Mathew Magno
12. Michael Schultz
13. Nader Pourmand
14. Noah Schochet
15. Peter Mullner
16. Robert Freishtat
17. Rodney Markin
18. Victoria Scott
19. Visar Berisha and Julie Liss
20. Wayne Knox

Alexandre Albuquerque

Name of Nominee   **Alexandre Albuquerque**
University the Nominee is   **UC Berkeley Extension**
   representing
Email: alexalbuquerque@alquer.com
Phone number: 713 931-2633

Alexandre A. Albuquerque is a Senior Engineer with extensive experience in the Oil & Gas areas being the mentor for the first Drilling Simulator for PETROBRAS. He is also the Project Manager, Product Developer, and Proprietor of the ALQUER BCRSS-3D™ Ballast Control and Rig Stability Simulator Software System.

Q2: The nominee's position when they created the company. Describe the nominee's process with the university as they were creating the company. Be as detailed as possible.

The company was created for academic purposes. The ALQUER BCRSS-3D™ Ballast Control and Rig Stability Simulator, which was already in existence, was designed by the undersigned as a physical person in 1986. The UC Berkeley Extension Project Management Class highly contributed to re-edit this Entrepreneurial Technology, through the Students Work Groups formed during the Quality and Risk Management Classes in 2003. The workshop provided relevant expert insights, highly contributing to pave the way for the future endeavors. During one of the workshops, an Official Member of the USCG in the audience said that the presentation by Albuquerque and his team was the best on campus. Their technology has been currently developed to build an advanced SAAS platform global enterprise.

Q3: Describe the nominee's experience working with the university in creating the company. What were the challenges? What support did they receive? Be as detailed as possible.

The ALQUER BCRSS-3D™ Ballast Control and Rig Stability Software Project, which had been shelved for years, was revived to use the concepts at the UC Berkeley Project Management Program for the future recovery and implementation of the singular system. Albuquerque and his team were not expecting any support to recover and implement the technology, and become a final useful product for which it was designed. This is a proprietary technology with no parallel in the market. It can leverage, by far, the competence of semi-submersible platforms BCOs (Ballast Control Operators) exceeded others. This system will help protect lives, assets, and the environment; increasing the safety of offshore drilling operations outside the continental shelf. Some endeavors were done in the Bay Area with Maritime Engineering Companies, California Maritime Academy, among others, looking forward to building possible partnerships and/or obtain supplemental funds to invest in this project without returns.

Q4: What happened to the company the nominee created? Describe in detail where it is now and how is it doing. What is the history of the company? Be as detailed as possible.

The Master Software was shelved again and stayed dormant for years to come, until 2014, when Albuquerque decided to definitely bring it back when he acquired the book *Stability and Ballast Control* from Michael Hancox, the renowned author and expert in this area. After opening the communication channel through his editors in London and seeing the Simulator features; confirming that Albuquerque and his team could simulate the Ocean Ranger, P-36, and Thunder Horse Platforms. Michael Hancox quoted the team's technology as "a very fine use of modern technology to enhance operator skill". He added the team could use his book and formulas for their project. On 2014, the www.alquer.com website was built and a special page to Michael Hancox's book was added, as gratitude. Since then, several interesting accesses were logged, including universities, research institutions, and Silicon Valley High-tech Companies. On 2016, the team was invited by the Brazilian Petroleum Institute (IBP) to participate at the Rio Oil & Gas 2016 Conference, being granted with their chancel Seal. The team came to the rescue in December 2018, after a cyclone semi-submerged the Orlinda Star the Semi-submersible Olinda Star off India's coast, Techstars Energy Accelerator Program from Norway invited the team for a video call on February 2019 to discuss their project and encourage them to submit a funding application during the same calendar year.

Anna Knapinska

Name of Nominee	**Anna Knapinska**
University the Nominee is representing	**Florida Atlantic University**
Email:	ania.knapinska@fau.edu
Phone number:	561 799-8140

Dr. Knapinska received her PhD in Molecular and Cellular Pharmacology from Rutgers University, New Brunswick, NJ, where she was an IGERT Fellow on Biointerfaces. She completed her postdoctoral experience at The Scripps Research Institute in Ultra-High Throughput Screening. She is currently a Research Professor and Associate Director for the Center of Molecular Biology & Biotechnology at Florida Atlantic University, as well as the CEO and President of MMP Biopharma, Inc.

Q2: The nominee's position when they created the company. Describe the nominee's process with the university as they were creating the company. Be as detailed as possible.

When MMP Biopharma was created in March 2017, Dr. Anna Knapinska was (and still is) a Research Professor in the Department of Chemistry & Biochemistry at Florida Atlantic University (FAU) and Dr. Gregg Fields was (and still is) Chair of the Department of Chemistry & Biochemistry at FAU. FAU set up a conflict of interest committee to review work performed by Drs. Knapinska and Fields as it related to MMP Biopharma interests. In April 2017, MMP Biopharma applied for the "Tech Runway" competition sponsored by the FAU Research Park. MMP Biopharma was one of the finalists. This position allowed MMP Biopharma to enter into the year-long entrepreneurship program, which concluded in June 2018.

Q3: Describe the nominee's experience working with the university in creating the company. What were the challenges? What support did they receive? Be as detailed as possible.

During the year of training with Tech Runway, MMP Biopharma received mentorship support, entrepreneurship training, networking, and presentation opportunities, as well as some legal and marketing support. MMP

Biopharma was offered free space to work for the duration of the entrepreneurship program and discounted space rental rates after the program development.

Q4: What happened to the company the nominee created? Describe in detail where it is now and how is it doing. What is the history of the company? Be as detailed as possible.
MMP Biopharma has existed for 1.5 years. MMP Biopharma is now raising funds and applying for SBIR grants. MMP Biopharma has pitched to numerous potential investors. The main focus of MMP Biopharma has been repositioned and the advisory board adjusted based on networking feedback. Dr. Fields has filed subsequent patent applications which will be licensed by the company. MMP Biopharma will be negotiating with FAU for laboratory space. The Center for Molecular Biology & Biotechnology (CMBB) at FAU leases space to local startup companies. MMP Biopharma will relocate to CMBB and join four other startup companies presently operating there.

Cedric Francois

Name of Nominee	**Cedric Francois**
University the Nominee is representing	**University of Louisville**
Email:	cedric@apellis.com
Phone number:	502 241-4114

Dr. Francois is the co-founder of Apellis Pharmaceuticals, Inc., and has served as a member of the Board of Directors, and as the President and Chief Executive Officer since September 2009. Prior to co-founding Apellis, Dr. Francois co-founded Potentia Pharmaceuticals, Inc., or Potentia, a private biotechnology company. Dr. Francois has served as President and Chief Executive Officer at Potentia since 2001. Dr. Francois received his MD from the University of Leuven in Belgium and his PhD in Physiology from the University of Louisville. Following postgraduate training in pediatric and transplant surgery, Dr. Francois was a member of the research team that performed the first successful hand transplantation and of the Louisville Face Transplant Team, whose work supported hand transplantation in Lyon, France in 2005.

Q2: The nominee's position when they created the company. Describe the nominee's process with the university as they were creating the company. Be as detailed as possible.

Cedric Francois received his medical degree from the University of Leuven in Belgium and his PhD in Physiology from the University of Louisville. Dr. Francois was a Fellow in Plastic and Reconstructive Surgery at the University of Louisville prior to his faculty position. Following postgraduate training in pediatric and transplant surgery, Dr. Francois joined the research team that performed the first successful hand transplantation and the Louisville Face Transplant Team, whose work supported the first human face transplantation in Lyon, France in 2005. He has published numerous publications and is the principal author on the clinical report on the first four human hand transplantations. He is an inventor of many biotechnology patent applications, including all of Potentia and Apellis's proprietary patent applications.

Dr. Francois led Potentia to become the first to test complement-inhibiting drug candidates for age-related macular degeneration, now an established procedure for that disease. In October 2009, Alcon, the world's largest ophthalmology company, entered into a licensing and option to purchase agreement with Potentia Pharmaceuticals who took over all of its operations. Dr. Francois is currently President and CEO of Apellis Pharmaceuticals.

Q3: Describe the nominee's experience working with the university in creating the company. What were the challenges? What support did they receive? Be as detailed as possible.

Dr. Francois worked with multiple universities at the start of his entrepreneurial ventures. As a fellow and faculty member at the University of Louisville, he started his companies in Louisville, KY, and also licensed his technologies to the University of Pennsylvania.

Q4: What happened to the company the nominee created? Describe in detail where it is now and how is it doing. What is the history of the company? Be as detailed as possible.

Dr. Francois has founded multiple companies, including Potentia Pharmaceuticals, Apellis Pharmaceuticals, Liberate Medical, and Revon Systems. Potentia Pharmaceuticals (Potentia) was founded in 2003, 2 years after winning the Harvard Business School business plan competition. Potentia was founded to commercialize a complement inhibitor to treat a variety of diseases, including macular degeneration. In 2009, Potentia entered into a strategic licensing and purchase agreement with Alcon, Inc. Apellis was founded in 2010 as a spin-off of Potentia to continue development of the lead compound for non-ocular indications. Subsequently, Apellis purchased the rights to the ocular indications from Alcon and secured more than $168 million in venture capital investment prior to completing an IPO in 2017. The IPO raised $150 million and the valuation at the time of IPO was $689 million. Apellis is currently evaluating their pipeline of products through several late-stage clinical trials. Dr. Francois is the President and CEO. He is also an Adjunct Professor at the University of Louisville.

Dean Sicking

Name of Nominee	**Dean Sicking**
University the Nominee is representing	**University of Alabama at Birmingham**
Email:	dsicking@uab.edu
Phone number:	402 4506295

For more than 30 years, Sicking has been a leading figure in highway safety research. His designs have reshaped guardrails and other roadside barriers throughout the United States. He was also one of the developers of the Steel and Foam Energy Reduction (SAFER) barriers that are used on NASCAR and Indy Racing League tracks around the world. In 2012, Sicking joined the UAB School of Engineering as a Professor and the Vice President of Product Development.

Q2: The nominee's position when they created the company. Describe the nominee's process with the university as they were creating the company. Be as detailed as possible.

Safety by Design was created in 1996 in affiliation with the University of Nebraska–Lincoln (UNL). Dean Sicking was one of four co-founders of the company which aims to improve roadside safety by developing innovative energy management systems. At the time, Dean was an Associate Professor with tenure at the university. The university had little involvement in the process of creating the company, but provided the support detailed in Q3.

Q3: Describe the nominee's experience working with the university in creating the company. What were the challenges? What support did they receive? Be as detailed as possible.

The university provided graduate students to help prepare a business plan and help to identify potential investors. UNL provided space in their business incubation center for a year until the company began generating positive cash flow. After which, Safety by Design graduated from the incubator and acquired their own space. Challenges with the university were minimum, but the biggest challenge was ensuring there were no conflict of interest between extramural research and the company's business.

Q4: What happened to the company the nominee created? Describe in detail where it is now and how is it doing. What is the history of the company? Be as detailed as possible.

Safety by Design continues to survive and thrive today. Since 1996, the company has developed six proprietary products that are sold globally. Their current annual royalty revenue is over 5 million/year with a gross sales revenue of over 70 million/year.

In 1997, Safety by Design Inc., (SDI), introduced a new energy-absorbing guardrail terminal. This product proved to be the safest terminal on the market and it quickly gained about 25% of the total market. This device, called the Sequential Kinking Terminal (SKT), generated approximately $1.4 million in royalties for SDI annually. In 1999, SDI introduced the first flared energy-absorbing guardrail terminal and marketed it as the FLEAT. This product added 5–10% market share which raised SDI's royalty earnings to about $2 million per year. The SKT and FLEAT proved to be extremely effective in attenuating high-speed impacts. In fact, on several occasions, these guardrail terminals were able to thwart suicide attempts by safely decelerating vehicles to a stop.

Over the next 12 years, SDI introduced other innovative highway safety devices, including the BEAT, a box beam guardrail terminal, the SSCC, a low-cost crash cushion, the MFLEAT, a safety treatment for median barriers, and the first of its kind trailer-mounted attenuator, called the TTMA. Although each of these products is profitable, none of them was successful on the scale of the SKT and FLEAT. SDI generated approximately $2.5 million annually in royalties on these eight products.

In 2014, SDI's primary competitor was forced to take its most successful guardrail terminal off of the market. As a result, SDI's market share increased to almost 90% and its revenue rose to over $5 million annually. Dr. Sicking has used much of this increased revenue to develop three new highway safety products that represent a paradigm shift in the guardrail terminal and crash cushion markets. For the last 24 years, Safety by Design has been the leading innovator in the roadside safety market and it is poised to carry this title into the future for many years to come.

Derek Sakata

Name of Nominee   **Derek Sakata**
University the Nominee is   **University of Utah**
   representing
Email: derek.sakata@hsc.utah.edu
Phone number: 801 5816393

Dr. Sakata is Professor and Vice-Chair of Anesthesiology at the University of Utah. He currently holds a Leland O. and Avanelle W. Learned Endowed Professorship in Anesthesiology. He is the Executive Medical Director of Ambulatory Anesthesiology and the Executive Medical Director of the Ambulatory Southern Service Area. He is Director of Anesthesia services for the John Moran Eye Center and holds adjunct Professorships in Bioengineering and Ophthalmology. He is founder of the CRNA care team at the University of Utah. He also is founder of Anecare LLC and Dynasthetics LLC. He is currently the Chief Medical Director for Dynasthetics LLC.

Dr. Sakata received his Bachelor of Science degree in Electrical and Computer Engineering from the University of California, Irvine, and his medical degree from Loma Linda University, Loma Linda, CA. Further, he completed an internship at Arrowhead Regional Medical Center, Colton, CA and a residency in anesthesiology at the University of Utah School of Medicine in Salt Lake City, UT. He served as the chief resident in his final year of residency at which time he decided to continue as faculty at the University of Utah.

Q2: The nominee's position when they created the company. Describe the nominee's process with the university as they were creating the company. Be as detailed as possible.

First company: Anecare: Resident/Instructor

Process with the university: Collaborated for the initial idea and the studies, and then Independent for the capital-intensive founding of the company.

Second company: Dynasthetics: Associate Professor
Process with the university: Independent

Q3: Describe the nominee's experience working with the university in creating the company. What were the challenges? What support did they receive? Be as detailed as possible.

The experience working with the university, when basic science research was being accomplished; was a collaborative relationship. The challenges were the intersection between entrepreneurism and traditional academia. This was exhibited by the funding of the company in the areas of IP protection, FDA approval, product manufacture, marketing, sales, and company operations. Additionally, promotion within the traditional academic system was and still is challenging. Initial financial support was obtained from the individual's department for his graduate student and then from the Society for Technology in Anesthesia. Also, the individual, as well as his partners, contributed financial equity as well as sweat equity during the capital-intensive founding of the company.

Q4: What happened to the company the nominee created? Describe in detail where it is now and how is it doing. What is the history of the company? Be as detailed as possible.

The first company, Anecare, still sells its original product. This company was founded while the nominee was a resident/instructor in the Department of Anesthesiology at the University of Utah. The second company, Dynasthetics, has two products on the market and sells into about 1,000 health care facilities in the US and approximately 12 countries around the world. Dynasthetics is presently working on its third product submission to the FDA.

Heloise Anne Pereira

Name of Nominee · **Heloise Anne Pereira**

University the Nominee is · **University of Oklahoma Health**
representing · **Sciences Center**

Email: · anne-pereira@ouhsc.edu

Phone number: · 405 271-6593

Dr. H. Anne Pereira serves as the Dean of the Graduate College. She has been a member of the University of Oklahoma Health Sciences Center since 1992 when she joined the faculty of the Department of Pathology. She rose through the ranks to Full Professor with tenure in Pathology, and in 2009 was appointed Professor of Pharmaceutical Sciences and Associate Dean for Research, College of Pharmacy. In 2018, Dr. Pereira was named the Herbert and Dorothy Langsam Chair in Geriatric Pharmacy and the David L. Boren Professor. Dr. Pereira received her PhD in Pathology from the University of Melbourne in Australia and then served as a Postdoctoral Fellow/Senior Research Associate at Emory University in Atlanta, before accepting her position at the University of Oklahoma. She has the distinction of being named a Fellow by the American Association for the Advancement of Science (AAAS) and a Fellow of the American Association of Colleges of Pharmacy (AACP) Academic Research Program. She is a renowned scientist in the areas of antibiotics and anti-inflammatory therapeutics and has had a longstanding record of federal funding. Dr. Pereira is the holder of several US and foreign patents and is the co-founder and Chief Scientific Officer of Biolytx, an OU spin-off company responsible for the commercial development of an antibiotic which she developed. She was named a Fellow of the National Academy of Inventors in 2015 for her highly prolific spirit of innovation in creating or facilitating outstanding inventions that have made a tangible impact on the quality of life, economic development, and the welfare of society. In conjunction with her scientific achievements, she has been an outstanding mentor for junior faculty, postdoctoral fellows, and high school, undergraduate, summer, medical, and graduate students over the past 25 years.

Q2: The nominee's position when they created the company. Describe the nominee's process with the university as they were creating the company. Be as detailed as possible.

Dr. Pereira established Biolytx Pharmaceutical Corp. in 2005 while she was an Associate Professor at the University of Oklahoma Health Sciences Center. She worked diligently with the technology transfer office to enter into appropriate agreements necessary to license the technology to Biolytx.

Q3: Describe the nominee's experience working with the university in creating the company. What were the challenges? What support did they receive? Be as detailed as possible.

To receive new funding for Biolytx, Dr. Pereira has continued to work with the Office of Technology Development on licensing agreements, filing of new patents, and partnering options. Challenges experienced have been the lack of partnering opportunities, cost of patent filing for a startup company, and procuring investor funds. Finding a suitable and experienced management team also has been a challenge. Non-dilutive funding was obtained through Oklahoma State agencies such as the Oklahoma Center for the Advancement of Science and Technology and the Economic Development for Generating Excellence. More recently, with the assistance of Oklahoma's innovation to enterprise (i2E) organization, a seed/angel round of funding was obtained to complete additional preclinical studies.

Q4: What happened to the company the nominee created? Describe in detail where it is now and how is it doing. What is the history of the company? Be as detailed as possible.

Biolytx continues to develop anti-microbial peptides for various applications (Website: www.biolytx.com).

Biolytx functions in a virtual capacity and is developing a suite of antimicrobial peptides for the treatment of severe Gram-negative infections that are difficult to treat with current antibiotics due to multidrug resistance. Studies are currently in the preclinical phase with plans to submit an IND within the next 18 months.

Kavun Nuggihalli

Name of Nominee	**Kavun Nuggihalli**
University the Nominee is representing	**Temple University**
Email:	knuggihalli@considercode.com
Phone number:	+14848868957

Q2: The nominee's position when they created the company. Describe the nominee's process with the university as they were creating the company. Be as detailed as possible.

Kavun Nuggihalli was a freshman in college when he created ConsiderCode LLC. He was good at writing software, and unlike other students, he had gotten a summer job at Dell coming straight out of high school. The problem was, he was an engineer and had no experience in business. He had some really great ideas in college but knew nothing about marketing, sales, or business development, so none of his ideas really took off at first.

As college was very expensive, trying to launch a business remained a second priority for Nuggihalli, his first priorities being his classes, jobs, and study time. He was lucky that his parents could help pay for some of the tuition fees, but rent and food required him to work 20 hours a week as a software engineer. In the summers, he worked full-time at SAP as a Business Analyst while living with his parents to save up enough money to try to launch the product he invented.

By sophomore year, he was a full-time student, working two jobs and putting together a business plan for a competition Temple University was hosting. The competition was called BYOBB or "Be Your Own Boss Bowl". Funding valuing $250k would be provided to the best startup on campus. Nuggihalli submitted his application in junior year and was rejected.

Q3: Describe the nominee's experience working with the university in creating the company. What were the challenges? What support did they receive? Be as detailed as possible.

Nuggihalli had created a software that was being used by hundreds of students on campus, but he had no way of letting the university know. When junior year started, he availed a loan to cover his tuition, rent, and living expenses, conducting only two classes to retain his part-time status at Temple University. It was the scariest time of his life, but he devoted every moment he could to network with anyone he could at Temple University. Eventually, he ended up speaking with the CIO of the university who decided to sign a contract to pilot his application at Temple University. That year, he applied to BYOBB again and walked away with $15k in funding.

In his senior year at Temple University, he was still conducting 1–2 classes a semester to continue scaling this business. The number of students using his software has gone up from a few hundred students to over 4k. The startup Nuggihalli set up has started pilots at 11 different universities and the team is representing Temple University in the Philadelphia Alliance for Capital and Technology.

It took him 3 years of networking to get to where he is today. Today, he is giving lectures at Temple University to show others how to scale their ideas in an academic environment. He is representing his school through his business and attends conferences each year to promote education software and technology.

Q4: What happened to the company the nominee created? Describe in detail where it is now and how is it doing. What is the history of the company? Be as detailed as possible.

Currently, ConsiderCode LLC is seeking funding to develop Artificial Intelligence systems for the higher education market. They started out by making apps that students could use on campus to be incorporated into the classrooms to be piloted by universities. They have a small development team and sales force which is constantly growing. Starting next year, they will be building computers for students and educators to use for documentation of research.

Laurence Hurley

Name of Nominee   **Laurence Hurley, PhD**
University the Nominee is   **The University of Arizona**
   representing
Email: hurley@pharmacy.arizona.edu
Phone number: 520-626-5622

Q2: The nominee's position when they created the company. Describe the nominee's process with the university as they were creating the company. Be as detailed as possible.

When the team created their startup, Dr. Laurence Hurley was serving as the Howard Schaeffer Chair in Pharmaceutical Sciences at the College of Pharmacy at the University of Arizona. He and his partner in research, Dr. Vijay Gokhale of the UA's BIO5 Institute, have been investigating gene expression and how it is controlled by molecular switches called C- and G-Quadruplexes. Drs. Hurley and Gokhale are the leading experts in drug targeting.

Dr. Hurley worked closely with Tech Launch Arizona (TLA), the UA's commercialization office, to disclose and protect the intellectual property behind the technology. He was paired with Rakhi Gibbons, TLA's Director of Licensing, who facilitated the work of protecting the IP and served as the team's point of contact throughout the process.

TLA's Director of Venture Development, Joann MacMaster, and her team also helped, bringing additional advisers and expertise to the table via their Commercialization Partners program (detailed in Q3).

In all, TLA provided services to define, protect, and license the intellectual property; bring the team together; and develop a business strategy for the startup. Reglagene was formed in November 2016 and licensed the technology in September 2017.

Q3: Describe the nominee's experience working with the university in creating the company. What were the challenges? What support did they receive? Be as detailed as possible.

Tech Launch Arizona has a Commercialization Partner program — of a network of over 1,500 experts — they have brought together 26 experts and entrepreneurs who collaborate with TLA on a weekly basis, providing expert feedback and industry perspectives on new technologies stemming from UA research.

Through this program, in 2016, Dr. Hurley was introduced to commercialization partner Dr. Richard Austin, a 24-year veteran of the pharmaceutical industry. Dr. Austin served as a medicinal chemist with GlaxoSmithKline and worked for Sanofi in Tucson. He holds a Doctorate in Organic Chemistry and an MBA in Pharmaceutical Management. Dr. Hurley served on Dr. Austin's PhD committee in the 1980s at UT, Austin, and the two reconnected through their association with TLA.

Dr. Austin became a TLA commercialization partner, and at a meeting of that group in May 2016, Dr. Hurley delivered a presentation about the DNA quadruplex technology. It was then that Dr. Austin was sold on the idea of leading Reglagene.

As the team started to form, TLA facilitated opportunities for them to further develop and present their ideas for their venture to a network of strategic partners, collaborators, and future investors. In addition to meetings on campus, TLA facilitated startup presentations for Reglagene at the April 2017 TechCode Showcase in Mountain View California, as well as at the October 2017 Regional Innovation Showcase in San Diego. Through networking, the company connected with industry experts and advisors, strengthening their venture ideas and building a strong business case to move Reglagene forward.

Q4: What happened to the company the nominee created? Describe in detail where it is now and how is it doing. What is the history of the company? Be as detailed as possible.

From the start, the team was positioned for success. They received the prestigious Flinn Foundation Biosciences Entrepreneurship Program grant, which provides $30k in funding and connects recipients to Arizona bioscience, academic, and policy leaders. Realizing they would need continued support after the IP was licensed, they applied to, and were accepted into the Arizona Center for Innovation technology incubator located at the UA Tech Park.

Reglagene is raising the capital needed from public and private sources to accelerate its progress. Recently, on the public side, the National Cancer Institute (NCI) alerted Reglagene that NCI is awarding a

$300,000 STTR award. At the same time, Reglagene is pursuing dilutive investment via the sale of equity in the company. A total of $500K has been raised to date with many more investors and groups in the pipeline.

Reglagene is in the process of ramping up operations. It is in the final stages of establishing a lease arrangement with the University of Arizona that will allow it to use lab space and equipment. Reglagene also plans to hire its first employees in October.

Marija Gajdardziska-Josifovska and Carol Hirschmugl

Name of Nominee	**Marija Gajdardziska-Josifovska and Carol Hirschmugl**
University the Nominee is representing	**University of Wisconsin-Milwaukee**
Email:	mgj@uwm.edu
	cjhirsch@uwm.edu
Phone number:	414 229-2937

Dean Marija Gajdardziska-Josifovska has led the Graduate School of the University of Wisconsin– Milwaukee since January 2014. She is active in research and an entrepreneurial Physics Professor who is the co-founder of a high-tech startup company (SafeLi LLC).

Dean Gajdardziska has extensive governance, managerial, and leadership experience, from Chair of Physics, through directorship of an interdisciplinary center of excellence, and two Associate Deanships in the College of Letters and Science and the Graduate School, respectively. She is a graduate of the 2009 Management Development Program at the Harvard Institute for Higher Education.

Dean Gajdardziska's interests in leadership for graduate education and research are rooted in her own studies of Physics that have spanned three continents. She received a B.Sc. in Engineering Physics from Ss. Cyril and Methodius University in her native Macedonia (research in atomic and molecular laser physics), an M.Sc. degree from The University of Sydney in Australia (in solar energy), a PhD and Postdoc from the Arizona State University (in nanoscience through electron microscopy). Upon joining the University of Wisconsin–Milwaukee, Professor Gajdardziska established the Laboratory for High Resolution Transmission Electron Microscopy where she images atoms to discover and develop advanced materials. She has received and managed more than $5.4 million in grant funding, published more than 140 peer-reviewed papers, presented at numerous conferences, and is most recently pursuing patents. She currently serves on the Editorial Board of *Microscopy and Microanalysis* (the journal of the Microscopy Society of America).

Select awards and honors that she's received include the following: Fellow of the Microscopy Society of America (2014), Woman of Influence award of *The Business Journal* (2014), visiting faculty at Oxford University (2009), Research Corporation Research Opportunity Award (2004), the White House/National Science Foundation Presidential Faculty Fellow Award (1995) and many more. The awards she received during her student years include the Herman E. DeMund Scholarship (1990; one a year for ASU), Australian–European Graduate Award (1985; one a year for Europe), and the Best Undergraduate Student in Physics for 10 years (1976–1986).

Carol Hirschmugl is Professor of Physics at the University of Wisconsin at Milwaukee, Principal Investigator at the Synchrotron Radiation Center, and Director of the Laboratory for Dynamics and Structure at Surfaces. Most recently, she co-founded SafeLi LLC and is its first CEO.

She received her B.Sc. in Physics from the State University of New York at Stony Brook in 1987 and her PhD in Applied Physics from Yale University in 1994. She has received an Alexander von Humboldt grant, a University of California President's Postdoctoral Fellowship, multiple National Science Foundation Grants, a Research Corporation Research Innovation Award, and a UWM Research Growth Initiative. She is notable for her research in applications of infrared microspectroscopy in biological specimens and materials science at the Lawrence Berkeley National Laboratory, Brookhaven National Laboratory, and the Synchrotron Radiation Center.

Results from her research have revealed a complex interplay between the electrons in a metallic substrate and the vibrations in molecules adsorbed on the surface. For example, Hirschmugl found that when certain vibrations of the adsorbate relax (decay), they create electronic excitations in the metal. Previously, it had been believed that these decaying vibrations would only create other vibrations.

Professor Hirschmugl held visiting scientist positions at ANKA, FZK (Karlsruhe, Germany) in 2004 and at ESRG (Grenoble, France) in 2005. Hirschmugl's awards include Fellow of the American Vacuum Society "For longstanding instrumental and scientific contributions to synchrotron-based infrared spectroscopy and micro-spectroscopy, including its applications to surface science, materials science, biophysics, and cultural heritage" (2014), three from the National Science Foundation, and the Research Corporation Research Innovation award.

Q2: The nominee's position when they created the company. Describe the nominee's process with the university as they were creating the company. Be as detailed as possible.
Dr. Marija Gajdardziska-Josifovska and Carol Hirschmugl are both professors in the University of Wisconsin–Milwaukee's Physics Department; in addition, Dr. Gajdardziska-Josifovska is also the Dean of the UWM Graduate School.

Q3: Describe the nominee's experience working with the university in creating the company. What were the challenges? What support did they receive? Be as detailed as possible.
Marija and Carol have decades of work in condensed matter physics — they had one of those "gee, that's funny" moments when studying diffraction patterns from their electron microscope. They had created a new form of graphene — graphene monoxide. The material is essentially the first solid form of carbon monoxide known to mankind at ambient conditions. It is a two-dimensional crystal with promising applications as carbon-based semiconductors, as nanosensors, and most immediately in lithium ion batteries. The UWM Research Foundation pursued a patent on the work and their research team received two awards from the Catalyst Grant Program to help them characterize and scale-up the material. Marija and Carol entered the NSF I-Corps program (through the Milwaukee I-Corps site) and conducted 40 customer interviews (with companies including Tesla, Samsung, and Apple) as part of this intense 4-week program that uses the "lean launch" methodology. They continued on to the national I-Corps program and to the state SBIR Advance program, conducting more than 250 customer interviews to identify their likely market entry point — the anodes for lithium ion batteries (where innovations have not kept up with cathodes or electrolytes) for immediate use in power tools and ultimate use in electric vehicles and consumer electronics. The team has launched a company, SafeLi, LLC which has licensed the technology from the UWM Research Foundation.

Q4: What happened to the company the nominee created? Describe in detail where it is now and how is it doing. What is the history of the company? Be as detailed as possible.

SafeLi LLC was formed on December 15, 2016. The team has worked closely with UWM's entrepreneur-in-residence (a former venture capitalist) and have recently been awarded two SBIR grants, one from the Department of Energy and the other from the National Science Foundation being used to conduct key validation tests. They are starting discussions with investors as well as incubator groups to help them accelerate the company development.

Matt Bilsky

Name of Nominee	**Matt Bilsky**
University the Nominee is representing	**Lehigh University**
Email:	matt@mattcomp.com

Dr. Matt Bilsky is a licensed Professional Engineer, Postdoctoral Research Associate, and Adjunct Professor in the Mechanical Engineering and Technical Entrepreneurship programs at Lehigh University. He has a PhD in Mechanical Engineering from Lehigh University that focused on smart product development, technical entrepreneurship, mechatronics, and engineering education. Matt won second place in the 2016 Lemelson/MIT invention competition for his work in snake-like robotics. He is also the recipient of the 2017 John B. Ochs Award for Faculty Achievement in Entrepreneurship Education and the Pocono Whitewater 2018 River Guide of the Year. A portfolio of his work is available at Mattbilky.com

Q2: The nominee's position when they created the company. Describe the nominee's process with the university as they were creating the company. Be as detailed as possible.

Graduate school was not originally on Dr. Bilsky's radar. A professor under whom he had taken a smart product development course recognized Dr. Bilsky's abilities and engineering skillset, and recruited him to be a researcher while pursuing a master's degree. This initial funding did not work out and Dr. Bilsky realized that the only way to get a funded graduate degree was to pursue a PhD. He started by following the "conventional" route — finding an advisor who had funded research and would fund him as a research assistant for his entire program. Toward the end of the first semester in the program, it became clear to that Dr. Bilsky was not in love with the work, which is a fundamental requirement for successfully earning a PhD. Then a phone call happened. His department chair was in need for someone who could help as an instructor and teaching assistant for the first-year engineering programming class, something that Dr. Bilsky was uniquely suited for in the department. The professor he was working for reluctantly agreed. This was the decision that changed the course of his life. At that time, he realized that his graduate funding was no longer tied to the professor since now the university was paying for his full tuition and stipend in exchange for his teaching services. He then looked for other research opportunities that might have better suited his interests in smart product development, robotics, and mechatronics; he found another advisor who was doing work that seemed to fit the bill. But, at the end of a second semester working for someone else, it became clear to both the professor and Dr. Bilsky that he needed to let his entrepreneurial spirit run free. That was when he approached Professor John Ochs, who directed the Technical Entrepreneurship program in the Mechanical Engineering department at Lehigh and explained: If the university is paying Dr. Bilsky to teach "full-time" (which is 20 hours per week on top of courses in graduate school math), then any research he does is essentially volunteer. Given this assumption, the following questions came to Dr. Bilsky's mind: Why can't I do my own research and TA my way through a PhD? More specifically, why can't I start a company, develop a project, and fund my research through startup grants? Prof. Ochs responded: "Why can't you?" and then you?" — and then over the the next 5 years Dr. Bilsky created a program called an Entrepreneurial Minded Dissertation (EMD) where he TA'd his way through his PhD in exchange for his full tuition and a stipend. He then founded the company, Impossible Incorporated LLC, through which he applied for grants to fund his research. The university's IP policies state that if a researcher was to fund the research by himself/herself and is paid to teach, not conduct research (which is the case here), then the researcher own his/her intellectual property. Around 3.5 years after Dr. Bilsky started with Prof. Ochs, in January of 2017 (after 4.25 years in graduate school) he graduated from Lehigh University, having completed both a Master's of Engineering and Doctor of Philosophy in Mechanical Engineering. His primary area of research, and the foundation of his company, revolved around his work as a contractor and property manager, which supported him during the summers since he initially only received a 9-month salary. Having renovated over 30 plaster and lathe houses, he saw the need for a device that could drive, drill, and see inside walls to run wires without a mess. This led to his invention: a 1-inch-diameter snake-like robot. He has invented a number of mechanisms, including the world's smallest, strongest gearboxes and a novel robotic architecture. All of these inventions are patent pending and Dr. Bilsky is the sole owner of the intellectual property. About half way through the program, he became heavily involved in entrepreneurial engineering education research through national organizations such as the Kern Entrepreneurial Engineering Network (KEEN), whose goal is to instill an entrepreneurial mind-set to accompany the engineering skillset in every engineering undergraduate. Membership in this organization started to fund his summers because he could work full time on the robot. Additionally, it got Dr. Bilsky involved in pedagogy development and studying how students learn. He also became a faculty mentor and leader in the KEEN program that now includes half of the engineering faculty at Lehigh (75 people). All of this experience enabled him to earn his current position at Lehigh: Postdoc, Adjunct Professor, Innovator, and Entrepreneur. Dr. Bilsky became a full-time faculty member of the university at age 26 while writing his dissertation. He taught three classes including both the undergraduate and graduate integrated product development courses (undergraduate being called the Technical Entrepreneurship or TE capstone). He runs the day-to-day operations for the TE capstone course, which has 200 students working on 31 teams for 21 corporate sponsors doing real-world, customer-driven engineering design in a business context. They are the capstone course for mechanical, materials, and bioengineering students along with supply chain management students. He was also the instructor for the senior dynamics/smart products engineering lab course in the mechanical engineering department. Upon graduation in 2017, he entered the "Lehigh Incubator" as a postdoctoral research associate (and the other titles listed above). In exchange for teaching the TE capstone and senior mechanical engineering courses, he received a commensurate salary, benefits, and full access to university resources including a multimillion-dollar machine shop and lab space. His research has been and continues to be the snake-like robot (i.e., working for my company). Along the way, Dr. Bilsky has raised over $162K in non-dilutive funding through internal and external pitch competitions, startup grants from the South Bethlehem Keystone Innovation Zone, and programs such as Pennsylvania Infrastructure Technology Alliance (PITA) where he is the industry partner and his colleagues are the academic researchers. This has funded his research and enabled over 50 capstone, undergraduate, and graduate students, interns, and researchers to work on the project, while allowing Dr. Bilsky to retain full ownership of the intellectual property. In April 2018, he turned down the offer of a full-faculty position from the Dean of the College of Engineering to pursue his robot invention full-time. December 31, 2018 was Dr. Bilsky's last day at Lehigh. He has gotten far more than his three degrees in his 10.5 years at the university. *P.S.*: Along the way, because of how Dr. Bilsky structured his program, he was also able to satisfy the 4 years of industry experience requirement to earn the Professional Engineering (PE) license, most likely making him one of the youngest PhD, PEs.

Q3: Describe the nominee's experience working with the university in creating the company. What were the challenges? What support did they receive? Be as detailed as possible.

As detailed in the founding story, Dr. Bilsky has been intimately involved with the university on numerous levels throughout the process. As mentioned, he retained full ownership of the intellectual property and about half way through the program, he was ready to file the initial provisional patents so he could enter competitions such as the 2016 Lemelson-MIT invention competition (which he had tied for second place, first loser in). Dr. Bilsky approached the technology transfer office at Lehigh to see if they would be interested in pursuing the patent if he were to offer them a licensing fee (i.e. give them 5–10% to cover costs). This was not something they had encountered before and it did not work out. Nevertheless, he is the proud owner of a signed letter from the Director of the Office of Technology Transfer confirming that he does own the IP. He also competed in the EUREKA! Pitch competition at Lehigh run by the Baker Institute, where he won the first place in the Levin Advanced Technology Competition, which came with a cash award along with two capstone teams to work on his project. In the subsequent year, Dr. Bilsky won the legacy prize in the EUREKA! competition which also came with two capstone teams. As a research-active faculty member, he also had a number of students work on the project as an independent study and/or a work-study, developing a two-way relationship with the university. This also permitted access to the robust research ecosystem at Lehigh that supports spaces like the student machine shop. Dr. Bilsky's colleagues, who have expertise in a number of areas, also helped him throughout. With the grants from the PITA program, Dr. Bilsky became the industry sponsor and is working with two of his colleagues (on two different grants), which allows their graduate students to get real-world experience by working on the projects. Dr. Bilsky is working with Professor Brandon Krick, who is an expert in tribology, the study of friction and wear, and Professor Subhrajit Bhattacharya, an expert in robotic path planning. Through tenacity and strong relationship building, Dr. Bilsky became known across the campus from the president to the custodians and has been able to use all the resources available to the fullest. Likewise, his experience has paved the way for others to pursue their own EMDs and also led to the formation of educational programs to help the university clarify gaps such as how to fund student startups despite the university being a non-profit entity.

Q4: What happened to the company the nominee created? Describe in detail where it is now and how is it doing. What is the history of the company? Be as detailed as possible.

Dr. Bilsky has quit Lehigh University to concentrate on Impossible Incorporated LLC. All the grants that he received have funded students and materials but not his salary. He is working with organizations such as NCET2 along with multinational companies and individual investors to fund the company so that he can continue his work. The goal of Dr. Bilsky's startup is to integrate and license the technologies developed during his PhD program (the gearbox, extension mechanism, robotic architecture, wall mapping system, etc.) to strategic partners who can commercialize them.

Every day and every meeting is getting Dr. Bilsky closer to his goal and he claims that he sleeps well at night, despite the uncertainty of funding, by knowing this is indeed possible. Dr. Bilsky would appreciate reader referral to any strategic partners to whom he should be talking.

Mathew Magno

Name of Nominee   **Mathew Magno**
University the Nominee is   **University of California, Davis**
  representing
Email: mathewmagno@japa.one
Phone number: 909 5611970

Mathew Laurence Magno moved to Davis from Southern California. He ventured North to study computer science and technology management at the University of California, Davis and proceeded to work on multiple projects relating to parking and augmented reality. Passionate about entrepreneurship and the tech industry, the move to Northern California was a natural fit. He has an amazing background of management with titles from Project Manager to Kitchen Manager. With encouragement from friends and family, Mathew helped co-found Japa, a software company dealing with parking.

Q2: The nominee's position when they created the company. Describe the nominee's process with the university as they were creating the company. Be as detailed as possible.

CEO Mathew Magno is a first-generation student that put himself through college. He founded the company while attending an entrepreneurship course at UC Davis. From there, he and his co-founder developed their products, thereby immediately gaining traction. He would initiate meetings and stand in front of city officials or decision-makers to move the process forward. As a student, he was able to leverage huge partnerships, manage fundraising, and grow the business while completing his degree in computer science with a minor in technology management. He encompassed his whole life around entrepreneurship which is evident in his passion toward the company and others.

Q3: Describe the nominee's experience working with the university in creating the company. What were the challenges? What support did they receive? Be as detailed as possible.

The challenges were based around balancing school, work, and home life. How does one overcome the obstacles of school and growing a business? He says it's about passion, resilience, and transparency. He was never afraid to ask for help and embraced all of the failures along his way. The university was a tremendous support in terms of workspace, incorporation and legal work, mentors and advisors, seed capital, workshops, competitions, IP help, creating a community of like-minded entrepreneurs, and most of all, the encouragement and support of the staff and students. With everyone believing in the team, it made it easier to be extra passionate about what they were doing.

Q4: What happened to the company the nominee created? Describe in detail where it is now and how is it doing. What is the history of the company? Be as detailed as possible.

Since the start of the company, the student co-founders graduated from UC Davis and now are 2 months into working full-time on the startup. They have partnered with SIEMENS and Paysafe Group with installations at two universities, one hospital, one factory, and one city. They are in the process of fund-raising to cover the cost of development and hiring. The company started in a classroom at UC Davis. The student founders decided to solve the problem of parking since parking caused them to be late for class sometimes. What went from a class assignment quickly became one of the leading smart parking companies.

Michael Schultz

Name of Nominee	**Michael Schultz**
University the Nominee is representing	**University of Iowa**
Email:	michael-schultz@uiowa.edu
Phone number:	865 356-1861

Michael K. Schultz, PhD, is co-founder and Chief Science Officer of Viewpoint Molecular Targeting, Inc. Dr. Schultz is an academic entrepreneur and is also an Associate Professor of Radiology and Nuclear Medicine in the Free Radical and Radiation Biology Program at the University of Iowa. Dr. Schultz is an internationally recognized content expert in radiopharmaceutical sciences and inventor of key intellectual property that comprises the backbone of Viewpoint's approach to cancer therapeutics and companion diagnostics. Dr. Schultz has been invited internationally to speak on topics related to his technology as well as on the topic of academic entrepreneurship.

Q2: The nominee's position when they created the company. Describe the nominee's process with the university as they were creating the company. Be as detailed as possible.

Michael K. Schultz was a non-tenure track Associate with the University in the Department of Internal Medicine. His research interests were primarily in radiopharmaceuticals, and he joined the Department of Radiology as an Assistant Professor in 2009 on the tenure track. This coincided with the establishment of his company, Viewpoint Molecular Targeting. Dr. Schultz was successful in securing several NIH and other external sources of funding to support his research and was promoted to Associate Professor with tenure in 2014. His company secured exclusive licenses to technology for his company from the technology transfer office (University of Iowa Research Foundation), which has assisted in the IP protection (patent filings) and strategy. This technology has received over $7 million in Small Business Innovation Research and NIH R01 grants and contracts, which has provided a basis for equity investment in the company.

Q3: Describe the nominee's experience working with the university in creating the company. What were the challenges? What support did they receive? Be as detailed as possible.

The University of Iowa Research Foundation provided assistance with patent filings for Dr. Schultz's inventions and assistance with strategy in maintaining these patents. The UIRF and university provided seed funding in the form of prizes for elevator pitch and business plan competitions. These prizes have amounted to approximately $95,000 toward technology and business development via the UIRF or OVPR at the university. The university also provided consulting from local entrepreneurs in the form of the Faculty Innovators program, which functions much like the NIH ICORP program. The experience with the Faculty Innovators program effectively prepared nicely for the NIH ICORP experience.

Q4: What happened to the company the nominee created? Describe in detail where it is now and how is it doing. What is the history of the company? Be as detailed as possible.

Viewpoint began with IP generated in the laboratory of Michael Schultz and the company is entering the clinical trial stage of development. The company has been awarded over $4 million in NIH Small Business Innovation Research grants and contracts and is collaborating with the University of Iowa on a recently awarded R01 grant ($3.7 million). The company has also secured the State of Iowa Economic Development Authority and Wellmark Fund loans and has been awarded matching funds by the Iowa Innovation Corporation. At the time of this writing, the company has partially completed a seed round of $2 million (convertible notes) to prepare the company for IND for its first clinical trial. The clinical trial will commence in 2019.

Nader Pourmand

Name of Nominee **Nader Pourmand**
University the Nominee is **University of California Santa**
  representing **Cruz**
Email: pourmand@soe.ucsc.edu
Phone number: 831 502-7315

Dr. Pourmand received his MS and PhD from the Karolinska Institute in Stockholm, Sweden, in Experimental Medicine and Rheumatology in 1997 and 1999, respectively. He joined the Stanford Genome Technology Center in 1999 as a postdoctoral fellow working with Ronald Davis to develop new technologies, during which time he co-developed MagArray technology and developed the charge-based DNA sequencing, which is the underlying technology for Ion Torrent system.

Dr. Pourmand co-founded MagArray Inc. in 2005, BioStinger in 2014, Pinpoint Sciences Inc. in 2016, and Hipic Inc. in 2017. In 2008, he joined UC Santa Cruz as a faculty member, and with his team he has been developing innovative tools that enable sweeping advances in knowledge. His research falls into two distinct but interrelated areas that share the common thread of leveraging the interface of bioelectronics and DNA sequencing to advance studies in the field of nanogenomics. In short, his team successfully developed a new RNA/DNA sequencing protocol from a minute amount of nucleic acid (less than 1% of a single cell content), which they can aspirate from cells with their newly developed nanopipette. The nanopipette provides an approach to insert or retrieve minute amounts of material from single cells using a precise, controllable manipulator in a suitable end-effector that can perform desired tasks without damaging the cells. The innovative RNA extraction methods allow them to amplify mRNA from as little as 1 mg of total RNA from a single cell. This can provide a platform to conduct very sensitive whole-transcriptome analysis (WTA) of single cells. This remarkable technology also provides spatial resolution by targeting individual cells in a mixture of many other cell types. The technology was recently described in *Nature Nanotechnology* as a major advancement in single-cell genomics and was recognized by the NIH, with Dr. Pourmand being awarded the first place and winning the first prize for Phase 1 and 2 in the NIH's "Follow that Cell Challenge" for the development of this single-cell nanogenomic technology.

Q2: The nominee's position when they created the company. Describe the nominee's process with the university as they were creating the company. Be as detailed as possible.

Dr. Pourmand is a serial entrepreneur and has some experience licensing technologies from universities. Before serving at UCSC, he cofounded a company, MagArray Inc. After joining the UCSC faculty team as an assistant professor in 2008, he started working on the nanopipette technology for single-cell interrogations. In 2014, when he was an Associate Professor of Biomolecular Engineering, he started another company, BioStinger Inc., for single-cell applications. BioStinger Inc. is in the process of being acquired by another, larger company. In addition, the nanopipette technology has been recognized by the NIH and described in *Nature Nanotechnology* as "a major advance in Single Cell Genomics," and has been awarded the Phase 1 Prize (2015) and Phase 2 Prize (2017, first place) from the NIH's "Follow That Cell Challenge."

Q3: Describe the nominee's experience working with the university in creating the company. What were the challenges? What support did they receive? Be as detailed as possible.

Starting a company has always been a challenge, no matter which university one is associated with. UCSC's Office of Technology Licensing was initially not set for spinning off companies and was literally run by a one or two people. As a result of Dr. Abosalam's leadership and by adding more manpower to that unit, it improved tremendously. One of the challenges as an entrepreneur is that universities require upfront payment for licensing, usually at exorbitant rates. In Dr. Pourmand's opinion, this methodology that UCSC is taking discourages a person from starting a company. Instead, the university could license more individual technologies for smaller bits of equity, without a cash fee; this would reduce negotiation times by standardizing and simplifying terms and ultimately increase net output.

Q4: What happened to the company the nominee created? Describe in detail where it is now and how is it doing. What is the history of the company? Be as detailed as possible.

Magarray Inc. is a company that is more than 10 years old and is based on GMR sensors with products in the market and is supported by Hitachi Hihtech.

BioStinger Inc. is 4 years old and has applications in single-cell interrogation. This company is one of the four spin-offs using the same platform, Nanopipette. BioStinger is in the process of being acquired by a big company.

Pinpoint Sciences Inc. is 3 years old, focusing on developing handheld and real-time detectors using the nanopipette platform. It has raised some seed funding and is in the process of raising series A funding.

Hipic Inc. is almost 2 years old and develops hand-held and real-time detection of drugs, both elicit other drugs and on the roadside that will be used by law enforcement to have safer roads.

Nanopore Bio Inc. is nearly 1 year old, using the nanopipette platform for measuring glucose, and related biomarkers for diabetes, stress, and inflammations.

Noah Schochet

Name of Nominee	**Noah Schochet**
University the Nominee is representing	**Princeton University**
Email:	noahas@princeton.edu/
Phone number:	972 8166228

Q2: The nominee's position when they created the company. Describe the nominee's process with the university as they were creating the company. Be as detailed as possible.

Noah Schochet arrived on campus having founded three previous startups and was eager to start a new one. He then joined a student accelerator and met a cofounder within a few weeks of the first day of college. He and his co-founder, Todd Baldwin, began working on creating a fitness startup. Their friend, Ayushi Sinha, was the President of the Entrepreneurship club. When a contest for social entrepreneurship was announced, they came up with a different idea and began to work on both startups at the same time. The social entrepreneurial startup, WellPower, won several competitions and gained traction. WellPower is essentially an innovative solar water filtration system that purifies drinking water combined with an Uber-like distribution model to deliver the water via a smartphone app. They won just enough money to build a prototype and bought plane tickets to Kenya, where they ran a pilot program.

Q3: Describe the nominee's experience working with the university in creating the company. What were the challenges? What support did they receive? Be as detailed as possible.

Schochet is of the view that the university is not well suited to help current students start companies. He and his friends had to Uber to Home Depot and pooled the money by themselves to buy every tool that they would need. Initially, they had a hard time getting lab space, so they built their first prototype in a study room in the middle of the night, sawing and hammering and running water hoses and pipes. They had to rent a car to transport the prototype to the competition in which they emerged as a finalist (Hult Prize, $1 million for winner). They were not old enough to rent a car, and the university refused to pay for or provide transportation. After a few months, they launched their water filtration system in Kenya. They have tried to raise the funds in every possible way — angel investors, their personal savings, GoFundMe with family and friends, and even reached out to alumni. Eventually, after thousands of emails and meetings, they convinced the university to grant them the necessary funding.

Q4: What happened to the company the nominee created? Describe in detail where it is now and how is it doing. What is the history of the company? Be as detailed as possible.

As a result of their water purification system, 1,000 people in Kenya are drinking clean water. They plan to raise money from an angel investor and return to Kenya to set up many such water purification systems. They have currently employed two people in Kenya. They have been incorporated as a C corporation in Delaware. They are currently testing a third-generation hardware prototype and are building a smartphone app. They also met with the CEO's and management of the top 25 relevant startups and companies in Kenya to learn about the business ecosystem and forge potential partnerships. Currently, they have a terms sheet for $200,000.

Peter Mullner

Name of Nominee	**Peter Mullner**
University the Nominee is representing	**Boise State University**
Email:	petermullner@boisestate.edu
Phone number:	208 426-5765

Peter Mullner is a Distinguished Professor at Boise State University. He earned his undergraduate and graduate degrees in Materials Science at ETH Zurich, Switzerland and served as postdoctoral researcher at the University of Illinois at Urbana–Champaign, at the Max Planck Institute for Metals in Stuttgart, Germany, and at ETH Zurich, Switzerland. In 2004, he joined Boise State University as Associate Professor of Materials Science and Engineering and was promoted to Professor in 2009. In general, he likes microstructures of crystalline materials. He studied the formation of microstructures, phase transformations, crystal defects, and defect interaction. The objectives of his study included structural materials and functional materials; metals, ceramics, intermetallics, and semiconductors; materials in bulk form and thin films. He always liked to ponder on the formation of crystallographic twins and their description in the language of dislocations and disclinations. In his current research, Mullner studies the magneto-mechanics of magnetic shape memory alloys and he develops devices utilizing these materials. In 2015, Mullner founded the Shaw Mountain Technology LLC with the goal to commercialize the technology evolving from his research. Shaw Mountain Technology prioritizes keeping product development, manufacturing, and company operations located within Idaho. Mullner's teaching interests evolved with his scholarly activities. Early courses focused on crystallography, mechanical properties, and electron microscopy. Around the year 2000, Mullner developed an interest in the lives of inventors, engineers, and scientists, for the impact of society on the emergence of inventions and technology, and for the impact of inventions and discoveries on culture, politics, and economy. These interests translated to courses on the history and sociology of invention, materials for society, and innovation. Dr. Mullner summarizes his mid-term career goals with these words:

"Magnetic Shape Memory (MSM) technology transfer. I envision the Treasure Valley as the home of (i) the first company that commercializes MSM technology and (ii) a growing new industry of smart material micro-devices. My scholarly activities in teaching, research, and service will support this vision."

Q2: The nominee's position when they created the company. Describe the nominee's process with the university as they were creating the company. Be as detailed as possible.

Peter Mullner is a Distinguished Professor of Material Science and Engineering (MSE) at Boise State University. Mullner formed Shaw Mountain Technology in 2015 while he was serving as the Department Chair of Materials Science and Engineering. OTT worked with Mullner and the Idaho SBDC, Boise State Compliance and the College of Engineering to facilitate the startup process, including preparation of internal COI forms and licensing arrangements.

Q3: Describe the nominee's experience working with the university in creating the company. What were the challenges? What support did they receive? Be as detailed as possible.

Shaw Mountain Technology is Mullner's second startup from Boise State University and currently the only startup still in business that is making great strides toward commercialization. As they do not have a lot of infra-structure to support startups (such as an endowment to provide funds in exchange for equity or an incubator), Mullner has done an amazing job of bootstrapping to capitalize on the resources he does have at hand.

Q4: What happened to the company the nominee created? Describe in detail where it is now and how is it doing. What is the history of the company? Be as detailed as possible.

The company is still up and running and Mullner has taken a sabbatical this semester to focus on the commercialization of the IP. In March of 2016, Shaw Mountain Technology was awarded an SBIR/STTR Phase 0 grant from the Idaho Small Business Development Center for developing an STTR Phase I proposal, which was successfully funded in July 2016. Shaw Mountain Technology competed in the Idaho Entrepreneur

Challenge, a statewide competition where entrepreneurs vet their business ideas to three separate panels consisting of seasoned business-people, industry experts, and technology developers. The judges awarded a cash prize, donated by Zions Bank, to Shaw Mountain Technology for winning the technology category. In the Fall of 2016, Shaw Mountain Technology was one of three finalists for the Early-Stage Innovation of the Year (Idaho Innovation Awards). The nominated innovation was the Magnetic Shape Memory μPump, a new microfluidic technology for research and medicine. In the Spring of 2017, Shaw Mountain was awarded The Prototyping Grant from uFluidix (Toronto, Canada), a manufacturing company specialized in the scalable manufacturing of lab-on-a-chip and microfluidic devices. This grant will cover production and development costs at uFluidix where the MSM Micropump will be redesigned using professional, scalable manufacturing practices. Shaw Mountain was also awarded a second SBIR Phase 0 grant from the Idaho Small Business Development Center for developing an SBIR Phase II proposal. Shaw Mountain will use these funds to optimize the MSM micropump and develop manufacturing infrastructure in Idaho.

Robert Freishtat and Evan P Nadler

Name of Nominee

Robert Freishtat MD, and Evan P Nadler MD

University the Nominee is representing

George Washington University and Children's National Health System

Email:

Rfreishtat@childrensnational.org

enadler@cnmc.org

Phone number: 202 4765669

Robert J. Freishtat, MD, MPH is Senior Investigator in the Center for Genetic Medicine at the Children's Research Institute and is Chief of the Division of Emergency Medicine at the Children's National Health System in Washington, DC, USA. He is a Professor with Tenure in Pediatrics, Emergency Medicine, and Genomics and Precision Medicine at the George Washington University School of Medicine and Health Sciences. He received his MD from the University of Maryland School of Medicine and residency training in Pediatrics at the University of Rochester Medical Centre — Strong Memorial Hospital. This was followed by a clinical fellowship in Pediatric Emergency Medicine at Children's National. During this time, he completed an MPH in Epidemiology and Biostatistics at the George Washington University School of Public Health and Health Services. He has remained a faculty at Children's National for almost two decades during which time he has served in a joint clinical and applied research role. Since 2003, Dr. Freishtat's research has been continuously funded by the National Institutes of Health. He is the principal investigator for international collaboratives studying injury/repair in the lung and systems biology investigations in obesity. He has authored or co-authored over 100 articles and book chapters in the fields of lung injury, asthma, obesity, exosomes, and emergency medicine. Dr. Freishtat is Past-President of the American Federation for Medical Research and an active member of the American Thoracic Society and Society for Pediatric Research.

Evan P. Nadler, MD, serves as Co-Director of the Children's National Obesity Institute and is the Director of the Child and Adolescent Weight

Loss Surgery Program at the Children's National Health System. He is also a tenured Associate Professor of Surgery and Pediatrics, at the George Washington University School of Medicine & Health Sciences. Before moving to Washington, DC, he was the Director of Minimally Invasive Pediatric Surgery at the New York University School of Medicine where he participated in US Food and Drug Administration-approved studies using laparoscopic adjustable gastric banding in adolescents with obesity. He was recently part of a National Institutes of Health-funded study investigating the effect of surgical weight loss on executive functioning and cognition in adolescents. His other current research pursuits include obesity device development, bariatric surgery for monogenic forms of obesity, and adipocyte signaling via exosomes. Dr. Nadler is an international leader in the field of adolescent obesity, has multiple publications on the topic, and was one of the founding members of the Childhood Obesity Committee of the American Pediatric Surgery Association.

Q2: The nominee's position when they created the company. Describe the nominee's process with the university as they were creating the company. Be as detailed as possible.

Dr. Freishtat was Chief of Emergency Medicine at Children's National and a Professor of Pediatrics, Emergency Medicine, and Genomics and Precision Medicine at GW. Dr. Nadler was Director of Adolescent Bariatric Surgery at Children's National and an Associate Professor of Surgery and Pediatrics.

Q3: Describe the nominee's experience working with the university in creating the company. What were the challenges? What support did they receive? Be as detailed as possible.

They worked with the Director of Innovation and Technology Commercialization after he arrived to ensure the IP was protected and to negotiate terms for licensing the IP from the hospital. Company creation was done outside of university help, basically with the guidance of a previous mentor who had started his own company.

Q4: What happened to the company the nominee created? Describe in detail where it is now and how is it doing. What is the history of the company? Be as detailed as possible.

The company won an NCET2 competition and participated in its University Startup Demo Day where one of the organizers joined the company to help take the next steps. They have found a new business adviser who will help them raise the $30 million needed for research and development of the products. NIH grants and internal funding are allowing them perform the science, but they are in need of funding for commercialization.

Rodney Markin

Name of Nominee	**Rodney Markin**
University the Nominee is representing	**University of Nebraska**
Email:	rmarkin@unmc.edu
Phone number:	402 690-3175

Dr. Rodney S. Markin is currently Associate Vice Chancellor for Business Development and Director of UNeTech at the University of Nebraska Medical Center and a Professor of Pathology and Microbiology; David T. Purtilo is a Distinguished Professor of Pathology and Microbiology, Courtesy Professor of Surgery, and Courtesy Professor of Psychiatry. Dr. Markin's professional and academic research interests have focused on clinical laboratory automation, which include but are not limited to, robotics, information systems, medical utilization management, and outcomes optimization. Dr. Markin received his Bachelor's Degree in Chemistry with a minor in mathematics and physics from Nebraska Wesleyan University in 1977; Doctor of Philosophy (PhD in Biochemistry) from the University of Nebraska–Lincoln in 1980; and Doctor of Medicine (MD) degree from the University of Nebraska Medical Center (Omaha) in 1983. Dr. Markin completed his residency in pathology and laboratory medicine at the University of Nebraska Medical Center. Dr. Markin is board certified in Anatomic and Clinical Pathology and he founded LAB-InterLink, a spin-out of the University of Nebraska Medical Center that provided products for hospital-based laboratory automation systems. Dr. Markin is also a director on the Boards of Trovagene, Mikroscan, PerceptiMed, and Afaxys and on the Board of Trustees for Keck Graduate Institute.

Q2: The nominee's position when they created the company. Describe the nominee's process with the university as they were creating the company. Be as detailed as possible.

Dr. Markin was Professor of Pathology at the University of Nebraska. He foresaw the need to develop automated systems to handle laboratory specimens — this was over 20 years ago. Such systems save money and deliver results more quickly. The company, LAB-InterLink was the pioneer in this field, employing 157 people (at its peak), generating considerable intellectual property and establishing standards for the emerging Laboratory Automation industry through CLSI (NCCLS). The company also acquired a competitor based in Canada, LABOTIX that operated mainly in Europe and Canada. The US Company was sold to Abbott Laboratories (Abbott Park, IL) and the Canadian Company was sold to Cerner (Kansas City, MO). The technology created by NU, LAB-InterLink, and LABOTIX had approximately 6,000 automation systems that had been incorporated several times around the world.

Q3: Describe the nominee's experience working with the university in creating the company. What were the challenges? What support did they receive? Be as detailed as possible.

Dr. Markin worked closely with the university and the university's Technology Transfer Office, UNeMed to license out the NU technology. Prototypes of the system were deployed in the UNMC hospital laboratory. In-kind support was provided by NU during the startup phase of the company. Dr. Markin raised outside funds to grow the company through Angel funding and Series A, B, and C funding. The company developed the prototypes into viable products and created a production facility. The company also was the index case for FDA 510K clearance for laboratory automation interfaces with clinical laboratory instruments. The essence of the product line was the Process Control Software which allowed the technologically automated specimen-handling devices (Specimen Carrier, Transportation System, Loading Station, Decapper, Aliquoter, Instrument Interfaces with Instruments, Recapper, and Storage and Retrieval systems) to interoperate. One of the key features of the software was the routing algorithms based upon Graph Theory and the introduction of STAT specimen routing.

Q4: What happened to the company the nominee created? Describe in detail where it is now and how is it doing. What is the history of the company? Be as detailed as possible.

Dr. Markin continued to work at the university throughout the history of the company. At some point, the size of the company and the intellectual property portfolio made Lab-InterLink a target for acquisition. However, after the acquisition, Dr. Markin continues to work for the university, mentoring startup companies. The LAB-InterLink technology and intellectual property portfolio were incorporated into the Abbott Laboratories ACCELERATOR Product Line. The LABOTIX technology and intellectual property were located in Peterborough, Ontario, Canada for several years and subsequently moved to a location in the Kansas City area to be closer to Cerner Headquarters. Several of the original LABOTIX employees retired prior to the move to Kansas City. Cerner continues to offer the Cerner Automation Products to its customers.

Victoria Scott

Name of Nominee	**Victoria Scott**
University the Nominee is representing	**Princeton University**
Email:	vscott@alumni.princeton.edu
Phone number:	646 5921319

Victoria Scott is a leader on the Cloud Platform Innovation Team at IBM where she is learning how to positively transform companies with the latest and most innovative cloud solutions.

Victoria graduated from Princeton University with a Bachelor of Science in Engineering in computer science and has extensive experience in entrepreneurship, front-end web development, and design.

Victoria has a strong technical background, and her preferred programming language is Python. In addition to Victoria's technical background, Victoria has an entrepreneurial mind-set, is a fast learner, a challenger, is flexible, and adapts quickly to change.

Prior to joining IBM, Victoria helped to co-found WellPower, a sustainably sourced and portable water filtration system that will bring clean water and energy to those who do have access to clean water and energy. She used her entrepreneurial skills to help secure funding and used her technical background to build the company's website.

Q2: The nominee's position when they created the company. Describe the nominee's process with the university as they were creating the company. Be as detailed as possible.

When the company was created, Victoria was a senior at Princeton University. She was finishing her computer science studies and applying to post-graduate job opportunities. Her co-founders, Noah Schochet, Ayushi Sinha, Todd Baldwin, and Bethwel Kiplimo, were all Princeton University engineering students and were at the time (and still are) balancing their rigorous engineering curriculums with the challenges of starting a company.

It was a busy time and a time of great transformation. Thankfully, Victoria and her four co-founders had a strong passion for entrepreneurship and implementing change in the world. In order to get the company off the ground, the team leaned on university entrepreneurship resources: The Keller Center and the Entrepreneurial Hub (the E-Hub). They gave them the space to work and helped them connect with the alumni, who were able to provide advice and funding. They also participated in university-pitching competitions to receive initial funding so they could purchase the materials and tools needed to build a prototype of the filtration system.

Q3: Describe the nominee's experience working with the university in creating the company. What were the challenges? What support did they receive? Be as detailed as possible.

There are many challenges in starting a company; however, those challenges are amplified if you have created a company while in school or if you are working full-time. Some of these challenges Victoria faced are highlighted in a Medium article (https://bit.ly/2GOZLTI).

Q4: What happened to the company the nominee created? Describe in detail where it is now and how is it doing. What is the history of the company? Be as detailed as possible.

The company is still going strong. They had successfully piloted the water filtration technology in a small village in Kenya. Now the team is focused on scaling the technology to other villages in Kenya by the end of the summer and getting investor interest to fund their future projects.

The company was started in late 2017, and Victoria joined the team as a co-founder in February 2018.

WellPower is a team of Princeton Engineers that has identified a problem that they are uniquely equipped to solve. Members of the team have experience working for solar manufacturers, social enterprises focused on renewables, water management facilities, and energy storage research labs. Their team has developed expertise in solar and battery systems, water purification technologies, distribution channels, NGOs, and sustainability. They first met on campus at Princeton as friends who had similar interests in sustainable energy and entrepreneurship. Together they have built a sustainable solution that will have a broad and lasting impact.

Visar Berisha and Julie Liss

Name of Nominee

University the Nominee is
   representing

Email:

Phone number:

Visar Berisha and Julie Liss

Arizona State University

visar.berisha@asu.edu
julie.liss@asu.edu
480-747-6455; 480-965-9136

Julie Liss is a Professor of Speech and Hearing Science and Associate Dean for the College of Health Solutions at Arizona State University. Her research, supported primarily by NIH-NIDCD, has focused on communication disorders secondary to neurological injury and disease. Dr. Liss has expertise in the neuroscience of speech production and perception, which she has studied through acoustic and perceptual analysis of disordered speech. Her work seeks to translate laboratory findings into the clinical domain, where speech and language analytics can offer a window to evolving neurological health. She is co-founder and Chief Clinical Officer of a faculty startup company, Aural Analytics, which was founded to accomplish this translational goal.

Visar Berisha is an Assistant Professor with a joint appointment in the College of Health Solutions and the School of Electrical, Computer, and Energy Engineering. His research resides at the intersection of speech production and speech analytics and is primarily supported by the National Institutes of Health, Office of Naval Research, and Industry. He is also the co-founder of Aural Analytics.

Q2: The nominee's position when they created the company. Describe the nominee's process with the university as they were creating the company. Be as detailed as possible.
Visar Berisha is an Assistant Professor with a joint appointment in the College of Health Solutions and the School of Electrical, Computer, and Energy Engineering. His research resides at the intersection of speech production and speech analytics and is primarily supported by the National Institutes of Health, Office of Naval Research, and Industry. He is also the co-founder of Aural Analytics.

Q3: Describe the nominee's experience working with the university in creating the company. What were the challenges? What support did they receive? Be as detailed as possible.

Faculty at ASU receive support throughout the tech transfer and venture creation process. They met the CEO of the company through an ASU Mentors Network program.

Q4: What happened to the company the nominee created? Describe in detail where it is now and how is it doing. What is the history of the company? Be as detailed as possible.

The company needs revenue and is raising venture capital funds to scale up their processes.

Wayne H. Knox

Name of Nominee	same
University the Nominee is representing	**University of Rochester**
Email:	wknox@optics.rochester.edu
Phone number:	585 281 396

Wayne H. Knox, PhD, is a Professor of Optics, Physics, Material Science, and Visual Science at the University of Rochester. His previous academic positions at UR include Associate Dean of Engineering and Director of The Institute of Optics. He started at Bell laboratories in 1984 as a post-doctoral researcher, advancing to Director of the Advanced Photonics. Research Department, a leading researcher in the field of ultrafast laser technology, science and applications when and has received numerous awards including the NAS W.O Baker Award, AAPT Richtmyer Award, and the R.B. Goergen Teaching Award. He has published over 150 publications and holds 50 US patents and 153 international patents. He is Chief Science Officer of Clerio Vision, Inc., a startup company that he co-founded and is Fellow of the Optical Society of America, Fellow of the American Physical Society, and Fellow of the National Academy Inventors.

Q2: The nominee's position when they created the company. Describe the nominee's process with the university as they were creating the company. Be as detailed as possible.

Wayne Knox was a Professor of Optics at the University of Rochester when he started research into femtosecond laser micromachining of ophthalmic polymers, working with Bausch and Lomb Corp (B+L) in Rochester around 2004. The work was successful, and the project continued to grow until in 2013, they negotiated an agreement to develop the technology commercially with B+L. Prof. Knox took a 1-year leave of absence to facilitate the tech transfer. Just as his leave started, Valeant Pharmaceuticals announced that they were acquiring B+L. They immediately canceled all university research contracts and he quickly switched gears into planning a startup company. He made many plans, including brainstorming potential products, technology roadmaps, customers, etc. He also started contacting potential new large companies to gauge their interest. But what he was really missing was a business team. Then in the Spring of 2014, he was introduced by his tech transfer office to an experienced business team and they put together the plan for the startup company: Clerio Vision Inc., which started in late 2014. Prof. Knox is the Chief Science Officer, retaining his full-time Professor position at the University of Rochester, where he is now Professor of Physics, Materials Science, and Vision Science as well.

Q3: Describe the nominee's experience working with the university in creating the company. What were the challenges? What support did they receive? Be as detailed as possible.

The University of Rochester greatly facilitated this startup in many ways. First, UR arranged a $10 million research agreement with B+L over a 5-year period. That was what attracted Prof. Knox to the field of Ophthalmology, which he quickly entered, having a background in optics, laser physics, optoelectronics, system design, semiconductor physics, and materials science. Furthermore, a somewhat unique NY State-funded program at UR called Center for Emerging Innovative Sciences (CEIS) provided matching funds and reduced overhead rates to help the research advance with relatively small corporate funding about ($60,000/year) until the technology could be convincingly demonstrated. When his B+L funding was cut, he applied for and received an internal research award of $250k over 2 years that kept the company running until Clerio Vision could get new startup funding in place. That was awarded by the Center for Translational Sciences Initiatives, by the science advisory committee (SAC). Then a miracle happened. UR told Valeant/B+L that it would like to have all of the I.P. returned to UR, and for Valeant to assign all of their rights to UR, at no charge. They did so. Clerio Vision Inc. then licensed all of the patents from the university. Clerio Vision now supports Prof. Knox's UR research group with an ongoing series of research grants, all with continued CEIS-matching funds. The company now has individual as well as Institutional Conflict of Interest plans, and everything is being managed very good on both sides. Prof. Knox is constantly filing new patents and currently has 50 US patents and 153 international patents. He has recently been recognized as a Fellow of the National Academy of Inventors.

Q4: What happened to the company the nominee created? Describe in detail where it is now and how is it doing. What is the history of the company? Be as detailed as possible.

As of 2018, more than 60 people work for Clerio Vision Inc., in different capacities. The UR team includes several other professors, and eight PhD students, various undergraduates, and six or seven laboratories. Labs and offices at 1255 University Ave are bustling with more than 20 full-time employees, and another 20 or more international consultants and industry advisors act in a consulting capacity. Their funding includes partially venture-backed funds worth around $15 million, more than $2 million initially invested by B+L, NSF STTR Phase 1, 1b, and 2, and they just received a Phase 2b STTR award. They are currently raising another $18 million. The basic technology of localized refractive index modification (we now call LIRIC, for Laser Induced refractive Index Change) is being deployed in three technology areas. They have developed a new kind of custom contact lens that provides excellent presbyopia correction, and it is currently in human clinical trial testing. They are on the lookout for a nearby building to lease, in order to build a manufacturing plant. For laser-based noninvasive adjustment of intra-ocular lens power, they have signed a partnership with a major vision company and are testing their materials. For direct-write of refractive corrections into the cornea, they have signed a partnership agreement to commercialize with a European partner. For the FIH (First in Human) clinical trial, they formed a Canadian subsidiary of Clerio Vision and partnered with Starfish Medical to build a fully quali-fied internationally shippable prototype surgical machine. Their FIH study was approved in October 2018, after successfully demonstrating the tech-nology in live cats and rabbits as well as cornea tissue from human cadavers. Academically, three PhD students have already graduated under Prof. Knox's guidance. One was actually an MD and PhD, the first in the history of the University of Rochester to do so with an MD and PhD in Optics from the URMC Medical School. So far, the company is highly successful and has promising new technology, a large patent portfolio, and strong business partnerships. We have a CEO (Michael Totterman), CFO (Alex Zapesochny), EVP (Alexandra Latypova), CSO (Wayne Knox), and President (Scott Catlin). Prof. Knox has been working on this since 2004 and is very proud of these accomplishments. He did a lot of team building as a department head at Bell Laboratories, Holmdel, NJ, and as Director of The Institute of Optics for 10 years from 2001 to 2011, but this is a very different kind of team building. Prof. Knox and his team have built quite a unique company in a great environment in Rochester, where there has always been a strong culture of innovation and entrepreneurship, particularly in Medical and Optics fields, and particularly so in the Vision Science area.

Index

innovation accelerators, 200, 202
innovation districts, 43
innovation economy, 37
innovativeness, 97
Instagram, 49
installment loans, 154
institutional capacity, 29
institutionalizing, 162
Intel, 162
intellectual mission, 4
interdisciplinary research, 263
international collaboration, 63
International Trade and Export Working Capital loans, 157
IPO, 45, 106, 175–176, 274
IP portfolio, 87, 198
IP protection, 2, 64, 66, 86–88, 278, 297
IPrime, 39
Isenberg Daniel, 26
IUPAC, 121

J

Johnson Controls, 39
joint inventors, 68

K

Kauffman Foundation, 11, 112–113, 190
Kendall Square, 44
Kennedy Edward, 178
key partners, 122–123
key resources, 122–123
Kickstarter, 160
Knapinska Anna, 271
Knox Wayne H., 317
Koyo, 39
KPCB, 48

L

labor-surplus, 182
land-grant universities, 41
launch strategy, 110
LEGO, 80
LIBOR rate, 157
Lightspeed Ventures Summer Fellowship Program, 48
limited liability, 183, 240–241
limited partners, 161–162, 165, 182–183
limited term, 64–65
line of credit, 154
Liss Julie, 315
living spaces, 32
localized entrepreneurial ecosystem, 30
long-term loans, 154

M

3M, 162
management by deviation, 126
Magno Mathew, 298
marketability, 221
marketing plan, 45, 103, 109, 134–135, 137, 227
marketing variables, 102, 222
market opportunity, 99, 102, 166, 221
market segment, 134–136
Markin Rodney, 310
Martinez Javier Barcia, 119
mass merchandisers, 149
Master of Engineering in entrepreneurship, 238
Master of Science in entrepreneurship, 238
McKinsey Global Institute, 28

mechanical mixture, 67
memorandum, 168
mental processes, 68
mentorships, 32
MESBICs, 162
Michelin, 39
Microsoft, 75
Miller Christopher, 145
Miller Phineas, 73
Minova, 39
mission statement, 134, 260
modern concepts, 10
molecular nanotechnology, 121
monopoly, 161
Monsanto, 162
Motorola, 75
Mullner Peter, 304
Musial David, 21
mutual evaluation, 170

N
NACIE, 28, 30
Nadler Evan P, 307
NAI, 33, 61
nanotechnology, 42, 98, 121, 201,
 299–300
National Venture Capital Association,
 168
NBIA, 200
NCET2, 61, 176, 207–210, 294, 309
need determination, 102, 222
need-to-know basis, 81
negative cash flow, 105
negotiations, 170
Nestle, 122
network security, 81
Newman, 10
NIH, 48, 181, 234, 297–300, 309, 315

Nokia, 54
non-disclosure agreements, 82, 244,
 264
non-provisional filing, 65
Nortel, 76
NSF, 2, 42, 48, 60, 178, 181, 234,
 288, 319
Nuggihalli Kavun, 281

O
Obermeyer Arthur, 178
OICs, 84
one-stop-shops, 35
operationality, 221
opportunity, 107
opportunity assessment plan, 93, 109,
 222, 224, 226, 232
ordinary innovation, 15, 97, 104
organizational plan, 109, 140
ORGS, 35–36
OTL, 46, 248
outsourcer, 126

P
Papal Decree, 5
partial ownership, 246
patents for invention, 69
Patent Wall of Fame, 33
Pereira Heloise Anne, 279
PETA, 79
philanthropic venture funds, 163
pivotal role, 51, 262
postdoctoral vita, 86
potassium chloride, 67
Pourmand Nader, 299
preferred stocks, 243
preliminary investigation, 170
prevailing interest, 148, 156

venture capital process, 161, 165, 167
venture creation, 96–97, 237, 316
Venture Incubation Program, 207
vesting, 247
Voor Michael J., 233

W
3 Ws, 244
Wall of Fame, 34, 36, 61, 87
Walt Disney Co., 78

Whitney Eli, 73
World IP Day, 34

X
Xerox, 81, 162
Xtandi, 38

X
Zuckerberg, Mark, 44

CPSIA information can be obtained
at www.ICGtesting.com
Printed in the USA
BVHW040732200320
574806BV00013B/16